The steamboats served as links between the thriving railheads in the river towns and the overland wagon lines. But as the railroads reached more points on the river and penetrated into the region beyond, they choked off the steamers' business and brought about their decline.

In the last years of the nineteenth century, the colorful steamboats were replaced by prosaic gasoline packets. These continued to move cargoes on the upper river until the construction of dams halted long-range commercial boating forever.

For *A History of Steamboating on the Upper Missouri River,* Dr. Lass has made liberal use of contemporary reports and records. In telling the story of the steamboats, he has also introduced the men who owned and operated them. There are vivid accounts of what life on the river was like and personality sketches of prominent figures. In addition the book contains an abundance of economic data bearing on all aspects of steamboating as a commercial enterprise.

A NOTE ABOUT THE AUTHOR

William E. Lass was born in Beresford, South Dakota. He completed his undergraduate study at the University of South Dakota and earned the masters degree there. He received the Ph.D. degree from the University of Wisconsin. During intervals in his scholastic career he served two two-year periods in the U. S. Army.

From 1957 until 1960 Dr. Lass taught at Southwestern State College in Weatherford, Oklahoma. He is at present assistant professor of history at Mankato State College, Mankato, Minnesota. In his research, Professor Lass has cultivated a special interest in the history of transportation in the Midwest.

A HISTORY OF STEAMBOATING

ON THE UPPER MISSOURI RIVER

A History of

Steamboating on the Upper Missouri River

WILLIAM E. LASS

University of Nebraska Press : Lincoln

Publishers on the Plains

UNP

MANUFACTURED IN THE UNITED STATES OF AMERICA

To Marilyn

Preface

THE ROMANCE of the steamboat has led historians to deal with many aspects of steam navigation—the technological development of it, the adaptation of the steamboat to both eastern and western rivers, and the part it played in the economic development of areas drained by the rivers. There has been no attempt, however, to tell in detail the story of steam navigation on the upper reaches of the Missouri River.

The Upper Missouri drains a wide basin which historically constituted a large portion of the last frontier. The river, despite the limitations of low water and seasonal use, gave the best access to the area. The vanguards of the last frontier—the traders, explorers, and military men—traveled by water and built their major installations along the river. The most important towns in the early agricultural history of the Upper Missouri region were the river towns, because of the area's dependency upon the river and the steamboats. In fact, the economic development of portions of the Upper Missouri depended upon river navigation for over a century.

The Upper Missouri River, as described by the Upper Missouri Outfit of the American Fur Company, consisted of that portion of the river above the mouth of the Big Sioux. The Outfit chose this designation because the Missouri turns sharply northwestward at that point. This geographic division of the river was adopted by the first steamboat men, and when Sioux City, located near the mouth of the Big Sioux, succeeded St. Louis as the steamboat port of the Fort Benton–bound boats, the demarcation of the river into Upper and Lower became even more firmly established. The term Upper Missouri was so commonly used to describe the portion of the river above Sioux City that it was employed by army engineers when they began work on the river, and it remains in use today.

This study traces the development of commercial navigation on the Upper Missouri from 1819, when the first steam vessel entered the waters of the Missouri, until 1936, when the last commercial navigation company on the Upper Missouri went out of existence. During this period the steamboat was the primary mode of river transportation, although it was augmented by the mackinaw and ultimately replaced by the gasoline packet. Steamboating was particularly important before railroads reached the Upper Missouri, but it remained important even after that time. Too often steamboat studies are concluded at the point of time when the railroads reached the river. To say that railroading killed steamboating does not explain the long years of competition and cooperation between these two modes of transportation.

On the Upper Missouri, steamboat men made good profits for nearly two decades after the first railroad reached Sioux City in 1868 by cooperating with the railroads and operating between railheads. In fact, the most active period of navigation on the Upper Missouri came after towns on that portion of the river became steamboat ports by virtue of becoming railroad termini. Commercial boating on the Upper Missouri lasted for sixty-eight years after the arrival of the first railroad. When it did die, it was for a complex of reasons, of which railroading was only one. Improved roads which enabled motor trucks to directly challenge boats, and the crop failures of the 1920's and 1930's, also contributed to the death of commercial navigation on the Upper Missouri.

Acknowledgments

I AM SINCERELY grateful to the people who contributed time and knowledge toward the preparation of this study. My thanks go first to Dr. Vernon Carstensen of the University of Wisconsin, who read and edited the entire manuscript in its early form and made many helpful suggestions concerning both source material and style. I also owe thanks to Dr. Herbert S. Schell, Professor of History and Dean of the Graduate School at the University of South Dakota, who stimulated my initial interest in the topic and in the study of the American Frontier.

I am particularly indebted to Miss Margaret Rose, Librarian of the North Dakota Historical Society, who devoted hours to locating materials during my months at Bismarck. Her familiarity with the historical records of the Upper Missouri greatly facilitated the research project. Mr. Ray H. Mattison, Historian in the Region Two Office of the National Park Service, Omaha, Nebraska, generously provided copies of his studies of the military frontier on the Upper Missouri and helped in locating other research material. Miss Lucile Kane, Director of the Manuscripts Section of the Minnesota Historical Society was most cooperative during my investigation of the Davidson Papers and the Hubbell Papers. I am also indebted to members of the Bureau of Indian Affairs and Old Army Sections of the National Archives who helped locate many transportation contracts, and to staff members of the Library of Congress who helped in the location of newspapers and secondary sources. I am grateful, also, to Mrs. R. E. Walpole, Yankton, South Dakota; Mr. and Mrs. Willard Leach, Bismarck, North Dakota; and Mrs. Melvin Welsh, Bismarck—all of whom provided information about the role they or their relatives played in boating on the Upper Missouri.

The work of my wife, Marilyn, deserves special mention. She edited portions of the manuscript, assisted in proofreading, and did all of the typing.

Contents

TABLES

MAPS

A Section of Photographs Follows Page 112

*A History of Steamboating
on the Upper Missouri River*

I

The Missouri River

THE MISSOURI RIVER, the longest waterway in North America, flows 2,945 miles from its source in Red Rock Creek, Montana, to the Mississippi.[1] The navigable portion of the river below the Great Falls makes up most of this distance. Above the falls, the gradient of the river is extremely steep, in some places averaging as much as seven feet per mile. Although in the 1890's several small steamers navigated the 130-mile stretch of river between Stubbs Ferry (near Helena) and the town of Cascade, navigation on the river above the falls was the exception rather than the rule.[2]

Historically, only that part of the river below Fort Benton has been of great importance to navigators. Fort Benton (known as Fort Lewis until 1850) throughout the era of navigation on the Missouri River was considered the head of navigation because the thirty-seven miles of river above Benton to the falls were, for all practical purposes, unnavigable.* The navigable part of the river down from Fort Benton to the mouth is composed of two distinct geological sections—the short, 172-mile "Rocky River" reaching from Benton to Cow Island, and the "Sandy River" stretching from Cow Island to the mouth.[3]

The Rocky River, so called because the stream cuts through solid rock formations, flows swiftly in a narrow, straight channel. The gradient of this portion of the Missouri is steep, averaging approximately 2.07 feet per mile, and consists of a series of drops which form rapids.

---

*There is a record of at least one steamboat going above Fort Benton. In July, 1868, Captain Burke, commanding the *Tom Stevens,* took a pleasure party within six miles of the Great Falls. The trip, despite high water, was arduous because of the 350-foot increase in elevation in the first sixteen miles above Fort Benton. (Michael A. Leeson [ed.], *History of Montana, 1739–1885* [Chicago: Warner, Beers & Co., 1885], p. 395.)

Loose boulders, rocky reefs, and permanent sandbars are also common in the Rocky River. The waters are clear and free of timber debris because of the barren, rocky nature of the banks.[4]

The 2,113-mile Sandy River, in contrast to the Rocky River, flows through an area of alluvial, easily eroded soil which muddies the waters of the stream. Since the banks are unstable and readily undercut, it is only natural that the river curves, or meanders. The current alternately attacks one bank and then the other, always cutting and depositing and always forming sandbars downstream and opposite the undercut bank. These sandbars, formed by the deposit of the current's load when it ricochets off the undercut bank, push the current out farther and farther, thereby exaggerating the river's meandering. Many of the curves eventually become extravagant loops, miles around and only a few hundred yards across. During floods, when it attacks the undercut bank with increased severity, the current commonly cuts through the meander necks and forms a new channel, or a chute.[5] The combination of the loose soil and the active river contributes to the unpredictability of the channel from one season to the next.

The ever-shifting, devious channel of the Sandy River is primarily responsible for the great length of the Missouri River. It was not uncommon for river distances between two points to be several times greater than the straight-line distance. Steamboat men on the Missouri naturally measured the river by following the curves; thus they computed the distance from the mouth to Fort Benton to be about 3,100 miles.[6] Army engineers, however, measured across the meanders and considered the distance from the mouth to Fort Benton to be only 2,285 miles.[7] The meanders of the Sandy River were not wholly inconvenient; they did serve to reduce the gradient of the stream. The climb from the mouth of the river up to Cow Island was barely perceptible, averaging only 8.5 inches to the mile and spiraling gradually all the way, since the channel was devoid of rapids.

The banks of the Sandy River, unlike those of the Rocky River, were heavily timbered, especially with cottonwood. The collapsing banks continually dumped large trees into the stream, where they became sawyers or snags, or part of a log jam or raft. Sawyers, trees with the roots moored to the bank and the tops extending out into the stream, were not particularly troublesome, since they could be easily spotted and avoided. If necessary, a boat could brush against a sawyer without ill effect. Snags, or tree parts with one end securely anchored in the river bottom, were the biggest menace in the Sandy River. Snags were immobile and hard to see, for many times they were broken off below the water surface.

The outstanding peculiarity of the Missouri River was its shallowness. The river for much of its course flows through the northern Great Plains region, an area of comparatively light precipitation. The waters of the Missouri begin either as melting snows or as runoff from spring and early summer rains. The normal snowfall at most points in the northern Great Plains is a scant twenty inches. The deepest snow of the river basin is found in the limited area near the headwaters of the Missouri and its principal tributary, the Yellowstone. Snow in these high altitudes of the Rockies may amount to two hundred inches during a winter. Rain, the second source of moisture, occurs mostly on the level plains region bordering the river. Generally, the amount of rainfall increases at successive downstream points. For example, the average annual rainfall is about twelve to fourteen inches near Fort Benton, twenty-six inches at Sioux City, and about forty inches near the mouth of the Missouri.[8]

The two annual rises of the Missouri, a peculiarity of the river, are both a combination of the melting snows and the rains. The first, or April rise, occurring anywhere from mid-March to mid-April, is caused by the melting of snows on the lower slopes of the Rockies and in the northern Great Plains and by the early spring rains which occur from the Dakotas southward. The April rise has but a minimum effect above the mouth of the Yellowstone, but increases steadily as it is fed by the downstream tributaries such as the Yellowstone, the Cheyenne, the Niobrara, Big Sioux, Platte, and Kansas rivers.

The April rise, which usually declined in mid-May on the Upper Missouri, was followed by the second, or June rise. This rise, caused by the melting of the high-altitude Rocky Mountain snows and the late spring rains on the plains, occurred anywhere from mid-May to around July 1. This second rise was particularly important to those who navigated the Rocky River, since it was the primary source of water for the extreme Upper Missouri. The strength and duration of the June rise on the Rocky River was directly proportionate to the amount of snow in the mountains; it could last anywhere from a few days to several weeks or more.

The condition of the Missouri River in spring could vary from that of no rise, as in the season of 1863, to that of uncontrollable floods, as in 1881. Most normally, however, the two rises were moderate, providing an almost continuous navigation season from mid-March to late June. After the June rise, the river dropped sharply, and the ordinary late summer and fall were without significant rainfall. While the aridity was felt along the entire length of the Upper Missouri, it was most severely felt on the Rocky River, where nearly every season navigation was closed by inadequate water, rather than by the fall freeze-up.

On the Sandy River the navigation period, although longer than that on the Rocky River, was still relatively short. The long period of closed navigation because of ice gave the Upper Missouri river trade a decidedly seasonal nature when compared to that of the Lower Mississippi and other southern rivers. The breakup on the Upper Missouri came anywhere from March 20 to April 15, and oftentimes was accompanied by destructive ice floes, ice jams, and local flooding. The permanent closing of the channel usually took place in late November or early December on the Upper Missouri, although during the last half of November the river was many times temporarily closed by ice floes.

Not all of the problems of navigating the Upper Missouri were attributable to the river. The high prairie winds, a feature of the plains country, would often blow steadily throughout the course of a day at twenty to thirty miles an hour. Such winds would occasionally blow boats onto sandbars or into the banks, would force officers to tie boats up for fear of capsizing, and would ripple the water, making the channel difficult to follow by obscuring snags and sandbars. During the rainy season, storm fronts capable of spawning tornadoes were not infrequent.

The Missouri River was used by six or seven generations of navigators; each of these generations learned the river through trial and error, and through the experience of their predecessors. Early navigators, with their simple, maneuverable craft, worked predominantly with the stream; later navigators, attempting to transfer advanced craft from eastern streams to the unpredictable Missouri, were confronted with what seemed to be almost insurmountable problems. The solution to the problems lay not only in understanding the Missouri but in adapting the boats to it. Once navigators learned to cope with the Missouri's eccentricities, they plied its shallow waters for over a century.

II

The Extension of Steamboating from St. Louis to Fort Benton

THE HISTORY of pioneer steamboat navigation on the Missouri began in 1819 with the government-sponsored Yellowstone Expedition and lasted until 1860, when the first boat reached Fort Benton, the head of navigation. The first attempt to extend this established means of transportation to the Missouri came from the federal government. Although the government failed in its initial effort to navigate the Missouri with steamers, privately owned fur companies seized upon the idea, and with their broader knowledge of the river, managed to employ the steamboat practically on the Missouri. The final extension of steamboating to the head of navigation must, however, be indirectly credited to the federal government. It was vigorous government activity in the area of the headwaters of the Missouri and the promise of lucrative government transportation contracts that made the idea of navigating to Fort Benton attractive to Pierre Chouteau, Jr. And even then, it took more than Chouteau's intimate knowledge of the river to make the attempt successful; the boat that Chouteau managed to push to the head of navigation was a carefully designed "mountain boat," a steamer much different from any of those employed by the ill-fated Yellowstone Expedition.

The Yellowstone Expedition, hurriedly organized in 1818 and early 1819, had as its principal objective the construction of posts at the Mandan villages and the mouth of the Yellowstone to serve as a bulwark against British penetration into American territory. It was Secretary of War John C. Calhoun who decided to use steamboats to carry the supplies and the scientific party that was to accompany the expedition, despite the fact that steamers had never been used on the Missouri River.[1]

5

Of the four boats used on the expedition, only one, the *Western Engineer*, was specially designed for shallow-water navigation. This government-built boat, constructed at Pittsburgh over the winter of 1818/19, was only seventy-five feet long and thirteen feet wide, and drew only nineteen inches. The other three vessels were supplied by a civilian contractor, James Johnson of Kentucky, and had been built for use on the Ohio River.[2] The expedition was handicapped not only by unsuitable boats but also by the lack of experienced Missouri River steamboat pilots. Prior to the Yellowstone Expedition, only one steamer, the *Independence*, had ventured upon the waters of the Missouri. And that boat, under the command of a Captain Nelson of Louisville, had ascended only to the villages of Franklin and Chariton, about two hundred miles above St. Louis in May of 1819.[3]

Since the government made no real attempt to secure shallow-draft boats for the expedition, it would seem that it would have made every effort to take advantage of the spring rises. Such was not the case. The expedition did not start up the Missouri until June 21, fully three months after the desirable starting time.[4] This late start was probably due to underestimating the nature of the river and to the many unforeseen delays encountered in assembling the *Western Engineer*, the Johnson boats, and the 1,100 escort troops and supplies in St. Louis.

Stephen H. Long, the commander of the expedition and the navigator of the *Western Engineer*, managed to steam his boat as far as the Council Bluff in an ordeal which lasted from June 21 to September 19. Despite its slow progress, the *Western Engineer* was easily the most successful of the four boats. The first of the Johnson craft managed to struggle just past the mouth of the Kansas River, the second to just below the mouth of the Kansas, and the third got only as far as the mouth of the Osage. The contractor's boats were so slow moving that the troops pulling keelboats constantly ran ahead of them.

The *Western Engineer* ran aground time and time again; within two miles of the mouth of the Missouri, she grounded twice on the same sandbar. This continual grounding was not due to the draft of the boat, but can be attributed to the navigator's ignorance of the stream. The boat also had trouble stemming the rapid currents in chutes. Most of the time it was necessary for the crew to cordelle, or tow, the boat across the bars and through the main currents.[5]

The steamer's boilers repeatedly clogged with mud and sand. Often they had to be cleaned more than once a day, which meant that a stop had to be made so the boilers could cool down enough for a man to enter and clean them. Long soon devised a method of blowing the boilers out with a tube, a convenient expedient, but still time-consuming. And there were other troubles. The abrasive action of the sandy water damaged the engine valves, and Long had to stop six days at Franklin to make repairs. Obtaining fuel was yet another problem. Since wood was available at only an occasional settlement, the boat often had to halt so the crew could go ashore to gather or cut wood. Had this problem been foreseen, wood could have been cut and stockpiled earlier, saving Long valuable time. Not only was there a problem of getting wood but there was the problem of getting the right kind. After much experimentation, Long discovered that the most satisfactory fuel, when it could be found, was dry mulberry wood.[6]

The failures of steamboats on the Yellowstone Expedition are understandable. It is amazing that the War Department expected so much from them on their trial run on the Missouri. Neither the boats nor the men who operated them were ready for the Missouri River in 1819. The boats, with the exception of the *Western Engineer*, were heavy draft and cumbersome. Moreover, their engines were not powerful enough to overcome the current in the Missouri River chutes. The navigators encountered obstacles that could have been avoided with experience.

The government within a few years undoubtedly would have been able to navigate the Missouri if it had chosen to continue the experiment. Instead, the failures of the expedition, and the scandals connected with it, were so humiliating that the government made no more attempts to use steamers on the Missouri River until the fur companies proved them adequate. In fact, a second Yellowstone Expedition, authorized by Congress in 1824, relied exclusively on keelboats to transport its men and supplies upriver.

Although this first effort by the government to navigate the Upper Missouri with steamers failed, traffic on the Lower Missouri flourished. The river continued to serve as the access road for the undeveloped western area. Reaching out from St. Louis, the fur business rapidly expanded, and settlement moved west along the Missouri Valley to Independence and Westport. Hundreds of emigrants passed through St. Louis, traveling upriver to Independence, the jumping-off point for the Oregon and Sante Fe trails. In 1829, regular steam packet service to Independence began. By 1831 there were five regular packets on the Lower Missouri; by 1836 the number had increased to fifteen or twenty.[7]

The fur trade, dominated by the American Fur Company and its successors, was the major business on the Upper Missouri from the late 1820's until 1862. The need to carry supplies into the unsettled region and the need for reliable downriver transportation of increasing quantities of furs initially interested the companies in the possibility of steam navigation on the Upper Missouri. First Kenneth McKenzie of the American Fur Company, then Pierre Chouteau, Jr., experimented with the steamboat.

The years from 1831 to 1860, during which the fur companies succeeded in extending steam navigation on the Missouri some three thousand miles to Fort Benton, can be divided roughly into two periods. The first period, 1831–c. 1853, was marked by a concentration of the fur trading activity at Fort Union. During this time steamers navigated the river to Fort Union, but keelboats and mackinaws were still used above that point. In the second period, c. 1853–1860, Fort Benton became the goal of the steamboats.

The American Fur Company, which controlled the fur trade during the 1830's, was dominated by Kenneth McKenzie, self-styled "King of the Missouri." Hiram M. Chittenden, a leading historian of the fur trade, described McKenzie as "the ablest trader the American Fur Company ever possessed."[8] McKenzie first appeared on the St. Louis scene in 1822 when he organized the Columbia Fur Company. McKenzie's company proved such a threat to the American Fur Company's Western Department that they offered to buy him out. In 1827 they managed to purchase the Columbia Fur Company, and took McKenzie into their organization. McKenzie, by virtue of his energy and driving ambition, succeeded in establishing the American Fur Company in the remote region of the Upper Missouri and Yellowstone in the five years from 1827 to 1832. It is not surprising that from McKenzie came the idea of cutting costs and enlarging trade by using steamboats to supply the posts on the Upper Missouri.[9]

Although McKenzie was aware of the difficulties of navigating the Missouri, he failed to realize that the steamboat, as it then existed, was designed for use on deeper eastern rivers, rivers which were placid and slow moving, and which maintained a good stage of water and a consistent channel during most of the navigation season. The steamboat was going through a series of improvements, modifications, and adaptations on the Mississippi and Ohio rivers at approximately the same time that the American Fur Company decided to experiment with a steamer on the Upper Missouri.

McKenzie was convinced, however, that steamers on the Missouri would be economical, speedy, and convenient, and he approached Pierre Chouteau, Jr., the company's principal St. Louis agent, with the idea. Chouteau, after some persuasion by McKenzie, presented the proposal in a letter to the company's headquarters in New York in August, 1830. In his letter, Chouteau recounted the losses, delays, and expenses incurred by the use of keelboats. He suggested that a small steamboat which would be able to navigate the Missouri could be built for about $7,000. The steamboat, Chouteau believed, could carry as much as several keelboats, which would mean that the number of voyageurs employed by the company could be decreased. The greatest difficulty, Chouteau assumed, would come from the breakdown of machinery, but this he proposed to remedy by providing the steamer with a complete blacksmith outfit.[10]

The plan to use steamboats was strenuously opposed by Bernard Pratte and J. H. Cabanne, prominent St. Louisians who had an interest in the American Fur Company, because they felt the Upper Missouri could not be navigated by heavy boats.[11] However, the New York officials were impressed with Chouteau's arguments, and immediately hired a Louisville contractor to build a vessel. The sidewheeler, constructed during the winter of 1830/31 and christened the Yellowstone, was 130 feet long, had a 19-foot beam and a 6-foot hold, and was powered by a single engine.[12] The Yellowstone drew six feet when loaded to seventy-five tons. It is surprising that the boat had such a heavy draft, because by that time most builders of boats for western rivers had recognized the need for light-draft vessels.

The Yellowstone was delivered to St. Louis on April 10, 1831, and preparations were hastily made for the intended trip to Fort Union at the mouth of the Yellowstone. A writer for the St. Louis Beacon ventured the opinion that "should the company succeed in reaching this point with their boat, we have good reason for believing that success will repay them for all the expense, and toil, and risk, which must necessarily attend them, and we shall have the pleasure of beholding it what was thought the other day, was reserved for the next generation."[13]

The *Yellowstone*, commanded by Captain B. Young, left St. Louis on April 20, 1831, with the annual supplies for the company posts. The boat proceeded rapidly upstream and passed the Council Bluff without serious incident. The first serious delay was experienced at the end of May near the mouth of the Niobrara River when low water caused a prolonged halt. Chouteau, who was a passenger on the boat, was greatly perturbed, and sent to Fort Tecumseh (about ten miles below the present Fort Pierre, South Dakota) for lighters to take on part of the *Yellowstone's* cargo. After being relieved of some of the cargo, the boat got under way again and reached Fort Tecumseh on June 19. The *Yellowstone* could not go above Fort Tecumseh. It returned to St. Louis on July 15 with a cargo of buffalo robes, furs, peltries, and ten thousand pounds of buffalo tongues.[14]

The limited success of the *Yellowstone* was disappointing to McKenzie and Chouteau. Pratte and Cabanne, who had opposed the scheme in the first place, referred to the experiment as an expense for nothing.[15]

The investment in the steamboat had already been made, however, and an effort to reach Fort Union was made again in 1832. The *Yellowstone* left St. Louis on March 26 with the artist George Catlin on board. Catlin left a vivid, if somewhat exuberant, record of his trip into Indian territory on board the *Yellowstone*. He described the steamer as "puffing and blowing, and paddling, and rushing" past the Indian villages along the river. Catlin recorded that the steamer carried one 12-pound cannon and three or four 8-pound swivels which were to be delivered to Fort Union. The American Fur Company was apparently very anxious to impress the Indians with a display of power, as the cannon and swivels were fired near every Indian village. Catlin noted that the discharge of the swivels "threw the inhabitants into utter confusion and amazement—some of them threw their faces to the ground and cried to the Great Spirit—some of them shot their horses and dogs, and sacrificed them to appease the Great Spirit whom they conceived was offended—some deserted their villages, and ran to the tops of the bluffs some miles distant."[16]

The *Yellowstone* traveled the 1,800 miles to Fort Union without great difficulty, arriving about June 17.[17] After the crew exchanged supplies for furs and peltries, they returned to St. Louis. The *Yellowstone's* success in 1832 was partially attributable to a much earlier start having been made than in 1831. This enabled the boat's officers to take advantage of both the April and June rises.

The *Yellowstone's* voyage of 1832 was an important landmark in Upper Missouri steamboat navigation. It established the practicality of steamboating to the satisfaction of the American Fur Company, and, in that year, the company approved the addition of a second steamboat, the *Assiniboine*, to the Missouri River trade. This boat was a single-engine stern-wheeler built under the superintendence of Captain Bernard Pratte, Jr., son of one of the company's owners. The *Assiniboine* joined the *Yellowstone* in the Missouri fur trade in 1833.[18]

In 1834, Astor sold his interest in the American Fur Company to Bernard Pratte, Sr., and Pierre Chouteau, Jr., both of whom had been associated with the Upper Missouri Outfit, a subdepartment of the American Fur Company. Pratte and Chouteau operated for the four-year period 1834–1838 as Pratte, Chouteau, & Company. In 1838 control of the company passed to Pierre Chouteau, Jr., and the company was reorganized as Pierre Chouteau Jr. & Company.[19] Chouteau became the leading force in the development of the Upper Missouri trade from 1838 until 1865.

During his twenty-seven years as head of the largest trading company on the Upper Missouri, Pierre Chouteau, Jr., did much more than engage in the fur trade. A vigorous, active businessman, Chouteau had an intimate knowledge of the river and of the Indians in the Upper Missouri area. His detailed knowledge was often sought by federal officials. Not only did the government seek information from Chouteau, but they also relied heavily upon his steamers for the delivery of Indian annuities and government supplies to points along the river.

After the success of the *Yellowstone* in 1832, Chouteau sent at least one steamboat a year to Fort Union, the fur trading capital of the Upper Missouri. Steamers rarely went above that point. As long as the fur trade was concentrated at Fort Union, there was no driving need to extend steamboating to the head of navigation. Most of the furs received at Fort Benton came in so late in the spring and in such meager quantities that it was much easier to ship them downstream to Fort Union by mackinaw than to try to navigate a steamboat between Fort Union and Fort Benton, the shallowest part of the Missouri.

During the years of the St. Louis to Fort Union trade, Chouteau and his fellow navigators learned a great deal about the nature of the Upper Missouri and the problems that had to be solved in order to successfully navigate it. Although Chouteau knew that the shallow-draft mountain boats were more efficient on the Upper Missouri, he apparently considered it more economical at that time to charter regular Mississippi River or Lower Missouri River boats than to build his own. After the *Assiniboine* burned in 1835 and the *Yellowstone* was no longer in use, Chouteau chartered steamers such as the *Robert Campbell*, the *St. Ange*, the *Highland Mary*, the *Banner*, and the *El Paso*. The annual boat usually did not leave St. Louis until in May, but in spite of this late start, managed to reach Fort Union each season. On occasion, if the river was exceptionally good when a boat reached Union, it would venture on upstream simply to see how far it could ascend. The highest point reached on the Missouri by steamer before 1859 was El Paso Point just past the mouth of the Milk River, about three hundred miles above the mouth of the Yellowstone. This point was reached in 1850 by the chartered steamer *El Paso*, commanded by Captain John Duroc.[20] The decision to steam beyond Fort Union was made as a result of Duroc's zeal to set a record, and Chouteau's desire to experiment during a period of advantageously high water.

It was no small achievement to navigate these heavy-draft boats to Fort Union. Navigators found it necessary to resort to warping, sparring, and even double-tripping to get their boats and cargoes upstream.

Warping consisted of tying a line to a tree or a "deadman," usually a large cottonwood log fixed firmly in the sand, and then pulling the boat forward by taking up the line with a small steam-powered winch colloquially called the "nigger engine." This particular process was slow and sometimes dangerous, as lines could snap and severly injure deckhands. In sparring, two poles, one on each side of the bow, were placed in the sand and angled toward the front of the boat. Each spar was connected to the steam winch by a line. By taking up the line, the boat was lifted up and pulled forward. Since a boat elevated above the sandbar by its poles resembled a squatting grasshopper, the spars were called "grasshopper poles" and the process of sparring was "grasshoppering." Each time a boat was moved forward, the poles would have to be reset and the entire action repeated. This process, too, could be dangerous, since there was no assurance that the wooden spars would hold the weight of the boat, and a broken spar could cause serious accidents or delays. In order for sparring and warping to work effectively, the sand had to be loose and easily moved.

In some places, where the stream was shallow and flowed over solid bottoms, warping or sparring would not work, since the boat could not be dragged over a hard bottom, nor the spars set into the bottom. Here steamboat men would have to either use their auxiliary boats or lighters, or else resort to double-tripping. Most steamboats carried from two to four flat-bottomed mackinaws for lifeboats; these were frequently used as lighters. In double-tripping, the mackinaws were used to remove part of the steamer's cargo to shore. The lightened steamer would then carry the remainder of the cargo beyond the trouble spot, where it would be unloaded on shore. The boat then returned and picked up the first half of its load. Sometimes two or three days were wasted in double-tripping. Most of this double-tripping took place near the mouth of the Niobrara, a notoriously difficult stretch on the Sandy River.

Debris in the channel and the gritty water of the Sandy River created other problems. Because of the prevalence of snags and sawyers, Upper Missouri steamboat men found that they could not normally navigate at night, as their contemporaries on the Lower Mississippi did. The only night-time navigation on the Missouri came during rare occasions of excellent water on a clear moonlit night. Missouri River navigators also had to contend with more plugged water lines and boiler valves then other steamboat men did because of the high silt content of the Missouri River. The continual need to clean boilers occasioned many delays.

Steamboat progress on the Upper Missouri was also slowed down by the lack of professional woodcutters. Since the country was uninhabited except for widely separated fur trading posts, the first steamboat men had to cut their own wood or else get their fuel supply by snagging driftwood from the river or gathering it on sandbars. There was a daily wood problem, as a steamboat used about twenty-five to thirty cords of wood for every twenty-four running hours.[21]

During the 1850's, a series of events occurred which marked the beginning of a shift in economic focus in the Upper Missouri area from Fort Union to Fort Benton. In 1853, the government sponsored the Stevens-Mullan Expedition to conduct a preliminary railroad survey; in 1855 an important treaty with the Blackfeet was concluded, the first step in an attempt to safeguard exploration and surveying in the area near the headwaters of the Missouri; in 1859, the government sent out the Raynolds Expedition on an exploring mission in the area. Chouteau was deeply interested in the government's activity in the Fort Benton area, for he had a virtual monopoly of the trade on the Upper Missouri and stood to profit heavily by cornering government transportation contracts. It was this government activity, combined with a simultaneous development of the fur trade in the Fort Benton region that led to the final conquest of the Missouri to the head of navigation.

The Congress of the United States, interested in the possibility of connecting the Mississippi River and the Pacific Ocean by transcontinental railroads, in March of 1853 appropriated $150,000 for the purpose of making railroad surveys.[22] Franklin Pierce and his Secretary of War, Jefferson Davis, both vitally interested in westward expansion, decided to conduct four surveys with the appropriation. Pierce appointed his friend and political supporter Isaac I. Stevens to head the Northern Pacific survey, or the Stevens-Mullan Expedition, which was to be conducted "from St. Paul or some eligible point on the Upper Mississippi, to Puget Sound."[23] This proposed route was to pass through Fort Benton. Government officials and traders alike assumed that Fort Benton would one day be reached by steamers, and the proposed railroad would then connect the Missouri with the Columbia River and the Pacific Ocean.

Stevens, who was also given the appointment of first territorial governor of Washington, organized his main party at St. Paul, but a detachment headed by Lieutenants Mullan and Donaldson started from St. Louis. Mullan's main responsibility was to superintend the transportation of supplies for the expedition. These supplies, along with Mullan's group, were transported on the Chouteau-chartered boat, the *Robert Campbell*. Mullan's detachment waited at Fort Union for the arrival of Stevens from St. Paul, and then the force attempted to take the *Campbell* to Fort Benton. The group managed to pilot the boat to a point about seventy miles above Fort Union. Here her progress was halted by sandbars. The expedition was then forced to proceed to Fort Benton on foot and by keelboat.[24]

In 1855, the government, interested in pacifying Indians in the headwaters area of the Missouri, scheduled a council to meet near Fort Benton. Chouteau was awarded the contract to deliver the goods for the council. These gifts were carried upriver in the spring of 1855 by the steamer *St. Mary* as far as Fort Union. At Fort Union, the goods were transferred to mackinaws. The slow progress of the supply-laden mackinaws led the government agents to change the assembly grounds to a point near the mouth of the Judith River. By October, some two thousand Indians had assembled. Blackfeet, Piegans, and Gros Ventres took part in the ten-day meeting, which was successfully terminated in late October with the signing of a treaty providing for the establishment of a Blackfeet Agency.[25]

The provisions of the contract of 1855 calling for the delivery of the goods to the Blackfeet Council were particularly profitable to Chouteau's company. Chouteau, who for a number of years had been transporting government Indian annuities to points between Fort Pierre and Fort Union, in 1855 was given four and three-fourths cents a pound on these regular annuities. But on the special goods destined for the council at Fort Benton, he was paid thirteen and three-fourths cents per pound. Since the word "destined" was used in the contract, Chouteau had only to make all necessary efforts to reach the head of navigation. He was not actually required to deliver the treaty goods at that point.[26]

In 1859, Chouteau made a real attempt to reach Fort Benton with a steamboat by constructing a "mountain boat," the *Chippewa*. The construction of this boat, the first specifically designed to reach the head of navigation, was immediately prompted by two government contracts awarded to Chouteau in that year. The first contract, with Acting Indian Commissioner Charles Mix, called for the delivery of annuities to Fort Union, Fort Sarpy, and Fort Benton (which had been designated as the Blackfeet Agency in 1855). Chouteau was to be paid $2.50 per hundred pounds on the freight from St. Louis to Fort Union, and $7.25 per hundred from Fort Union to Fort Benton.[27] The second contract called for the transportation of Major W. F. Raynolds' military reconnaissance party. Raynolds had been ordered to explore "the mountain region about the sources of the Yellowstone and Missouri, to ascertain the character of the routes leading south and west from the navigable parts of those rivers."[28] The apparent intention of the federal government in organizing the Raynolds Expedition was to encourage development of the Upper Missouri and

Yellowstone through a preliminary geographical study which would be of use to traders and settlers as well as subsequent military forces.

Raynolds organized his professional staff in Washington, D.C., before making further arrangements in St. Louis, and then completed his outfit at Fort Leavenworth and St. Joseph. Raynolds met the heavily laden Chouteau steamers, *Spread Eagle* and *Chippewa*, on June 4 at St. Joseph and began the first leg of his journey. The two boats, which had left St. Louis on May 28, were loaded with the annual shipment of supplies for Pierre Chouteau Jr. & Company, annuities for the Upper Missouri and Blackfoot Agencies, goods for the Sioux at Fort Pierre, supplies for Mullan's wagon road force, and Raynolds' complete outfit, including animals, provisions, and camp equipment.[29] The steamers traveled only during the day, and above Sioux City were forced to stop daily to procure wood.

Raynolds and his party left the Chouteau steamers at Fort Pierre and proceeded overland for Fort Sarpy on the Yellowstone. After Raynolds' party disembarked on June 18, the two steamers continued upriver to Fort Union, where Raynolds' supplies were unloaded and stored.

Charles P. Chouteau, son of Pierre Chouteau, Jr., had accompanied the steamers on the trip with the assignment of pressing on to the head of navigation if the condition of the river above Fort Union made the plan feasible. Chouteau made his attempt with the *Chippewa*. The boat was a small stern-wheeler, 165 feet long and 30 feet wide, with a tonnage of approximately 350. It drew only thirty-one inches when heavily loaded, and was equipped with a powerful high-pressure engine.[30]

By the time Chouteau had the *Chippewa* built, the pattern of light-draft steamers was well established on the Ohio and Mississippi rivers. Early steamboats, designed by engineers whose experience had been in the construction of ocean-going vessels, were extremely heavy and solidly built. Since river craft were not subjected to pounding ocean waves and wind, lighter construction was practical, and after the 1820's the boats intended for use on the western rivers were made as light draft as possible. Lightness of draft was achieved not only by using lighter construction materials but also by broadening the beam of the craft. Steamers were also lighter after the 1820's because of the diminished size and weight of engines.[31]

One of the most important advances in steam navigation was the conversion to the high-pressure engine. Early steamboats used low-pressure, condensing engines of the same type which were commonly used industrially. Such engines carried pressures of but a few pounds per square inch and were extremely large and heavy. The high-pressure engine was more compact than the low-pressure engine, more powerful, cheaper to build, and simpler to operate and maintain. The first boat described as a "regular high-pressure boat" was the *Washington*, designed by Henry Shreve and built in 1816. The performance of the *Washington* was amazing and after that time, the trend toward the use of high-pressure engines was rapid. By 1840, engines that carried pressures up to 100 pounds per square inch were in common use.[32]

Although some critics claimed that high-pressure engines were more dangerous than low-pressure engines, navigators felt that the treacherous nature of western rivers made the more powerful engine a necessity. They realized that the high-pressure engine had more reserve power than the low-pressure engine, making it possible to stem the rapids and contend with the numerous sandbars in the shallow rivers.[33]

Chouteau's *Chippewa* was a stern-wheeler, as were, eventually, most of the mountain boats. The builders of steamboats went from side-wheel to stern-wheel back to side-wheel. The opinion which finally emerged from this cycle of experimentation was that the side-wheels were more graceful in appearance, contributed to the balance of the boat, and made the boat easier to maneuver in most instances, whereas the stern-wheel was a "working" boat's wheel. Stern-wheels proved particularly advantageous on small steamers used primarily for cargo purposes in the shallower, narrower rivers such as the Missouri, and on certain parts of the Mississippi. Stern-wheelers had the obvious advantage of narrower construction, and their paddle wheels were less apt to be damaged by snags and floating objects. The stern-wheel was also advantageous on the cargo boat because it left more space for cargo and made loading easier.[34]

For his trip above Fort Union, Charles Chouteau made careful preparations. He chose John LaBarge, one of the company's key men, as captain of the *Chippewa* and carefully selected a crew of ninety-five men, many of whom were experienced voyageurs well acquainted with the Upper Missouri. Chouteau also had two ninety-foot mackinaws of forty-five tons capacity lashed to the sides of the *Chippewa* to serve as lighters in the event they were needed.[35] One hundred and sixty tons of freight had been transferred by the crew from the *Spread Eagle* to the *Chippewa*, and Chouteau ordered the captain of the *Spread Eagle* to wait at Fort Union for the return of the smaller boat.

LaBarge started the *Chippewa* upriver for Fort Benton on July 1. Five days later, at three o'clock on the afternoon of July 6, the boat passed the mouth of the Milk River and shortly thereafter reached El Paso Point.[36] The water was so shallow near El Paso Point that the *Chippewa's* crew spent much of the afternoon of July 6 and most of the next day in lightening the steamer and sparring. Despite the obstacles encountered at El Paso Point, the men on board the *Chippewa* demonstrated their joy upon entering virgin steamboat waters by shouting and firing the cannon.[37]

The remainder of the voyage to Fort Brule was difficult. The river was choked with snags, and the two cumbersome mackinaws had to be shifted many times. After the steamer entered the Rocky River, rapids presented the greatest problem; LaBarge's men spent two entire days, July 13 and 14, negotiating the dangerous Dauphin's Rapids. After dropping one of the mackinaws on July 15 and the second the next day in order to lessen the drag, the *Chippewa* struggled to the mouth of the Marias River by 8 A.M. of July 17, and by early afternoon reached Fort Brule, only twelve miles below Fort Benton.[38]

Fort Brule was the highest point reached by the *Chippewa* in 1859. On the afternoon of July 17 Chouteau visited Fort Benton. The following day he returned to the steamer in a skiff, and he noted that there was but three and one-half feet of water in the deepest portion of the river. Chouteau also reconnoitered timbered points but found the wood too green for fuel. Since the only supply of dry fuel was a considerable distance downstream, Chouteau abandoned any hopes of actually reaching Fort Benton and ordered the *Chippewa* to unload at Brule. After leaving instructions that quantities of cordwood be prepared for the next season, Chouteau headed the *Chippewa* downstream at 2 P.M. on July 18.[39]

On its descent, the *Chippewa* was nearly wrecked on boulders at Dauphin's Rapids, and some fifty miles farther downstream, at Bird's Rapids, the boat was again pounded and beaten by the current. The battered, leaking vessel was hung up time and time again on sandbars and was tormented by high winds on the remainder of the trip.

After reaching St. Louis, Charles Chouteau optimistically summed up the *Chippewa's* voyage in his report to the Secretary of War. Chouteau wrote: "by my present experience I have arrived at the conclusion that with suitable boats and the removal of boulders here and there obstructing the channel and forming the rapids, that the navigation of the Upper Missouri can be made just as safe and easy as the Upper Mississippi and Ohio rivers, and I have no hesitation in affirming that the trip from Saint Louis to Fort Benton can be easily accomplished within thirty-five days."[40]

The next year, Pierre Chouteau Jr. & Company's two steamers, the *Chippewa* and *Key West*, reached Fort Benton on July 2, thereby establishing the navigability of nearly three thousand miles of the Missouri River.[41] Navigation on the Upper Missouri, however, was never as safe and easy, nor as speedy, as Charles Chouteau envisioned it, and it changed radically in character over the years. Nevertheless, it remained the backbone for the economic development of portions of the Upper Missouri area for nearly eighty more years.

III

The Expansion of Steamboating
on the Upper Missouri, 1861–1864

WHEN CHOUTEAU sent his first steamers to Fort Benton, he did so because he was interested not only in the fur trade but also in the profitable business of supplying and transporting goods for the military activity near the headwaters of the Missouri. Within five years after the first boat reached Benton, events transpired which changed even further the nature of the transportation business on the Upper Missouri River. In 1859 Dakota Territory was opened, and the land seekers moved into what is now southeastern South Dakota. In 1862, the Sioux Uprising took place in western Minnesota, followed by extensive military campaigns in the Upper Missouri area. By the end of the campaigns, the gold rush into Montana was underway. Steamboats on the Upper Missouri had then to serve not only the fur companies and the military, but also the miners and settlers who moved westward.

In the 1850's, the agricultural frontier was extended into western Iowa, and with the farmers came investors, realtors, lawyers, and town planners. The men who platted Sioux City in northwestern Iowa in 1855 chose its location carefully. The city was located at the eastern edge of the Indian lands and at the farthest extreme of surveyed land. It was also located at a point on the Missouri where the river channel bends to the northwest and the Big Sioux enters from the north. This river location promised a firm economic foundation for the city. Once Dakota Territory was opened, Sioux City would be the supply base for settlers in the area to the northwest of the city.

The Sioux City area was first surveyed by a government party under Dr. John K. Cook in 1854. After the completion of the survey,

Cook chose to settle in the area and, in 1855, became a member of the land syndicate that platted the town of Sioux City. This syndicate, known as the Sioux City Company, had some influential members: Iowa senators Augustus C. Dodge and George E. Jones, Congressman Bernhart Henn, and former territorial official, Jesse Williams.[1]

Sioux City grew rapidly; within a year after its platting it had a population of about four hundred and approximately ninety buildings had been erected.[2] The influence of the members of the Sioux City Company contributed greatly to the rapid growth of the city. A land office was established in Sioux City by Congress on March 3, 1855, and it opened in the fall of that year with Dr. S. P. Yeomans, a member of the Iowa legislature and a personal friend of Senator Jones, as register. The two senators also used their influence in 1856 to secure a land grant in aid for a proposed railroad from Dubuque to Sioux City.[3]

Sioux City was incorporated by the Iowa legislature on January 16, 1857, and by that time the town was a significant trading center for the Upper Missouri. Most of the provisions were brought in by steamboat from St. Louis for local wholesalers who traded up the Missouri from Sioux City. The most important trading firms in the town were those of Tootle & Jackson and Frost & Todd.

James A. Jackson, who had stores with Milton Tootle at Omaha and Council Bluffs as well as at Sioux City, was the first Sioux City businessman to employ a steamboat to carry freight from St. Louis. In 1856 Jackson went to St. Louis, where he chartered the *Omaha*, commanded by Captain Holland, for a sum reported to be $24,000. The *Omaha* arrived at the Sioux City levee with a cargo valued at $70,000, which included a sawmill, furniture, dry goods, hardware, and groceries.[4]

Only four steamers arrived at Sioux City in 1856, but the next year, thirty steamers docked at the town levee at the foot of Pearl Street. The average time for a trip from St. Louis to Sioux City was eight days and eighteen hours.[5] By 1860, the steamer *Florence*, commanded by Captain John Throckmorton, was running as a regular packet from St. Louis to Council Bluffs, Omaha, Sioux City, and Fort Randall.[6] Fort Randall, the terminus of the St. Louis packet service, was the only permanent military post on the Upper Missouri in 1860. The post was established in 1856 by General William S. Harney for the purpose of safeguarding the overland trails and pacifying the

Sioux.[7] This installation, located on the Missouri thirty miles above the mouth of the Niobrara, depended on steamboats for many of its supplies throughout its thirty-six-year history.

The largest wholesaling firm in Sioux City was Frost, Todd & Co. Frost and Todd not only engaged in local merchandising but also operated government-licensed trading posts on the Missouri as far as Fort Union and served as post sutlers at Fort Randall. The founders of the firm, David M. Frost and John B. S. Todd, pioneered the movement of settlers into the Indian lands above Sioux City. In 1857 they established trading posts at Vermillion and at the mouth of the James River,[8] and they were among the first to take up residency in Dakota Territory after it was officially opened for settlement in 1859.

The Upper Missouri Land Company, which was formed at Sioux City in February, 1858, was instrumental in the opening of Dakota Territory.[9] The company, comprised of many prominent Sioux City businessmen including Frost and Todd, Dr. Cook, and Dr. Yeomans, attempted to gain a cession of the Yankton Sioux Indian lands, and with the help of Charles F. Picotte, an educated French-Yankton half-breed, were successful in persuading the Yankton chiefs to cede most of their land east of the Missouri for a reservation tract and annuity payments.[10]

The Yankton Sioux signed an official treaty with the government in 1858, but Dakota was not officially opened to settlers until July 10, 1859.[11] Some of the Indians were reluctant to move from their village site, but possible conflict was averted when the Indian agent, Major A. H. Redfield, arrived with the steamer Carrier loaded with food, calico, blankets, plows, wagons, mowers, and a saw and grist mill. Redfield also carried large sums of money, reported by Kingsbury to be "many thousands of dollars in gold and silver coin"[12] to be paid to the Yankton Sioux as part of the government obligation under the treaty of 1858.

Redfield stopped the Carrier at the Yankton village for several hours but would not deliver the annuities. After the Indians agreed to move to the reservation about forty miles up the Missouri, the heavily laden Carrier proceeded to the agency at Greenwood, while the Indians traveled along the river banks within sight of the boat.[13]

The Upper Missouri Land Company was reorganized in 1859 as the Yankton Land and Town Company with Todd as president. The company immediately started platting the townsite of Yankton, which was named after the Yankton branch of the Sioux Indians.[14] Yankton was located at a point on the Missouri River where the banks were not steep and where the deep channel was next to the Dakota side of the Missouri. These conditions created a good natural landing which contributed greatly to Yankton's importance as a steamboat port for many years.

As soon as the area was opened and the town of Yankton platted, merchants and promoters began agitating for territorial organization. Todd lobbied in Washington in 1860 and 1861, and the Territory of Dakota was created March 2, 1861, when President Buchanan signed the organic act. Yankton was made the capital of Dakota Territory by the first territorial governor, a position it held until 1883, when the capital was moved to Bismarck.[15]

The men who promoted the establishment of Yankton anticipated immediate growth. The town, by virtue of being the point of settlement farthest west on the Missouri, was a natural distribution point for supplies for southeastern Dakota. However, the expected flood of immigrants was inhibited by two factors, the Civil War, which started a month after Dakota was organized as a territory, and the Sioux Uprising. The event which most directly discouraged settlement in Dakota Territory was the uprising. In 1862, the Santee Sioux of southwestern Minnesota, led by Little Crow, started a war which threatened portions of Minnesota, Iowa, and Dakota. The Santee were immediately challenged by volunteers, militiamen, and federal troops. The military campaigns of 1862 were extensive and the war destructive, but by 1863 the Santees had either been captured or driven westward to the Missouri River, and the leaders tried and ordered hanged at Mankato. The government then proposed to dispose of the Indian problem by first removing some of the Minnesota Indians to a reservation along the Missouri and then by using military force on the renegades under Inkpaduta who had escaped into Dakota. Both of these plans depended on the navigation of the Upper Missouri River.

The plan simplest in execution was the removal of hostile Santee Sioux and a group of Winnebagoes from the state of Minnesota. On March 3, 1863, Congress passed an act which provided that "the sum of fifty thousand and sixteen dollars and sixty-six cents be appropriated to enable the President of the United States to remove the Sioux Indians of the Mississippi beyond the limits of any state." The same act also appropriated $50,000 for the removal of the Winnebago Indians to a "suitable location outside the limits of any state." On April 16, Pierre Chouteau Jr. & Co. signed a contract with Clark W. Thompson, Superintendent of Indian Affairs of the Northern Superintendency, to transport the Sioux and Winnebagoes from St. Paul to a reservation area along the Missouri River. The reservation site chosen by Thompson was at the mouth of Crow Creek, upriver from Fort Randall in the south-central part of Dakota Territory.[16]

Chouteau agreed to transport the Sioux and Winnebagoes from St. Paul to their Missouri River reservation for $25 per person and to provide them "with provisions and sustenance while being transferred for the sum of ten cents per head for each day while making the journey." He was to allow each Indian free transportation on baggage up to one hundred pounds, and Indian agents were to be transported free of charge. Chouteau was also required to provide seaworthy boats in sufficient number "to give said Indians ample space for comfort, health, and safety. . . ."[17]

It is unlikely that the Indians were comfortable on the steamers Chouteau chartered to transport them. In May, 1863, the steamer *Florence*, loaded with 1,400 Indians arrived at Yankton, where it stopped for several hours. It was the opinion of some of the visitors "that there was not an Indian on board that could be said to be free from some malady."[18]

On June 10 the *West Wind*, commanded by Captain Hooper, stopped at Yankton with 800 Santee Sioux Indians on board. The *Florence* later made a second trip for Chouteau on which she transported a group of Winnebagoes to Fort Thompson. Chouteau, in the summer of 1863, moved a total of 3,251 Indians to the reservation with his steamers.[19]

The second phase of government action against the Indians was begun during the winter of 1862/63 when General John Pope, Commander of the Department of the Northwest, planned a campaign which had as its goal the final subjugation of Little Crow and Inkpaduta. Pope believed that the Indians were massed near Devil's Lake in northeastern Dakota Territory and therefore proposed to trap them with two armies: one from the east led by General Henry Sibley, and another from the south by way of the Missouri River, led by General Alfred Sully. Thus Pope hoped to crush the Indians between the two armies as they came together on the Upper Missouri.[20]

Sully's army was organized at Sioux City and was to be supplied by four steamboats which had been chartered in St. Louis. The boats were late in arriving at Sioux City, delaying the expedition so much that it was still not in the field by June 9.[21] Sully's progress upstream was slow. None of the boats had ever been on the Upper Missouri, and none of them had been built for shallow streams. To complicate matters, because of an extended drought during the summer of 1863, the Missouri was even more shallow than usual.

Sully's boats spent most of June and July resting on the sandbars between Fort Randall and Fort Pierre, and in desperation, Sully persuaded the captains of two mountain steamers, the *Shreveport* and the *Alone,* to join his forces. The *Shreveport* and one of the chartered boats, the *Belle Peoria,* finally reached Fort LaFromboise (several miles above present-day Pierre, South Dakota) on August 1. By August 12, after some double-tripping from Crow Creek, General Sully had all of his boats at Fort Pierre, and had sent the *Shreveport* and the *Alone* ahead with supplies for a depot at Swan Lake about one hundred miles upriver.[22]

Pope was displeased with Sully's slow progress and did not accept poor transportation as sufficient reason for the delay. On August 5 Pope wrote to Sully: "I never had the slightest idea you could delay thus along the river, nor do I realize the necessity of such delay." Pope asserted that Sully should have used some of his 120 wagons and gone overland in order to meet with Sibley. He concluded,

"I never dreamed you would consider yourself tied to the boats if they were obstacles in going up the river. As matters now stand, it seems to me impossible to understand how you have staid about the river, delaying from day to day, when time of all things was important, and when you had wagons enough to carry at least two months' subsistence for your command."[23]

Pope ordered Sully to load his wagons with subsistence rations and proceed overland, but Sully had already been so delayed that it was impossible for him to coordinate with Sibley. Sibley moved across the plains, reaching the site of present-day Bismarck on August 29, and then, short on supplies, began the return to Minnesota.[24]

Sully moved up the Missouri some one hundred miles and then eastward, where he defeated the Sioux at the Battle of White Stone Hill on September 3. After this battle, Sully used the steamer *Alone* to transport the wounded downstream. He also established a new military fort on the Missouri about five miles below Fort Pierre on the east side of the river, naming it Fort Sully.[25] The Sully and Sibley campaigns of 1863 did not remove the Indian menace, and during the following season the armies were again put in the field.

Pope, in the winter of 1863/64 drew up a new plan for operations in the Indian country along the Missouri River. He proposed the construction of four new military posts, one on Devil's Lake, a second on the upper extremities of the James River due west of Coteau des Prairies, a third on the Missouri near Long Lake, and a fourth on the Yellowstone River near the trading post of Fort Alexander.[26] The last three posts were to be placed on or near the proposed emigrant routes from the Upper Mississippi and Missouri to the gold mines of Montana and Idaho.

In conjunction with the establishment of these posts, Pope ordered a campaign against the Yanktonnais, Teton, and Uncapapa Sioux, whom he believed were concentrated on the Upper Missouri above Grand River. Sully was ordered to provide for the security of the Iowa frontier and then move up the Missouri with 1,300 cavalry and four companies of infantry. Despite the poor performance of steamers in 1863, Pope directed that Sully's supplies be again carried by steamboat because he wanted Sully to operate along the river to keep the water route open to the Montana mines.[27]

Pope anticipated a heavy emigration to the gold mines in the season of 1864, and on March 14 published a request that prospective emigrants not proceed up the Missouri ahead of Sully's army. He warned that the Uncapapa and Teton Sioux would probably try to obstruct river navigation and suggested that steamboat men "communicate with General Sully, on the Upper Missouri river, and do not attempt to pass in advance of his forces until notified by him that it will be safe. As many as possible of the boats carrying emigrants should go together, under some sort of organization; and it will be found judicious to protect the vulnerable parts of the boats, by planking them so as to be bullet proof."[28]

Hoping to avoid delays, Sully went to St. Louis himself to make transportation arrangements. About March 10 he began what proved to be the difficult task of chartering boats. Sully was well acquainted with the Upper Missouri and knew that it could best be navigated with the specially constructed mountain boats, operated by experienced Upper Missouri navigators. His first step was to talk to Pierre

Chouteau, Jr., and his son Charles. The reliability of the Chouteaus was above question; they had the boats and the knowledge to work on the Upper Missouri. They had proven themselves masters of the Big Muddy on many occasions. Sully wanted to make an arrangement awarding the entire military contract to Chouteau, who was willing to transport all of the Yellowstone River freight at four cents a pound.[29]

But Sully's plan to use Chouteau steamers was vetoed by the Army Quartermaster in St. Louis, who had charge of military transportation contracts. Just why the quartermaster did not honor Sully's request is not clear. Sully later implied that the quartermaster felt that chartering was more economical than giving Chouteau a special contract.

Sully and the quartermaster apparently had differences of opinion on several matters. After the disagreement over the use of Chouteau's steamers, the two men disagreed as to what type of boats should be chartered for the expedition. Many of the boats in the St. Louis harbor had been impounded for military purposes, and their disposition was dependent upon the quartermaster. Sully felt that mountain steamers were essential for the maneuver, but the quartermaster seemed to think that almost any steamboat could be used.

At the end of March, Sully was still tied up with quartermaster red tape and knew that he could not possibly get steamers to Sioux City by May 1 to assemble the expedition, as he had planned.[30] In the meantime, a number of boats bound for the Montana mines left St. Louis with the opening of navigation rather than wait for a military escort. Sully's delay in getting steamers meant that one of the purposes of the expedition, to run ahead of the miners, could not possibly be carried out.

Sully spent nearly two months in St. Louis before his chartered steamers were loaded and ready to proceed to Sioux City. The delay in leaving St. Louis, according to Sully, was due not only to the slowness of the quartermaster but also to poor weather, which hindered the loading of the boats.[31]

In Sioux City, Sully met contingents of the Minnesota and Iowa militia and then started for the next assembly point at Farm Island, about four miles below present-day Pierre, South Dakota. Sully's original force of about 2,200 men had, as part of their equipment, two batteries, or twelve pieces, of artillery, and took with them three hundred teams and three hundred beef steers.[32] The major part of this force moved along the banks of the Missouri while the supplies were carried by steamers.

Sully succeeded in getting the boats and his party to Farm Island without serious incident. The island, on the edge of hostile territory, was the point where Dakota militiamen joined Sully and it also served as a supply depot. After supplies from the quartermaster at St. Louis were delivered there, Sully's force moved upstream in order to establish the first military post.

In a matter of eleven days, Sully moved by land and by river from Farm Island to the outlet of Long Lake, a distance of about two hundred miles. On July 7, Sully located Fort Rice—one of the four posts ordered constructed by Pope—on the west bank of the Missouri just above the outlet of Long Lake and about eight miles above the mouth of the Cannonball River. The supplies for Fort Rice were carried by seven steamers. After the boats were unloaded, Sully's men used them for three days to ferry Minnesota troops across the Missouri to the new fort. These troops had traveled overland from Minnesota in order to join Sully prior to his concerted move against the Sioux. While the troops were engaged in setting up the new post, Sully waited anxiously for the arrival of additional supplies from St. Louis. The quartermaster had made arrangements for the delivery of goods to the new post as part of a coordinated operation. This freight, however, was not delivered to Fort Rice, but instead, some one thousand tons of it were simply dumped on Farm Island. The supply situation was so confused that Sully claimed he did not know the names of the boats that had dumped goods at Farm Island or the nature of the cargoes.[33] Before Sully's troops could proceed, he had to send his steamers back down to Farm Island to pick up the supplies.

Sully spent nearly two weeks establishing Fort Rice and planning subsequent military operations. He planned to move to the northwest, marching his troops between the Heart and Cannonball rivers with the intention of engaging the Sioux near the headwaters of these streams. Sully then intended to come out on the Yellowstone River, where his army would be resupplied by steamers. Sully was aware of the fact that the Yellowstone had never been navigated by steamboats, but he also knew that the delivery of supplies was essential to his campaign. Sully had used the transportation provided by the quartermaster up to this point of the expedition, but he realized that only mountain boats would be able to navigate the Yellowstone. He therefore requisitioned the services of two of Chouteau's mountain boats, the *Alone* and the *Chippewa Falls*. Both vessels were very light draft; the *Chippewa Falls* drew only twelve inches light.[34] These boats were to be loaded at Fort Rice and were then to proceed immediately to the Yellowstone to await the arrival of the expedition.

While the steamers were moving upriver from Fort Rice, Sully was moving overland with a force of about 2,400 men. By the time he was ready to leave Fort Rice on July 18, he had a force of about 4,000. However, he left 1,600 men behind, some to remain as post garrison and some to serve as escorts for the *Alone* and the *Chippewa Falls*. Sully's expedition was complicated by a wagon train of about 250 emigrants which had joined him at Fort Rice. The emigrants, who were on their way to the Montana mines, were poorly equipped, and Sully was obliged to give them a military escort of about 400 men, leaving his actual tactical force at about 2,000.[35]

After leaving Fort Rice, Sully engaged the Indians in one decisive struggle, the Battle of Killdeer Mountain, fought on July 28. After this victory, Sully's major problem was to reach the Yellowstone River before he exhausted his supplies. During the last few days of the movement, the troops were rationed one hardtack a day, and the entire force realized that if the steamboats had failed to navigate the Yellowstone they would be reduced to near-starvation.[36]

On August 11, as the army was nearing the river at a point about ten miles below present Glendive, the soldiers heard the whistles of the *Chippewa Falls* and the *Alone*. The boats, which had succeeded in navigating the river by carrying only fifty tons of freight each, had been patrolling the river for two days signaling for the army. The *Island City*, an accompanying steamer loaded with corn, had snagged and sunk near Fort Union.[37]

Sully had entertained thoughts of campaigning northwest of the Yellowstone but had changed his mind because of the shortage of grass and the loss of the corn. The two steamers ferried the troops across the river and then moved downstream. The boats had difficulty descending the rapidly falling river and before they reached Fort Union freight had to be removed to Sully's wagons. On August 17 the troops reached the fur trading post, where the entire command was again ferried across the river. Sully stopped at the mouth of the Yellowstone long enough to select a site for the new Yellowstone River fort. Owing to the lateness of the season and low water, which would have prevented the shipment of building materials upstream to the new site, Sully did not attempt to construct the new post in 1864. In fact, the fort, to be named Fort Buford, was not constructed until 1866.

Because Sully had been instructed to safeguard the Missouri River route, he made arrangements with Pierre Chouteau Jr. & Co., owners of the fort, to leave one company of troops at Fort Union.[38]

The main body of troops was back at Fort Rice by September 11. In a summary of his campaign, Sully attributed most of the failures during the summer to the uncontrollable whims of nature:

". . . had the Missouri River commenced to rise in April, as it generally does, instead of June, the boats from Saint Louis would have got up to Sioux City and other points of starting sooner; the command would have been in the field sooner, boats would not have stuck on sand-bars, freight would not have been unloaded and loaded, whereby much of the stores were badly damaged. Had not two of the boats sunk and one become disabled, more supplies would be on hand, and if the usual amount of snow had fallen last winter the river would have been higher, the Yellowstone would have been navigable, there would have been grass and water, not alkali which has helped to kill off many of my animals, the post on the Yellowstone would have been established."[39]

Despite all of the difficulties he had encountered in carrying out his campaign, Sully felt that his forces had successfully broken the Indian combination, and "proved to them that in spite of their boasts and threats they were no match for the whites."[40]

Although some of the steamers performed poorly during the expedition, the army's use of steamboats helped promote further navigation of the Upper Missouri. Sully employed fifteen different boats on the river during the course of his campaign, making 1864 the busiest year on the Upper Missouri up to that time.[41] Because of the increased use of steamboats by the military, more and more navigators became acquainted with the upper reaches of the Missouri. The two new military posts, Fort Sully and Fort Rice, also contributed to the extension of navigation. Both were permanent posts and were supplied by steamboats.

Although he failed to establish a military post in the Yellowstone region as he had been instructed to do, the success of Sully's campaign coupled with the extensive government activity on the river, kept the routes into Montana open. The movement into the Montana gold fields, which had begun in 1862, increased steadily throughout the war years.

Gold had been found in Montana a decade before the operations of 1862. In 1852, François Finlay, or Benetsee, a Red River half-breed, discovered faint traces of gold along Gold Creek in western Montana. The next year members of the Stevens surveying party found gold along a branch of the Hellgate River. In 1856, a miner named Silverthorne, after prospecting in the mountains southwest of Fort Benton, brought his find into the fort and asked Alexander Culbertson, Chouteau's agent, for $1,000 worth of goods in exchange for the gold. Culbertson reluctantly accepted the dust and charged the trade goods to his own account rather than that of the company. The next year Culbertson sent the dust to a mint where it was coined into $1,500 in gold and $25 in silver.[42] Other miners found gold in the late 1850's, and an increasing number of California miners became interested in the possibilities of the region.

In 1862 miners moved into the Salmon River area from the west from Fort Walla Walla and from the east by way of the Missouri River. The strikes of 1862 were not spectacular but were large enough to attract more miners in 1863. In 1863 a group of prospectors discovered rich deposits of gold in Alder Gulch, where Virginia City was founded. During the first three years after the initial strike, $30,000,-000 in gold was taken from the gulch. In 1864, gold was discovered at Last Chance Gulch, where Helena was founded, and thousands of hopeful prospectors poured into the area.[43]

The first St. Louisians who entered the gold fields were members of the American Exploring and Mining Company. On March 22, 1862, H. M. Thompson, Josiah Fogg, Nicholas Wall, and several experienced miners formed the company. Fogg was elected president and Wall, a steamboat captain, was put in charge of supervising the initial expedition to the mines. The company was reported to have a capital of $10,000 and to be interested in operating a permanent line of packets from St. Louis to Fort Benton.[44] The American Exploring and Mining Company, however, never owned steamers, but relied on commercial boating companies for transportation of their goods.

The gold strikes of the early 1860's were clear indications that the Fort Benton steamboat trade would increase as the mining potential of Montana was realized, since the Missouri was a natural route from the mines to the east. Only small quantities of Montana gold were shipped down the Missouri in 1862, but shipments increased greatly in 1863 and 1864. Montana mining receipts in 1863 reached $8,000,000 and were doubled in 1864.[45]

As gold lured miners into the region, other steamboat owners appeared to challenge Pierre Chouteau Jr. & Co. on the Upper Missouri. Among the first was Joseph LaBarge, an employee of Chouteau's and a veteran navigator of the Missouri River. In 1862 LaBarge formed the transportation and contracting firm of LaBarge, Harkness & Co. The other members of the organization were James Harkness; John LaBarge, Joseph's brother; William Galpin; and Eugene Jaccard.[46]

This new transportation firm started with modest capital and equipment. Each of the five full partners put $10,000 into the company, and the firm purchased two light-draft steamers, the *Emilie* and the *Shreveport*. LaBarge intended to trade with Montana miners and also to transport supplies to Sioux City, Yankton, and the military forts and Indian agencies. The company started out auspiciously enough in 1862 when the two steamers started for Fort Benton with full cargoes of company supplies, and equipment belonging to the American Exploring and Mining Company.

The first indications of the bitter rivalry between LaBarge and Chouteau occurred while the steamboats were en route to Fort Benton. Chouteau started two steamers for the head of navigation, hoping they would arrive there before LaBarge's steamers. The effort of each company to be the first to reach Fort Benton resulted in a steamboat race between LaBarge's *Emilie* and Chouteau's *Spread Eagle* near the mouth of White Earth River. During the race the *Spread Eagle* collided with the *Emilie,* breaking her guards and causing some angry exchanges between the two crews.[47] LaBarge's two boats reached Fort Benton on June 17, three days before the Chouteau boats. All of the boats experienced difficulty the last few miles to Benton because of the unusually high water and rapid current. Bradley reported that in 1862 the Missouri River was so high that the flood plain was covered to a minimum depth of a foot and a half, and people were able to dip water by the bucketful at the front gate of Fort Benton.[48]

LaBarge and his partners held a business meeting soon after their arrival and selected a location for a trading post one and one-half miles above Fort Benton.[49] The new post, Fort LaBarge, was deliberately situated to take trade away from Chouteau. LaBarge traded with miners in 1862 and attempted to make a second trip from St. Louis to Fort Benton during the season. But the *Shreveport* only got as far as Yankton, where she delivered quantities of freight to several Yankton merchants.[50]

After establishing his trade in 1862, LaBarge planned to expand the following year by submitting a bid for the Indian annuity contract. In 1863 the government awarded LaBarge and his associates the contract for annuities for the agencies from Omaha to Fort Benton. The contract which LaBarge signed with William Dole, Commissioner of Indian Affairs, specified that LaBarge would be paid the following rates per hundred pounds:

St. Louis to Omaha	$ .75
St. Louis to mouth of Niobrara River	1.25
St. Louis to Yankton Agency	1.50
St. Louis to Fort Pierre	2.00
St. Louis to Fort Berthold	2.25
St. Louis to Fort Union or vicinity	2.50
St. Louis to Fort Benton or vicinity	6.00
St. Louis to Fort Sarpy or the mouth of the Milk River as the agent might direct	5.00[51]

LaBarge also had a contract in 1863 to deliver quantities of supplies for the American Exploring and Mining Company. In order to carry both the Indian and mining supplies, LaBarge planned to use two steamboats, the small, light-draft *Shreveport* and the large *Robert Campbell*. The *Shreveport* was put upon the river first with a cargo of goods for Fort LaBarge. The *Campbell* followed, carrying 650 tons of freight, 150 tons of which were to be deposited at Sioux City. LaBarge did not intend to take this large boat all the way to Fort Benton, but to unload 200 more tons of the freight at Fort Randall, then to proceed upstream to meet the *Shreveport* on its return from Fort LaBarge and transfer all remaining freight to the smaller boat.[52]

LaBarge's plans for getting the large cargo shipment to Fort LaBarge were practical, but river conditions made it impossible to carry them out. Kingsbury reported that the year 1863 was one of the driest on record; there was a period of fifty days without rain.[53] Even the *Shreveport* had great difficulty getting to Yankton, and LaBarge's experiences with the *Campbell* were still more discouraging.

The *Campbell* left St. Louis on May 12[54] and had difficulties even before reaching Sioux City. The boat ran aground time and time again; the crew was forced to spar repeatedly, and at times resorted to cordelling. The craft literally ground its way upriver, at times backing up and ramming its way through sand-blocked passages.

The boat discharged its Sioux City freight on June 10 and 11, and on the twelfth started for Fort Randall. The *Campbell* delivered the Fort Randall freight, then remained in the vicinity of the fort, carrying freight to and from the Yankton Agency. On June 22, the *Campbell* began moving upstream once again. It was not until July 2, somewhere above the mouth of the Cannonball River, that the *Campbell* at long last encountered the *Shreveport*.[55]

The *Shreveport*, which had carried a sizable cargo of mining equipment and eighty-five passengers, had not reached its destination but had had to discharge freight and passengers at Snake Point, some 250 miles below Fort Benton.[56] After the rendezvous with the *Campbell*, the two boats proceeded back upstream to a point just below the mouth of the Yellowstone, which was as far upstream as the heavy-draft *Campbell* could go. From that point, the *Shreveport* carried all of the *Robert Campbell's* freight to Fort Union to be stored, as by that time it was impossible for even the light-draft *Shreveport* to proceed beyond the fort. After the *Shreveport* made five trips to Fort Union with the freight, the boats turned about and began the return to St. Louis.[57]

LaBarge must have anticipated great profits from the business of 1863. In addition to what he stood to gain from the transportation of mining supplies and Indian annuities, the eighty-five passengers on the *Shreveport* had paid fares ranging from $125 for cabin passage with stateroom to $50 for deck passage.[58] However, it had been necessary for Robert H. Lemon, LaBarge and Harkness' agent at Fort La-Barge, to hire King and Gillette, Fort Benton freighters, to transport the provisions which the *Shreveport* had dumped at Snake Point by wagon to Bannack City. King and Gillette charged twenty-five cents a pound for this freighting, which must have taken a substantial piece of LaBarge's profits.

The delay in delivery of the mining company's goods cost LaBarge in more ways than one. Because of this delay, Wall of the American Exploring and Mining Company immediately brought a damage suit against LaBarge, Harkness & Co., and received a judgment against the firm. The next year Fort LaBarge and its equipment were bought by Pierre Chouteau Jr. & Co. at a sheriff's sale.[59] LaBarge later brought a countersuit against Wall and was awarded damages for the seizure of the fort and harm to the business, but the compensation was not sufficient to reinvigorate his transportation business.

Chouteau also failed to get boats through to Fort Benton in 1863, but since his company was large and established, one bad season did not affect him in the way it had LaBarge. Chouteau made every effort to keep pace with the expanding Fort Benton trade in 1864 by putting two new light-draft steamers on the Upper Missouri. Chouteau's trade in 1864 was based on the transportation of miners and mining equipment, the carrying of Indian annuities, and the shipment of some small quantities of furs. Chouteau combined the transportation of upbound mining equipment with the shipment of annuities. He had the contract to supply the agencies from Omaha to Fort Benton and also to carry the Flathead annuities to Fort Benton, and from there to the agency. William Dole, Commissioner of Indian Affairs, agreed to pay Chouteau the following rates per hundred pounds:

St. Louis to Omaha	$ 1.10
St. Louis to mouth of Niobrara	1.50
St. Louis to Yankton Agency	2.00
St. Louis to Usher's Landing	2.50
St. Louis to Fort Sully or Fort Pierre	3.00
St. Louis to Fort Berthold	4.00
St. Louis to Fort Union	4.50
St. Louis to Fort Benton	10.00[60]

Dole also agreed to pay Chouteau $9.00 a hundred for transporting the freight for the Flatheads from Fort Benton to the Flathead Agency.[61]

In 1864 Chouteau's transportation of mining equipment and supplies and Indian annuities completely overshadowed his fur trade. The fur receipts for the year were very light; the two Chouteau boats brought down only 1,700 bales of buffalo robes and some miscellaneous skins and peltries.[62]

Because of the traffic in mining equipment and passengers to the mines, another transportation company started operations in 1864. This company was headed by John G. Copelin, a St. Louis merchant who had operated a boat line on the Mississippi. Copelin sent the steamer *Welcome* to Fort Benton with seventy-one passengers and two hundred tons of freight.[63] Captain Tom Townsend managed to navigate as far as Fort Galpin, where it was necessary to transfer the provisions and passengers to a Chouteau boat, the *Benton*. Although Copelin failed to get his boat through to Fort Benton, he was sufficiently attracted by the possibilities of the trade to enlarge his business the following year. In 1865, Copelin and his father-in-law, John J. Roe, formed the Montana and Idaho Transportation Line, which became the largest steamboat company on the Upper Missouri during the boom after the Civil War.

In 1864 the future of steamboating on the Upper Missouri was promising. During the war years, steamboating supported and was supported by military activity, mining, and farming. The end of the war, with the accompanying release of men and capital, gave impetus to westward movement. In the five years after the end of the Civil War, there was an unprecedented boom in steam navigation on the Upper Missouri, based primarily on the move to the gold fields.

IV

The Peak of St. Louis Dominance
of Trade on the Upper Missouri 1865–1869

FOR NEARLY seventy years businessmen of St. Louis cultivated trade on the Upper Missouri and reaped annual profits from it. During the last half of the 1860's, the harvest was golden. St. Louis steamboat men had a virtual monopoly of the Upper Missouri and enjoyed unprecedented prosperity. The peak was reached in 1867, when over fifteen thousand tons of freight were carried on the Upper Missouri River by St. Louis–based steamboats. (See Table I for statistics on St. Louis steamboat trade to the Upper Missouri, 1860–1869.) This boom was based largely on the Montana gold trade and the reinforcement of the military frontier.

It was primarily the rush to the Montana gold fields that drew St. Louisians into the Upper Missouri River transportation business after the Civil War. During the late 1860's, thousands of miners poured into Montana, both by way of the Missouri River route and the Columbia River—Mullan Road route. Miners took millions from the Montana mines; receipts reached a high of $18,000,000 in 1865. In 1867 and 1868 minerals worth a total of $24,000,000 were taken out of Montana. Five-sixths of this mineral wealth, according to Major C. W. Howell, came down the Missouri River.[1]

The only competition St. Louis steamboat men faced during the first years of the Montana mining boom came from overland wagon routes. This competition was not hard for boatmen to meet in spite of the fact that steamboating was a seasonal business. The route to the mining regions by wagon was long and difficult, and passed through country infested with hostile Indians. Shippers and travelers were not only faced with discomfort and loss of time, they were faced with extremely high freight and passenger rates. Large numbers of shippers and travelers found it more convenient and economical to gear their movement to the navigation season, rather than rely on wagon transportation.

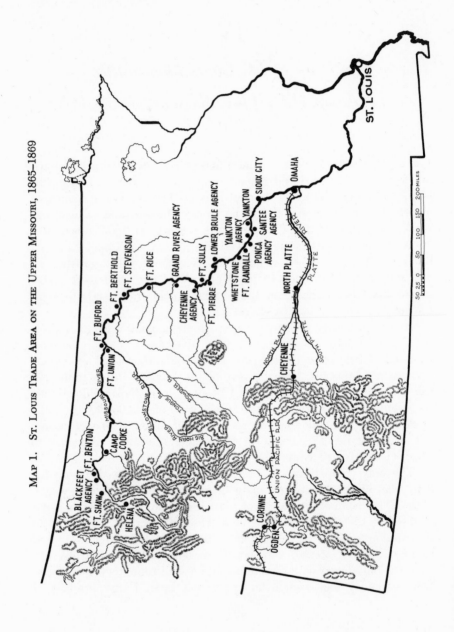

MAP 1. ST. LOUIS TRADE AREA ON THE UPPER MISSOURI, 1865–1869

The principal overland route from Missouri was by way of Atchison, Kansas, to North Platte and Fort Laramie. From Fort Laramie the trail went to Fort Hall and then northward to the mining camps at Bannack and Virginia City.[2] Missouri freighters sometimes went by way of Fort Riley, Kansas. The distance from St. Louis to Fort Riley was 420 miles, and from Riley to Virginia City, 1,520. It was

TABLE I

ST. LOUIS STEAMBOAT TRADE TO THE UPPER MISSOURI, 1860–1869

Year	Boats to Upper Missouri, including Fort Benton	Arrivals at Fort Benton	Total Tonnage
1860	9[a]	2[b]	Not available
1861	11[a]	0	Not available
1862	13[a]	4[b]	Not available
1863	18[a]	0	5,900[a]
1864	30[a]	2[b]	7,300[a]
1865	39[a]	4[b]	12,600[a]
1866	51[d]	31[b]	10,385[d]
1867	71[d]	37[b]	15,882[d]
1868	62[d]	25[c]	9,729[d]
1869	37[d]	24[b]	7,450[d]

[a] Moses K. Armstrong, *History of Dakota, Montana and Idaho* (Yankton, S.D.: George Kingsbury, 1866), in *South Dakota Historical Collections*, XIV, 63.

[b] "Steamboat Arrivals at Fort Benton, Montana and Vicinity" in *Montana Contributions* (1876), I, 317–323.

[c] According to *Montana Contributions*, there were actually thirty-five steamboat arrivals at Fort Benton in 1868. However, according to the *Montana Post* (Helena), September 18, 1868, ten of these trips were made by steamers based at Sioux City.

[d] *Trade and Commerce of St. Louis* (1870), p. 32.

reported by R. E. Strahorn that merchants supplied by way of the overland route received "only one stock of goods a year, hauled in wagons a whole spring, summer and autumn and often half a winter's journey, at a freight charge of 25¢ a pound. . . ." Wagon lines allowed passengers only twenty-five pounds of baggage free, all excess was carried at $2.00 a pound. At the same time, steamboat rates were approximately twelve cents a pound, and goods could be delivered in about two months. Passenger fare from Omaha to the mines overland was $350 one way, with meals extra at from $1.00 to $2.00 each, while steamers were carrying passengers for $150 to $200 from St. Louis to Fort Benton.[3]

Montana residents agitated for an improved wagon route into the territory, and in 1866 the Bozeman Trail was opened. For two years after its opening, the few emigrants traveling the trail were harassed by the Oglala Sioux under Red Cloud. With the signing of the Laramie Treaty in 1868, the government abandoned the land through which the Bozeman Trail passed, and the route was closed.[4]

When faced with the high cost of wagon transportation, the length of time the journey consumed, and the Indian problem, a majority of travelers from the east chose to go to Montana by way of the Missouri River. Major Howell recorded that in 1867, some ten thousand miners went to and from the Montana mines on Missouri River steamers.[5]

As the miners prospered, so did the steamboat trade to Fort Benton. Chouteau had controlled steam navigation on the Upper Missouri some twenty-four years until challenged by LaBarge, Harkness & Co. in 1862. LaBarge's first venture met with failure, but other challengers immediately rose in his place. St. Louis merchants organized steamboat companies to expand their business into the mining area and individual operators put boats on the river with the hopes of making immediate fortunes. These new navigators offered intense competition to Pierre Chouteau Jr. & Co. Then, in 1865, the government refused to renew any of Chouteau's licenses to trade with Indian agencies or military posts because of his Southern sympathies, and Chouteau withdrew from the river trade.[6]

In March of 1865, Charles Chouteau, who had recently succeeded his father as manager of the company, sold the posts and goods of Pierre Chouteau Jr. & Co. to James Hubbell and Alpheus Hawley, government contractors and Indian traders of Mankato, Minnesota.[7] Chouteau closed out his business on the Upper Missouri by sending the *Yellowstone* to Fort Benton to bring down the company's accumulated furs. The boat returned to St. Louis carrying nearly three thousand buffalo robes and over $250,000 in gold dust and then was sold by the company for use on the Lower Mississippi.[8]

Chouteau's successors, Hubbell and Hawley, with James A. Smith of Chicago and C. Francis Bates of New York, reorganized the company as the Northwestern Fur Company on March 23, 1865.[9] During its five-year history on the Upper Missouri, the company operated primarily as a fur company, maintaining five trading posts in Dakota and Montana, and running only one steamboat. Although the company dominated the declining fur trade during the late 1860's, it did not figure as prominently in the transportation business as Chouteau had.

The largest and most active company engaged in the Fort Benton trade during the mid-1860's was the Montana and Idaho Transportation Line. This company was formed during the winter of 1864/65 by John G. Copelin and John J. Roe. These two men had extensive capital at their command. Roe was one of the most prominent businessmen in St. Louis. He moved there from Cincinnati in 1840 while working as a steamboat captain. In St. Louis he operated a commission house, a boat line, and also developed the firm of John J. Roe & Co., which became one of the largest pork packing businesses in the country. Roe later extended his activities to include the organization of banks and insurance companies.[10]

Copelin and Roe bought and constructed steamers for the trade and also organized a wagon freight line from Fort Benton to the mines. With this combination, they could offer through bills of lading from St. Louis to any point in the mining area. To facilitate the handling of steamboat freight in the immediate Fort Benton area, in 1865 Copelin and Roe had the light-draft steamer *Deer Lodge* constructed in Pittsburgh. This boat was kept in the Fort Union area during the navigation season of 1865 and was used only between Fort Union and Benton as a lighter for the other boats. The next year the *Deer Lodge* engaged in the regular trade on the Upper Missouri. In 1865, the Montana and Idaho Line sent at least five boats to the Upper Missouri.[11]

Many of the boats which made the Fort Benton run were owned by the St. Louis & Omaha Packet Line, also known as the "O Line." This company, headed by Joseph Nanson of St. Louis, ran triweekly packets from St. Louis to Omaha. Boats were sometimes taken out of this trade and sent to Fort Benton. The *William J. Lewis, Henry Turner, Kate Kinney, Columbian, Glasgow, Virginia,* and *Peoria City* were among the boats of the O Line. The best-known O Line captains were James A. Yore, D. H. Silver, and Joseph Kinney.[12]

Other St. Louisians who entered the trade during this period were the Mepham Brothers, and John P. and C. W. Keiser. The Mephams ran at least three boats to Fort Benton in 1866. The Keisers, who had a large mercantile business in St. Louis, entered the trade in 1865 and during the next few years operated two or three boats in the Fort Benton trade. Among the prominent independent operators were Joseph and John LaBarge, Joab Lawrence, and Fred Dozier, each of whom participated in the trade with one boat.

In 1868, two Pennsylvanians, both owners of steamboating concerns on the Ohio and Mississippi rivers, entered the Upper Missouri trade. James Rees of Allegheny City, a manufacturer of steamboat parts and machinery, started business on the Missouri with five boats, all destined for Fort Benton. The second Pennsylvanian was William J. Kountz, also of Allegheny City. Kountz and Hiram K. Hazlett, his brother-in-law, set up an office in St. Louis after being awarded the contract for the transportation of United States Army supplies to the forts on the Upper Missouri for 1868.[13] Kountz operated his boats from there for three seasons and then moved his company to Sioux City.

The men who used steamboats on the Upper Missouri always found the river a poor servant. Since the river was high only during the early months of the season, St. Louis steamboat operators could usually make only one trip to Fort Benton a year. There are but two recorded exceptions to this: the *Deer Lodge* made two trips to Fort Benton in 1866 and the *Only Chance* reached Benton twice in 1867.[14] Operators ordinarily sent their boats out from St. Louis in mid-March for what was approximately a sixty-day trip to the head of navigation. Steamboat men counted on riding the June rise on the trip downstream. After making the Fort Benton trip, owners generally used the boats in the trade to military posts on the Missouri or entered them in the Mississippi trade.

During the comparatively short period from mid-May to mid-June, when most of the steamboats arrived at Fort Benton, the small village was a scene of accelerated activity. Benton was the break-in-bulk point between the river and the destinations in the Helena and Virginia City areas. Overland transportation from Fort Benton was provided by wagon lines, which were a vital link in the trade from St. Louis to the mines. The freighters had to work quickly to transfer goods from a boat to freight wagons or warehouses, since boat officers did not care to keep a steamer in Benton any more than a few days. Navigators were very well aware that a slight drop in the river could leave them stranded above the rapids, perhaps until the next spring rise.

By late June of 1868, twenty-six steamboats had delivered cargo to Fort Benton, and some 1,500 freight wagons were used to transport this freight to Helena and the neighboring mining camps.[15] The principal wagon lines were those owned by J. J. Roe & Co., J. T. Murphy, and King & Gillette.[16] The Roe wagons, under the management of Nicholas Wall, usually gave priority to the steamboat freight of the Montana and Idaho Transportation Line. Copelin and Roe had agents in all of the mining areas, and much of their success stemmed from their ability to offer through transportation of supplies and passengers both to and from the mines. Steamboat men also relied upon Fort Benton wagon lines to lighten boats which could not reach the head of navigation. It was fairly common for freighters to go 200 to 250 miles downstream to relieve boats that could not negotiate the rapids.

A trip to Fort Benton by steamer was never a pleasure cruise. It took about two months to make the 3,000-mile trip from St. Louis to Fort Benton, with most of the traveling being done in the daytime. Passengers sometimes got off the steamer when it stopped at posts and agencies, or when it stopped for fuel, but they never roamed far from the river. Most of them were not interested in possible encounters with wandering Indians.

A trip from St. Louis to Fort Benton on a steamboat in 1865 was described by E. W. Carpenter as "two months of life on a 'mountain steamer' with cracked roofs and warped decks, especially adapted to the broiling of passengers in fair weather and drenching them in foul; two months of life between a double wall of muddy bluffs bounding the river on either side and cutting off whatever scenery might lie beyond. . . ."[17]

Carpenter wrote that when the boat stopped for wood, it was frequently "visited by mass delegations of Indians, a precious set of 'bucks,' ringed, streaked and striped in visage, and equally in morals; talented in stealing and duplicity, in begging and loafing—emblems, according to some Eastern notions, of American liberty."[18]

The steamer Carpenter traveled on reached Dauphin's Rapids, 250 miles below Benton, where it was forced to stop because of low water. Carpenter attributed the low water to the fact that there had been next to no snow in the Rocky Mountains the preceding winter. One of Carpenter's fellow passengers, however, had yet another explanation for the lack of water, saying that the barkeeper "had taken so much water from the river for the dilution of his whisky" that the boat could proceed no farther. At any rate, Carpenter and his thirty-nine fellow passengers were forced to go overland the rest of the way to Fort Benton—the "nominal head of navigation on the Missouri," which in Carpenter's words consisted of "a dozen uncouth houses of logs and adobes."[19]

The discomfort of steamboat travel was also one of the favorite topics of General Philippe Régis de Trobriand, who traveled on the *Deer Lodge* from Omaha to Fort Stevenson in 1867. De Trobriand told of the frequent encounters with that scourge of the river—the mosquito. "The sun had scarcely set when millions of mosquitoes invaded the boat, and nothing could protect us from them. They were everywhere—on the deck, in the salon, in the cabins. No matter what was done, they slipped in under the mosquito netting. . . ." During the August heat, the steamer's supply of ice was depleted, so it was impossible to butcher and preserve the beef which had been brought along to provide fresh meat. Until more ice could be procured at the next post, the passengers were fed fried ham, potatoes, and corn cakes. The wine served on the *Deer Lodge* was so bad said De Trobriand, that it was better "to drink the yellow, dirty, unpurified, and tepid water of the Missouri."[20]

The down trips on the mountain steamers were often just as uncomfortable, although quicker. John Napton, who mined in Bear Gulch, Montana, during 1866–1867, left an interesting account of a rather unusual downstream voyage. Napton and his cousin, Lewis Miller, contemplated taking one of the three available steamers at the Benton levee, but then learned of the presence of the *Imperial* at Cow Island. The *Imperial's* agents represented the boat as a veritable palace, saying that if Napton and Miller would go down with them, they would have a "royal good time."[21]

After paying the $130 fare, Napton went downriver in a mackinaw to Cow Island, where he found the *Imperial*, a stern-wheel boat, large but hardly palatial in appearance. The agents of the *Imperial* had contracted to carry about 275 passengers, but had accommodations for only half that number.[22] The *Imperial's* trip was complicated by the fact that she was a heavy-draft steamer, not a regular mountain boat. Many times during the downstream run, the crew had to resort to sparring and warping. On one occasion, while working off a sandbar, a cable snapped and broke a deckhand's leg. There was no doctor on board, so the leg was set crudely and bound with splints. In spite of this attention, the injured man died.

The captain of the *Imperial* on occasion resorted to a unique method of working the boat off sandbars. A long chain, handled by three men at either end of it, was worked under the hull of the boat. The men then sawed back and forth with the chain. The action of the chain started the sand moving, which in turn caused the boat to slide off the bar.

It took a month for the *Imperial* to travel from Cow Island to Fort Buford. At one point on the descent, the captain tried to hire one of the pilots from the steamer *Benton*, but failed because he would not pay the $1,000 demanded by the pilot. Some passengers on the *Imperial* transferred to the *Benton*, but when they asked for a refund, were told by the captain that he had no money. It had all been forwarded to St. Louis on another boat. Napton wrote that after this occurrence, the passengers were "under the impression that the captain of the *Imperial* had some doubts about being able to make the trip, and had made his arrangements accordingly."[23]

By the time the boat reached Fort Buford she was out of supplies, and gave no promise that she could reach St. Louis. At this point Napton and twelve others left the *Imperial* and proceeded downriver by mackinaw.

The steamer was finally abandoned in the Missouri near Bon Homme, Dakota Territory, and the next year was sold at public auction for $2,205.[24] The *Imperial*, like many of the steamers entered in the race to Fort Benton during the post–Civil War boom, was not suited to navigation on the Upper Missouri. It is quite likely that the owners sent her to Fort Benton to make a quick profit and were not particularly concerned with getting the boat back to St. Louis safely.

Not many steamers were abandoned in the river as was the *Imperial*. But the channel did hold the hulls of steamers that had snagged and sunk, or burned and sunk. Many such hulls were noted by navigators as obstructions and were later removed as part of the government's river improvement program.

Individuals operating on the Upper Missouri recognized the risk involved in navigating the shallow stream. Most operators tried to insure both boats and cargoes, but many times boats could not meet the insurance underwriters' standards, which were higher than government steamboat safety standards. Boats frequently were not insured at full value either, as insurance rates on Missouri River steamers were always extremely high.

Newspapers throughout the era of steam navigation on the Upper Missouri carried frequent announcements of steamboat losses. In

April of 1865, the *Union and Dakotaian* noted that the Montana and Idaho Lines' *Bertrand* snagged and sank. The boat and cargo were valued at $100,000. The same spring, the *A. E. Stanard* snagged in DeSoto Bend and sank within five minutes of hitting the snag.[25]

In 1866, the *Leodora*, owned by three partners, burned and was totally destroyed in the river below Yankton. The boat was valued at $25,000 but was insured for only $15,000. In July, the *Pocahontas* sank above Fort Randall. In 1867, the *Sunset* collided with another steamer below Brownsville, Nebraska, and sank. The *Nora* also snagged and sank in May; the boat and cargo, including a $30,000 quartz mill, were a total loss.[26]

Steamboating on the Upper Missouri was risky from yet another standpoint. Navigators never discounted the possibility of attack from renegade Indians. The Indian menace was particularly severe from the time of the Sioux Uprising in 1862 to the conclusion of the Laramie Treaty of 1868. At any point above Fort Randall, boats were likely to be attacked by Sioux war parties. In 1865, George Merrick, the mate of the *St. Johns*, was killed near Fort Rice by a small party of Sioux who fired directly into the pilot house while the boat was running close to a bend.[27] In 1867, a band of Sioux fired into the *Silver Lake* forty miles above Fort Rice, wounding a son of the captain. During the same month, the *Antelope* was completely riddled with bullets by a Sioux war party.[28] Many boat owners resorted to armoring the pilot houses, and all boats were equipped with weapons. Pilot houses were usually armored with boiler iron, leaving only peep holes for the pilot to see through.[29] Boat owners were also authorized by the government to borrow guns and ammunition from the army quartermaster at St. Louis or from post commanders at any site on the Missouri if the need arose.[30]

While the threat of Indian attack was constant, the attacks themselves were infrequent and often ineffectual. When the Indians did attack, they usually laid in ambush at points along the river where the boats had to come close to the banks. This device was used by a large party of Sioux in what is known as the Tobacco Garden Skirmish in 1863. The Sioux detained the *Robert Campbell* and the *Shreveport* at a narrow place near the mouth of Tobacco Creek about ninety miles below the mouth of the Yellowstone. The Indians indicated a desire to negotiate with those on board, so Captain Joseph LaBarge of the *Robert Campbell* asked seven men to take a yawl to shore and bring some of the chiefs to the steamer. The Indians first made friendly gestures, then attacked the men in the yawl when it touched the bank. Three of the seven crew members were killed.[31]

The men on board the *Robert Campbell* had been warned that the Indians meant to attack by Alexander Culbertson, a veteran fur trader who was a passenger. Since they had howitzers and small arms ready, they were able to open fire on the Indians as soon as the yawl was attacked.[32] Pierre Garreau, the interpreter at Fort Berthold, reported later that the Indians lost eighteen men and twenty horses.[33]

Indians presented the greatest threat to steamboat crews when they stopped to cut wood. Sometimes extreme precautions were taken to insure the safety of the men. On one occasion in 1866, the crew of the steamer *W. J. Lewis* was ashore cutting wood somewhere above Fort Union when two of the group, who were acting as scouts, discovered signs of Indians. The men had cut down trees and were engaged in cutting them to proper lengths, intending to carry the wood aboard after dark. That night, huge fires were lighted in the work area, and volunteer guards formed a convex line from above the boat to below it, enclosing the wood piles, and the crew worked within the confines of the line. The men were ordered to fall back to the boat if a shot were fired. The threat from Indians was real—the line was forced to retreat to the boat once during the wooding procedure. After a wait of an hour or so, the formation was set up again. This time a roustabout panicked and attempted to sneak back to the safety of the boat. In the darkness he was not recognized and was shot at by the pilot. Once again the line dissolved and all retreated to the boat in confusion. After the officers of the boat determined the nature of that disturbance, they decided to cease wooding operations that night and finish by light of day.[34]

At the time that St. Louis trade on the Upper Missouri reached its peak, there were still comparatively few individuals who could qualify as Missouri River pilots and captains. Boats could not be transferred indiscriminately from the Mississippi and Ohio rivers to the Upper Missouri River; neither could boat navigators. Experience on the Missouri River itself was required before pilots or captains were granted licenses. Such a requirement was not unreasonable, but it did create a shortage of boat officers. The effect of this shortage was reflected in the high wages paid to Missouri River steamboat officers as compared to wages on the Mississippi and Ohio rivers.

Table II compares Missouri River steamboat officers' wages in 1866 to those of Ohio River officers.

TABLE II

COMPARISON OF

MISSOURI RIVER–OHIO RIVER STEAMBOAT OFFICERS' SALARIES, MAY, 1866*

RANK	MONTHLY WAGES	
	Missouri River	Ohio River
Captains	$400	$150
First clerks	250	150
Second clerks	125	50
Pilots	725	175

*Evening News, May 3, 1866. Deckhands, roustabouts, chambermaids, etc., received comparable wages.

An average mountain boat engaged in the Fort Benton trade employed approximately thirty-eight people. Steamers carried a captain, two pilots, one clerk, two mates, two engineers, a carpenter, a watchman, steward, two cooks, two cabin boys who often filled in as

TABLE III

WAGES PAID TO MISSOURI RIVER STEAMBOAT CREW MEMBERS, APRIL, 1866*

Crew Member	Salary
First mate	$225
Second mate	100
First engineer	225
Second engineer	125
Carpenter	150
Watchman	60
Steward	100
Cooks and assistants[a]	300
Cabin boys, each	30
Firemen, each	55
Chambermaid	30
Roustabouts, each	50

*Evening News, April 18, 1866. All wages were computed on a monthly basis and included room and board.

[a] Cooks were usually paid a sum of money out of which they paid wages to as many or as few assistants as they felt they needed.

galley boys, two firemen, a chambermaid, and about twenty roustabouts. Officers salaries are shown in Table II; typical wages paid to other crew members are given in Table III.

During the boom of the St. Louis to Fort Benton trade, most upbound steamers were loaded with mining supplies such as hardware and an occasional quartz mill, groceries and dry goods, furniture, provisions for military forces along the Upper Missouri, and passengers. In most instances the boats were not fully loaded, but would carry only 250 to 300 tons. Carrying partial loads lessened the draft of the boats and made the ascent speedier. On the return from Fort Benton, steamers usually carried gold dust, buffalo robes, miscellaneous furs, and passengers. Rates charged by steamboat owners varied from shipment to shipment, and usually lower rates were given on large consignments of goods than on small consignments. Freight rates were at their peak in 1865, but by 1867 had declined sharply because of increased competition in the Fort Benton trade.

John Mullan wrote that freight rates from St. Louis to Fort Benton were ten to twelve cents per pound in 1865, while the *Union and Dakotaian* of Yankton noted that some freight in 1865 was carried for as much as eighteen cents a pound, and that freight in 1866 brought eleven cents a pound. The entry of many boats in the trade brought the maximum rate down to ten cents by 1867, and the minimum rate as low as six cents. The average rate of 1867 according to the *Union and Dakotaian*, was nine cents.[35]

Carrying passengers was a most profitable part of the transportation business. Passenger rates, like freight rates, were very high. Throughout the period 1865–1867 the average fare to or from Fort Benton was $150. Occasionally boat owners would charge as much as $200, as Lockwood and Wider did for passage on the *Only Chance* in 1867. By early June of 1866, thirty-one steamers had started for Fort Benton with 1,500 passengers on board; in 1867, 10,000 passengers paid a total of $1,500,000 fare on Upper Missouri River steamers.[36]

Steamboat owners estimated in 1866 that they netted from $10,000 to $40,000 profits during the season from each boat in the Fort Benton trade.[37] The greatest profits were made by owners who were fortunate enough to receive gold shipments. Table IV contains a selective listing of steamers carrying exceptionally valuable downstream cargoes during the period 1865–1867.

Not all of the downriver traffic from the Montana gold fields was carried by steamboats. Throughout the 1860's and early 1870's, hundreds of miners came downstream in skiffs and mackinaws. The heaviest mackinaw migration usually occurred after the steamboat season closed.

The last steamer ordinarily departed from Fort Benton by the first part of July, and the levee was virtually deserted. In the fall,

TABLE IV

EXAMPLES OF VALUABLE STEAMER CARGOES OUT OF FORT BENTON, 1865–1867

Year	Name of Boat (and owner if known)	Nature and Value of Cargo	Annual Profits
1865	St. Johns[a] (Keiser)	$200,000 in gold dust 100 bales robes	
1865	Yellowstone[b] (Chouteau)	250,000 in gold dust 3,000 buffalo robes	
1866	Stonewall[c]	100,000 in gold dust 260 bundles robes	
1866	W. J. Lewis[c] (Copelin)	200,000 in gold dust large quantity furs and robes	
1866	Only Chance[d]	85,000 in gold dust 100 bales robes	
1866	Walter B. Dance[d]	109,225 (4,369 oz. gold) 9,450 in gold coin	
1866	Gallatin[e]	500,000 in gold dust 250 passengers	
1866	Lillie Martin[f]	4,500 oz. gold 73 passengers	
1866	Peter Balen[g] (Mepham Bro's.) Gold Finch[g] (Mepham Bro's.) Iron City[g] (Mepham Bro's.)		} $100,000
1866	St. Johns[g] (Keiser)		17,000
1866	Mollie Dozier[g]		50,100
1866	W. J. Lewis[g] (Copelin)		40,000
1866	Deer Lodge[g] (Copelin)		70,000
1866	Tacony[g]		18,000
1867	Cora[h]	$35,000 in gold dust belonging to passengers; large amount of gold dust consigned to St. Joseph traders; 500 packages furs and pelts.	
1867	Octavia[i]	$75,000 in gold dust and bars; large shipment furs; passengers.	

[a]Democrat, July 13, 1865.　[b]Ibid., June 20, 1865.　[c]Evening News, June 22, 1866.
[d]Ibid., July 2, 1866.　　　[e]Daily Dispatch (St. Louis), August 22, 1866.
[f]Evening News, July 21, 1866.
[g]Democrat, July 7, 1866, as quoted in the Union and Dakotaian, July 28, 1866.
[h]Morning Herald, June 16, 1867.　　　[i]Ibid., July 7, 1867.

however, the Benton levee once again was the scene of great activity reminiscent of the spring steamboat rush. Mackinaws were often constructed at or in the vicinity of the levee, and throngs of people were often present just before departures. Some of the craft could carry as many as fifty passengers. Some of the returning miners carried their gold in strong boxes which had buoys attached with a heavy rope, so that the treasure could be located in the event of a wreck. Bradley estimated that approximately two hundred mackinaws and 1,200 passengers left Benton each autumn during the gold rush years.[38]

Mackinaws were flat-bottomed craft constructed of cut lumber and they had pointed bows, squared sterns, and low gunwales. They ranged from forty to seventy-five feet in length, from eight to twelve feet in breadth, and had a draft of six to nine inches. This boat, used by French voyageurs in the Lake Superior region and named after the Straits of Mackinac, was first introduced to the Missouri River early in the nineteenth century. Mackinaws were ordinarily manned by five or six men, all of whom were rowers save the steersman, who handled the rudder from the stern and commanded the boat. The rowers were supposed to keep the boat in the strongest current and deepest channel; they depended upon the velocity of the current for their speed.

The mackinaw navigators who left Fort Benton during the late summer would try to reach St. Louis, but those who departed in the late fall often had to stop at Yankton or Sioux City because of ice and had to seek overland transportation. When the miners reached their destinations, they abandoned their mackinaws or sold them for lumber.

The mackinaw migration of 1866 was very heavy. Miners passed Yankton as early as mid-August; Kingsbury, the editor of the *Union and Dakotaian*, remarked that the river from Fort Benton to Yankton was "covered with returning miners." The *Union and Dakotaian* reported that most of the miners made good time, since well-built mackinaws could travel up to a hundred miles a day. According to Kingsbury, during October and November alone some two thousand miners stopped at Yankton, where many of them sold their boats and proceeded overland, usually by wagon or stagecoach.[39]

Steamboat owners who engaged in the Fort Benton trade also participated in the trade to military installations on the Upper Missouri. After the Civil War, the primary purpose of the army on the Upper Missouri was to protect the river route; consequently the major posts were located on or near the river. By the end of the Civil War, there were three posts along the river, Fort Randall, Fort Rice, and Fort Sully. Fort Sully was relocated in 1866, when it was moved upstream about thirty miles. In 1866 and 1867, four new posts were constructed to protect the Missouri River route; Fort Stevenson, above present-day Bismarck; Fort Buford, near the mouth of the Yellowstone; Camp Cooke, near the mouth of the Judith; and Camp Shaw, on the Sun River about twenty miles from its juncture with the Missouri.[40] Fort Dakota, at the site of present-day Sioux Falls, South Dakota, was built in 1865, and was supplied by way of the Missouri River. Supplies were delivered to Yankton and then carried by wagon to the fort.

The significance of the Upper Missouri military frontier is competently analyzed by Ray H. Mattison, a historian for the National Park Service, in his article "The Military Frontier on the Upper Missouri" (published in the September, 1956, issue of *Nebraska History*). Mattison wrote that Fort Randall, the oldest post on the Upper Missouri, had an average of 181 men stationed there from 1868 to 1891. The average size of Fort Sully from 1868 to 1894 was 183. From 1868 to 1878, Fort Rice was garrisoned with an average force of 233. Fort Buford, which was constructed in 1866, had an average strength of 274 men from 1867 to 1895. Camp Cooke, established in 1866, was abandoned in 1870 after the army decided the garrison was improperly located. In 1867–1868, this post had an average size of 428. Fort Benton, abandoned as Blackfeet Agency in 1869, in the same year was designated as a military post. Fort Benton from 1870 to 1880 had an average size of 51 men. Fort Stevenson had an average size of 132 from 1868 to 1882, and Fort Shaw had an average of 231 men stationed there from 1867 to 1890.[41] Fort Dakota, the smallest of the posts supplied by way of the Missouri, had accommodations for only 100 men.[42] In 1869, the Secretary of War reported 2,122 men stationed at twelve posts in Dakota and Montana Territories.[43] Nine of these posts were supplied directly by steamboats.

Carrying provisions and supplies for the soldiers alone provided substantial business for steamboat men, and the transportation of wagons, arms, ammunition, and construction supplies added greatly to their annual tonnages. The maintenance of the military posts also increased the passenger trade because of the numerous soldiers and dependents who traveled by steamboat. Some insight into the volume of the trade to military posts can be gained from Table V, which was compiled from records of the St. Louis Quartermaster for 1867.

As a rule, the bulk of military freight was shipped during the spring months. The most difficult posts to supply were those located near the head of navigation—Fort Shaw and Camp Cooke. Most supplies for these two posts were carried early in the boating season. Supplies for some of the lower posts could be carried later; cargoes to Fort Buford were sometimes delivered as late as September 30, and the posts below the Yellowstone were quite often supplied in October and early November.

TABLE V

FREIGHT CARRIED TO UPPER MISSOURI MILITARY POSTS BY STEAMER, 1867*

Destination	Tonnage
Fort Sully	1358.7
Fort Buford	1085.8
Fort Benton	1101.0[a]
Camp Cooke	993.3
Fort Randall	198.7
Yankton	195.6[b]
Fort Rice	1093.0
Fort Berthold	1828.0[c]
Fort Stevenson	326.5

* This table compiled from "Atkins' Logs, Appendix," reprinted from *North Dakota Historical Collections*, pp. 115–118. This appendix was reprinted from 40 Congress, House Executive Documents, Congressional Series 1368, p. 666.

[a] Freight to be delivered by wagon to Fort Shaw.

[b] Freight to be delivered by wagon to Fort Dakota.

[c] The garrison at Fort Berthold was moved to Fort Stevenson during the summer of 1867.

The army did considerable experimenting before adopting an established routine for supplying the posts. During the war years, and in 1866, the quartermaster at St. Louis signed special contracts with boat owners each time he had supplies to be delivered. In 1866 William McPherson was given a special contract to transport the supplies required by Fort Rice and Fort Buford throughout the season.[44] The other posts were also supplied by special contract or by chartered steamers. During the spring of 1866, a boom year in the Montana gold trade, boats were at a premium; the only way the government could get transportation was to charter steamers at exorbitant rates. The quartermaster chartered at least five boats for $530 each per day, and one for $600. The St. Louis *Evening News* called the rates excessive and referred to the chartering system as "the bleeding of Uncle Sam."[45] Late in the season when the Fort Benton trade was finished, boats were plentiful, and the quartermaster made contracts to ship goods to Fort Sully for $3.48 per hundred pounds, and to Fort Rice for $4.48 per hundred pounds.[46]

The high cost of the chartering system of 1866 led the army to adopt the system of letting season-long contracts after that time. In

1867 contracts for supplying all of the military posts were given to William McPherson and John Copelin.[47]

In 1868 the military contract for the Upper Missouri area was granted to Hiram K. Hazlett, who worked with William Kountz in delivering the wares.[48] This was the last year in which military contract goods for the Upper Missouri posts were carried solely from St. Louis. In 1869, the government designated Sioux City as the starting point for some of the military freight shipments.

The very forces which led to the expansion of St. Louis trade in the late 1860's led to its downfall by 1870. The Missouri River was but an indirect route to the Northwest. As long as it was the only economical route, it was supreme. The river served the fur traders, the military, the miners, and the settlers well, but once the first wave of settlement had passed into Dakota and Montana territories, speedier, more-direct transportation was desired. With the opening of the Montana gold fields, and the establishment of the military frontier, railroad interests projected themselves into the Upper Missouri region. With the extension of a railroad to Sioux City, and the completion of the Union Pacific in 1869, St. Louis' domination of trade in the Upper Missouri area ended.

V

Sioux City Replaces St. Louis as
Headquarters for Upper Missouri Navigators

ST. LOUIS remained the base of steam navigation until the Chicago &
North Western Railroad reached Sioux City in 1868. This railhead
above St. Louis gave merchants in the Upper Missouri area a direct
connection with Chicago and New York wholesalers, and cut nearly
a thousand miles off the river route. Sioux City navigation interests
presented even greater competition to St. Louis steamboat men when
the government started shipping contract goods from that point. The
first government shipments from Sioux City were made in 1868, and
by 1871 the government was channeling all of its business on the
Upper Missouri through Sioux City. Joab Lawrence capitalized on
the extension of the railroad by moving his steamboat company from
St. Louis to Sioux City in 1868. Most of Lawrence's trade was based
on the transportation of Chicago and New York freight up the Missouri.

While Lawrence at Sioux City was developing competition to St.
Louis steamboat interests, the Union Pacific Railroad was completed
to Corinne, Utah. The line, from that point, could compete for Fort
Benton trade. Goods sent to Montana by way of St. Louis steamers
took some two months to reach Fort Benton, and the transportation
season was limited. Goods sent from Chicago to Corinne took approximately eight days to reach their destination, and the route was
open year around. Although rail rates were high at first, and the
wagon distance from Corinne to the mining towns was four times
greater than was the distance from Fort Benton, shippers who had
large amounts of capital tied up in easy-to-transport goods could
afford to use the railroad–wagon line combination.

After the completion of the Union Pacific and the shift in activity to Sioux City, the base of the river trade changed from what was predominantly trade to the Montana gold fields to primarily trade with the military. There was, too, an increasing emphasis on the transportation of domestic goods for settlers and settlements. Although the river was "shortened," and freight rates decreased, steamboating intensified. Steamers from Sioux City carried goods to a rapidly expanding trade area. This expansion was a concomitant of further settlement of Dakota Territory and increased government installations along the river.

Sioux City promoters had begun agitating for a railroad as early as 1856. The long-awaited rail connection with Chicago was not completed until twelve years later when the Sioux City & Pacific Railroad was finished, connecting the town of Missouri Valley on the Chicago & North Western line with Sioux City. This seventy-five-mile line was then leased to the Chicago & North Western Railroad.[1] The first train, which arrived on March 9, 1868, was greeted by the Sioux City *Journal* with exuberant headlines, among them " 'Saved at Last' " and " 'All hail Chicago.' "[2] Sioux City was then a town of 1,030 inhabitants, with active merchandising firms and adequate port and landing facilities; Sioux City Chamber of Commerce members hoped to make the town the new "gateway to the west."[3]

One of the first individuals to realize what impact the railroad to Sioux City would have on the river transportation business was Joab Lawrence. As early as the fall of 1867, Lawrence began to organize the Northwest Transportation Company. Lawrence was an experienced promoter and enterpriser. During the summer of 1865, Lawrence and Charles E. Maurice operated the firm of Joab Lawrence & Co., cotton factors and commission merchants, in Mobile, Alabama. Lawrence also had the government transportation contract for the Alabama River. After the Civil War, Lawrence operated a steamer in the St. Louis–Fort Benton trade. The St. Louis *Democrat* once declared: "Joab Lawrence can't be beat. He is a whole team. We needn't wish him success. He always has it, whether he buys a steamer, runs a distillery or commands a regiment of city militia."[4]

Lawrence's Northwest Transportation Company was incorporated by the state of Iowa on November 11, 1867. The company had an authorized capital and stock of $150,000, which was to be sold in $100 shares.[5] Lawrence was named president and superintendent of the company, Samuel DeBow was the general agent, and Charles D. Woolworth the secretary. Because of the soon-to-be-completed railroad to Sioux City, Lawrence established company offices in New York, Boston, and Chicago.[6] By so doing, he could offer through bills of lading to any point on the Upper Missouri. Lawrence claimed that shippers to the Upper Missouri who used the railroad to Sioux City, and then Sioux City–based steamboats, would save "1000 miles, 20 days, and cut their insurance costs one-third."[7]

Lawrence made his preparations for the season of 1868 in St. Louis, where he readied his packets for the mountain trade by removing every stick of wood, plank, and deck not actually necessary. The *Bertha, Alabama,* and *Barker* were reported to be "extensively razed" while being remodeled.[8] In addition to being remodeled, each of the Northwest Transportation Company's boats was equipped with a twelve-pound howitzer and twenty stand of arms, and with two thousand rounds of ammunition, for protection against possible Indian attack.[9]

The company partially loaded its boats in St. Louis and then added to the cargo at Sioux City. In early March, Lawrence advertised that the *Deer Lodge* would leave St. Louis for Sioux City on March 25 loaded with one hundred tons, and would take on additional cargo at Sioux City for Fort Benton.[10] After each of his five steamers made the initial trip from St. Louis, Lawrence operated them out of Sioux City for the remainder of the season. Each of the boats made two trips to Fort Benton, the quickest time being made by the *Deer Lodge* on a voyage of twenty-two and one-half days.[11] Lawrence's steamers carried quantities of Indian annuities originating in New York to Fort Sully and Fort Berthold in 1868,[12] but most of his shipments originated in Chicago. Montana sales by Chicago merchants increased $4,000,000 in 1868 as a result of the railroad to Sioux City.[13]

In reviewing the work of 1868, the Northwest Transportation Company reported that it carried freight from Sioux City to Benton for five cents per pound; through-rates from Chicago to Benton were six cents a pound, and from New York, eight cents. The insurance rates before 1868 on Missouri River shipments from St. Louis to Benton were 6.4 per cent and insurance could not always be obtained, but the shipments from Sioux City were insured for 3 per cent because the hazards of one thousand miles of river transporta-

tion were avoided.[14] Passengers from Sioux City to Fort Benton paid
$150 cabin fare and $25 deck fare.[15] In 1868 the Northwest Transportation Company claimed they employed about four hundred men as
officers and crews of the five boats. This rather liberal estimate is
probably a total of all men employed for the season, including part-
time as well as full-time workers.

In spite of the fact that the company's boats each made two trips
to Fort Benton in 1868, Lawrence was unhappy with the performance.
He felt that a lightly loaded boat could reach Benton on the average
within twenty-five days and could thus make three trips a season instead of two. Lawrence announced that in 1869 the company's boats
would be limited to one hundred tons freight, which would enable
them to make a quick passage.[16] He made this declaration even
though his crews were forced to cut their own wood after reaching
a distance about three hundred miles above Sioux City.

In anticipation of a good season in 1869, the Northwest Transportation Company added five boats, thus doubling the size of its fleet.
The firm also constructed a dry dock at Sioux City for the purpose
of repairing and wintering boats. A correspondent for the *Chicago
Republican* noted that from forty to fifty carpenters worked on the
dock. This enterprise added substantially to the economy of Sioux
City during the winter of 1868/69.[17]

In 1869 Lawrence continued to transport freight for Montana
merchants and added to his business through two government contracts. In May the Northwest Transportation Company obtained a
contract to supply the Indian agencies on the Upper Missouri, and
the company was also given a contract to supply military installations. The Indian contract signed by G. T. Nutter, Lawrence's agent
in New York, provided that the Northwest Transportation Company
would receive all goods in New York, and then would provide transportation to the Upper Missouri agencies by way of Sioux City.[18]
The contract covered the period May 13 to July 12, 1869. Rates paid
to the company for transportation from New York are shown on
Table VI.

Lawrence's company shipped all of the Upper Missouri Indian
annuities for 1869, but handled only part of the military freight. The
army in 1869 let two contracts for the posts on the Upper Missouri:
to J. N. Bofinger for the business from St. Louis to Fort Benton and
way posts on the Missouri River, and to Lawrence for shipment from

Chicago to Sioux City by rail and then to Fort Benton and way points by steamer.[19]

Although the Sioux City port attracted business away from St. Louis, a certain amount of boating from the older port still continued in 1869. Lawrence left his ten boats at St. Louis in the winter of 1868/69, as his ways at Sioux City were not yet completed, and these boats all carried some cargo from St. Louis that spring. Rees and Kountz still operated out of St. Louis in that year, and the Bofinger contract goods also originated at St. Louis.

TABLE VI

RATES PAID NORTHWEST TRANSPORTATION COMPANY
FOR TRANSPORTATION OF FREIGHT TO UPPER MISSOURI INDIAN AGENCIES, 1869*

From New York City to:	Rate per Hundred Pounds
All points on the Missouri River between Yankton and Fort Sully, including both	$ 7.72
Fort Rice and all points between Fort Sully and Fort Rice	8.72
Fort Buford and all points between Fort Rice and Fort Buford	9.72
Musselshell and all points between Fort Buford and Musselshell	10.72
Fort Benton and all points between Musselshell and Fort Benton	11.72

*Contract between G. T. Nutter, Agent for the Northwest Transportation Company and E. S. Parker, Commissioner of Indian Affairs, May 13, 1869, in Bureau of Indian Affairs, Interior Department, National Archives.

The completion of the Union Pacific in May of 1869 dealt a blow to both the diminishing St. Louis trade and the expanding Sioux City business. Early spring shipments on the river were not affected, but within a year after its completion, the Union Pacific visibly affected the volume, nature, and pattern of steamboat traffic on the Upper Missouri.

Shortly after the opening of the railroad, Colonel C. A. Reynolds, Quartermaster Department, United States Army, announced that the government would establish an army depot at Corinne, Utah. Corinne, located about twenty-eight miles northwest of Ogden on the railroad angle that passed Salt Lake, was the most favorable point for supplying both Idaho and Montana from one general depot. A writer for the *Montana Post* reported that wagon freight would probably be carried from Corinne to Helena for six cents a pound and speculated that within a year the rate would be reduced to four and one-half or five cents a pound.[20]

In the spring of 1870, a reporter for the *Helena Herald* commented that most of the freight into Montana Territory would go by way of the Union Pacific and the wagon road from Corinne. He was of the opinion that river shipments, except for heavy freight, would definitely decline because of the railroad competition.[21] A spokesman for the *Union and Dakotaian* was unwilling to concede anything to the railroad, answering "our great water route from the Mountains to the sea is more than a match for the railroad, and from this [day] forward the importance of the Big Muddy as a commercial route will send forth its own praise by its thousands of steamers and cheap freight."[22]

This claim was no more than a hollow boast; during 1870 at least four wagon lines were carrying goods from Corinne to Helena: the Diamond R Line, the Far West Freight Company, S. Howe & Co., and a line operated by Lawrence's Northwest Transportation Company. Wagon trains advertised that they could deliver freight from Corinne to Helena in eight days, and on one occasion in 1871 the Diamond R Line brought freight from Corinne to Helena in seven days and twenty minutes. The usual charge for carrying goods from Corinne to Helena was about seven and one-half cents a pound. Although shippers paid more by the overland route than by the Missouri River, they had the advantages of speed and a much longer shipping season. The railroad-wagon combination induced steamboat owners to reduce their rates sharply. By the spring of 1872, rates were as low as three to four cents per pound from St. Louis to Fort Benton.[23]

. In 1872, Thomas P. Roberts, an engineer for the Northern Pacific, made a reconnaissance of the Upper Missouri River area with the assignment of determining the economic potential of the region and investigating the possibility of the Northern Pacific working in combination with steamboat lines to control trade to the military forts and Indian agencies. In his report, Roberts commented on the effect of the Union Pacific on Missouri River commerce. He noted that steamboat operators who started from St. Louis and Sioux City always kept their rates below the rail and wagon rates; consequently steamboat rates were reduced each time rail rates were lowered. Roberts claimed that steamboat freight from St. Louis to Fort Benton had been carried for as little as three cents a pound. Freight was taken from Benton to Helena by wagon, he wrote, for one and one-half cents, making a total of four and one-half cents a pound from St. Louis to Helena by way of the Missouri River. By rail and wagon from Omaha to Helena, noted Roberts, the rates were six cents a pound.[24]

The impact of the Union Pacific is suggested by the statistics of steamboat arrivals at Fort Benton. There were twenty-four arrivals in 1869, but the number declined to eight in 1870. There were six arrivals in 1871, thirteen in 1872, seven in 1873, and six in 1874.[25]

Captain William A. Jones, who investigated the possibility of a military wagon road from the Union Pacific into Montana, credited the success of the railroad to its definite advantage of speed as compared to steamboats. Jones wrote:

As the business of the country is now conducted, men can ill afford to have their money lying idle for months, or weeks, or even days, locked up in goods *in transitu*. Every day saved on goods, of whatever character, is the equivalent of money gained. It is this element of time and its money equivalent that underlies the astounding success of railroads as competitors with water-lines of traffic. . . .[26]

Fort Benton freight decreased after 1869 not only because of the railroad, but also because of a decline in mining activity. In 1865, at the peak of production, Montana mines yielded $18,000,000 worth of gold; by the mid-1870's, mine production was down to $4,000,000. In 1867, thirty-seven boats had arrived at the Benton levee. In 1874, only six boats landed at Benton.

With the decline of Fort Benton trade, steamboating on the Upper Missouri became more and more dependent upon the transportation of supplies to military posts and Indian agencies located on the stretch of river between Sioux City and Fort Buford. By the end of the Civil War, the Indian Service had established the Blackfeet Agency, the Yankton Agency, and the Lower Brule Agency No. 1 (abandoned in 1865). The Ponca Agency and two Santee agencies in northern Nebraska were added in 1867. The greatest increase in agency Indians occurred after the Laramie Treaty of 1868. This treaty between the government and the Teton Sioux provided for three additional Missouri River agencies, Whetstone, Grand River Agency, and Lower Brule Agency No. 2, all of which were supplied with government annuities. By 1870 there were 4,500 Indians drawing rations at the Whetstone Agency alone.[27]

The Laramie Treaty and the additional Indian agencies caused an expansion of the military frontier in 1870, when five new military posts were built near the agencies to keep peace. Fort Bennett at the Cheyenne River Agency had an average size of 108 men from 1870 to 1891. The post at the Grand River Agency had an average size of 245 from 1870 to 1897, and the garrison at Fort Hale (at the Lower Brule Agency) had an average size of 79 men from 1870 to 1883. Temporary posts were established at Fort Thompson and at Whetstone Agency in 1870, but both were abandoned within two years. One non-agency military post, Fort Abraham Lincoln, was constructed on the Upper Missouri in 1872 to protect the route of the Northern Pacific Railroad. This post was supplied from Sioux City by steamboat in 1872, but after that first year, supplies were delivered by rail to Bismarck and then ferried across the Missouri. From 1876 to 1890 the post had an average size of 163.[28]

By 1869, the first year that both military and Indian supplies were started from Sioux City, there were seven army posts and eight Indian agencies located on or near the Missouri. By 1872, the last year of Sioux City dominance of steam navigation on the Upper Missouri, there was a total of nineteen army posts and Indian agencies supplied by steamboats. It was these government installations along the Missouri River that accounted for most of the tonnage carried on the river during the years Sioux City controlled navigation on the Upper Missouri.

During the winter of 1870/71, Joab Lawrence sold his interest in the Northwest Transportation Company, and the company was reorganized under the same name. The chief stockholder in the reorganized company was the trading firm of Durfee & Peck. This firm, licensed to operate on the Upper Missouri, had purchased the posts of the Northwestern Fur Company after its dissolution in 1869, and in the absence of any organized fur companies, handled most of the fur business on the Upper Missouri after that time. After the trading firm became associated with the Northwest Transportation Company, most of the furs that came down the Missouri River were handled by Northwest Transportation Company boats. The largest shipments of furs came downriver with the first boats of the season; after that, shipments were sporadic and were handled as miscellaneous freight. In 1871, the early fur shipments provided important downriver business for the company. The *Ida Rees* brought down a cargo of 39,000 buffalo robes, called by a Sioux City *Daily Journal* reporter "the most valuable cargo of robes and peltries which probably ever came down the Missouri." The *Nellie Peck* alone brought down enough furs and hides to fill twenty-three railroad cars.[29]

The Northwest Transportation Company dominated steamboat trade on the Upper Missouri as long as the trade was controlled from Sioux City. The reorganized firm had its home office in Leavenworth, Kansas, with agencies at New York, Chicago, and St. Louis, but its general freight depot and shipping point was Sioux City. The officers of the company were E. H. Durfee, president; N. Springer of St. Louis, vice-president; S. B. Coulson of Sioux City, general superintendent; J. P. Dunlevy of Sioux City, general travel agent; and C. K. Peck of Keokuk, secretary. The directors of the company were Durfee, Peck, Coulson, William S. Evans of Allegheny City, Pennsylvania, and O. B. Taylor of Leavenworth, Kansas. Samuel DeBow, who had been associated with Joab Lawrence, held the position of New York agent with the new firm. Other agents were Erfort & Petring of St. Louis, John B. Dallas of Pittsburgh, H. Warfield of Chicago, I. G. Baker & Bro. of Fort Benton, and J. H. Charles of Sioux City.[30]

The Northwest Transportation Company was awarded the Indian contract in 1871, and both the Indian and military contracts in 1872. Both William J. Kountz and the Northwest Transportation Company submitted bids for the Indian contract of 1871. The Northwest Transportation Company's bid was accepted by E. S. Parker, Commissioner of Indian Affairs, who signed a contract with Peck in Washington on May 23, 1871. Kountz, bitter about the awarding of this contract to his rivals, attacked Commissioner Parker in his newspaper, the *Allegheny Mail*.[31]

The Northwest Transportation Company's contract provided for delivery of all goods purchased for the fiscal year ending June 30, 1872, and was to remain in effect until July 12, 1872. Provision was made that if goods could not be delivered by boat because of low water, the company would distribute the supplies by land routes at no additional charge.[32] Transportation rates from Sioux City to the various points on the Upper Missouri are shown in Table VII.

The company agreed that these charges would include "free warehouse privileges at Sioux City on all goods and supplies until such time as the boats may remove them. . . ."[33] On such goods as might originate in St. Louis, the charge by river to Sioux City was sixty cents per hundred.

The Northwest Transportation Company put six steamers on the Upper Missouri in 1871. All of the boats, the *Nellie Peck, E. H. Durfee, Far West, Esperanza, Ida Rees No. 2,* and the *Viola Belle,* were light-draft mountain boats built for the Fort Benton trade.[34] Two of the vessels, the *Durfee* and the *Nellie Peck,* came to Sioux City from Pittsburgh, and at least two others were wintered at St. Louis.[35] All of the boats carried some cargo up from St. Louis and then began to carry annuity goods.

TABLE VII

RATES PAID NORTHWEST TRANSPORTATION COMPANY
FOR TRANSPORTATION OF FREIGHT TO UPPER MISSOURI INDIAN AGENCIES, 1871*

From Sioux City to:	Rate per Hundred Pounds
Santee Agency	$ .18
Ponca Agency	.18
Yankton Agency	.18
Whetstone Agency—as at present located	.46
Brule in the Upper Missouri Agency	.53
Crow Creek in the Upper Missouri Agency	.63
Cheyenne Agency	.80
Grand River Agency	1.05
Fort Berthold Agency	1.48
Fort Peck	2.75
Musselshell	2.95
Fort Benton	3.36

*Contract between C. K. Peck of the Northwest Transportation Company and E. S. Parker, Commissioner of Indian Affairs, May 23, 1871, in Bureau of Indian Affairs, Interior Department, National Archives.

The first real rush of business began in June. On June 3, the *Esperanza* arrived from St. Louis carrying three hundred tons of sugar and bacon, bound for the Cheyenne Agency. The *Durfee* also carried three hundred tons of Indian goods up from St. Louis intended for the Grand River Agency. Both boats picked up additional cargo at Sioux City and then proceeded upriver.[36]

The spring rush was not difficult for the Northwest Transportation Company to handle. Agencies needed large quantities of annuities in the early spring to augment depleted winter supplies, and the river was in good condition for the delivery of such supplies. A large share of the annuities, however, did not reach Sioux City until in August, and these shipments were most difficult to deliver. It is understandable that the government should wish to send large quantities of supplies to the agencies before winter set in; it was unfortunate that such supplies often were not placed in the hands of steamboat companies early enough in the season for easy and sure delivery. In the season of 1871, the Northwest Transportation Company received a late shipment of annuity goods, and by August 25, they still had some 1,500 tons of Indian freight to deliver. The river was exceedingly low, and the company had already taken one of its boats, the *E. H. Durfee*, out of the Upper Missouri trade and had sent it to St. Louis to compete in the Mississippi River cotton trade.[37]

The company later received a large consignment of Indian supplies for the Whetstone Agency. In early November, the Northwest Transportation Company negotiated with Captain A. F. Hawley of the *Miner* for the transportation of 2,000 sacks of flour to the agency. The company resorted to dealing with Hawley because most of their boats had already been sent downstream. The negotiations were never successfully completed, and there is no indication as to how this freight was delivered.[38]

If the Indian agents urgently needed these goods, it is likely that the Northwest Transportation Company was forced to pay wagon freight on these late annuities. Otherwise, the company may have simply stored the goods for the winter, a contingency also in the contract, and delivered them in the spring.

The contract for transporting Indian annuities for 1871 did not expire until July 12, 1872, and in February of 1872 still more annuity goods arrived in Sioux City. On February 14, a writer for the *Sioux City Journal* reported that there were 6,729 sacks of flour at the Northwest Transportation Company's warehouse awaiting spring shipment.[39]

Although the Northwest Transportation Company was awarded the Indian annuities contract for 1871, they had earlier lost the contract for the transportation of supplies to military posts to William J. Kountz. Kountz was operating out of St. Louis, but after receiving the military contract for 1871 moved his headquarters to Sioux City, where he was represented by Hiram K. Hazlett.[40]

Hazlett signed the military contract on March 17 in Chicago, the headquarters for the Military Division of the Missouri. In the contract Hazlett agreed to

furnish all steamboat transportation required by the United States government, for officers and soldiers on the Missouri River, from Sioux City,
Iowa, Yankton Agency, Fort Randall, Whetstone, Lower Brules and Crow
Creek Agencies, Fort Sully, Big Cheyenne and Grand River Agencies, Fort
Rice, Stevenson and Buford, D.T. to Fort Benton, M.T. and from each to
any other of the above points, at any time from March 20th, 1871 to October 31st, 1871. . . . [41]

The contract contained explicit provisions pertaining to the accommodations for officers and troops. All officers were to be given
cabin passage, and were permitted to carry one hundred pounds of
baggage free. Enlisted men were to be given deck passage, eighty
pounds of free baggage, and were to be provided with a kitchen
room, cooking stoves, and bunks. The boat owners also had to provide
troughs and "proper conveniences for transporting and feeding horses,
mules and cattle."[42]

From the above reference, and from newspaper items of the time,
it is possible to visualize army life on a steamer. Officers with their
cabin passage would have the comforts of a private or semi-private
room, mattresses, sheets, and chambermaid service. Their fare would
include meals in the dining room.

The troops with all of their personal baggage, and their folding
cots or bedrolls, were relegated to the boiler deck, which many times
was shared with livestock. One can well imagine the morning dis-
array when dozens, and at times even hundreds, of men would pre-
pare for the day by dressing, folding their cots, and standing in line
with their tins for breakfast. These activities were sometimes nearly
impossible owing to the large number of troops. The *Western* was
once loaded with 500 officers and men as well as a considerable number of civilians and 250 tons of government freight.[43] Normally when
troops were moved, less than 200 would be put on a boat. But even
that number when increased by some civilians, the boat's crew, and
perhaps some livestock, could seriously crowd a vessel. It was probably a blessing to the enlisted men on the often crowded decks when
mechanical failures gave them an opportunity to disembark and pitch
their tents on some nearby levee or sandbar for a time.

The contract also provided that the Kountz Line would furnish only
such steamboats as were approved by the inspector of the St. Louis
Board of Underwriters and also by the quartermaster in charge of
transportation at Sioux City. In the event the company could not

make deliveries by river, it was obligated to deliver all goods by land at regular contract rates.

Contained in the contract also were certain provisions that regulated the tonnage and movement of the Kountz boats. The contractors agreed that no boat would be required to go above Sioux City with less than fifty tons of freight, and also that no boat drawing more than three and one-half feet of water would be allowed to go above Sioux City. No boat drawing over three feet was to navigate above Fort Buford.[44]

The contract gave the Kountz interests monopoly only of the military trade which originated at Sioux City. Provision was expressly made that the government could contract with anyone to ship from St. Louis, Fort Leavenworth, and Omaha. There was also a provision in the contract that gave the government the right to use any government-owned steamers if it should so choose and also to transport any forage which could be produced in the vicinity of any fort or post.

The schedule of rates to be paid the Kountz Line was drawn up in a tabular form showing rates to and from all points on the river. The same rates applied for both up and down freight and were to be in effect for the entire period of the contract, which was a departure from the usual practice of allowing higher rates during the late summer and fall months when the river was low. Table VIII is a condensation of the tabular statement showing only the rates from Sioux City to the various destinations.

Kountz, in his eagerness to get the contract, bid ridiculously low and incurred substantial losses in the transportation of the military supplies.[45] Probably because of the competition of the Northwest Transportation Company in 1871, Kountz cut his bid far below that of 1870, when he had been awarded the contract to deliver government provisions from St. Louis and Sioux City to military posts and Indian agencies. In 1870, the government paid Kountz $5.50 a hundred on goods from St. Louis to Fort Benton, and $4.50 a hundred on goods from Sioux City to Fort Benton. These rates were in effect through August and were doubled in September and October.[46] In 1871, Kountz's rates from Sioux City to Fort Benton were $1.12 per hundred less than the preceding year, and no provision was made for higher rates during the low-water months.

Throughout the season of 1871, Hazlett had difficulty keeping the company's boats busy. On July 8, he sent one, the *Carrie V. Kountz*, to St. Louis to enter in the Mississippi River trade. At the same time, three other Kountz boats, the *Peninah, Katie P. Kountz,* and *Andrew Ackley,* were lying idle near the government transportation warehouse in Sioux City. The boats made occasional trips upstream; in late August, the *Peninah* was dispatched to Fort Buford with a cargo of military stores and thirty-two recruits for the Seventh Infantry. All three of the boats were out on the river in October. The *Yankton*

TABLE VIII
RATES PAID KOUNTZ LINE
FOR TRANSPORTATION OF MILITARY FREIGHT TO UPPER MISSOURI POSTS, 1871*

From Sioux City to:	Officers	Soldiers	Pound Fr't per 100 lbs.	Horses, Cattle, Mules	Wagons, Ambulances	Carts
Yankton Agency	$ 5	$ 3	$ .20	$ 5	$10	$ 6
Fort Randall	10	4	.40	8	15	8
Whetstone Agency	12	5	.48	15	15	9
Lower Brules Agency	16	6	.55	15	18	11
Crow Creek Agency	20	7	.68	15	20	13
Fort Sully	25	8	.80	25	25	17
Big Cheyenne Agency	25	9	.82	27	27	19
Grand River Agency	28	10	1.07	30	35	21
Fort Rice	30	11	1.15	35	40	23
Fort Stevenson	40	13	1.50	40	45	24
Fort Buford	50	15	1.69	45	50	25
Fort Benton	70	17	3.38	50	75	50

*"Tabular Statement," from *Contract for Missouri River between Hiram K. Hazlett and Assistant Quartermaster General, Chicago, March 17, 1871,* in Old Army Division, National Archives.

Press reported that the *Ackley* had been several weeks in making the trip to Cheyenne Agency, a trip normally made in ten days on a good river. By the end of September, there were but thirty-two inches of water in the channel between Sioux City and Fort Randall. The *Katie P. Kountz,* which drew thirty-six inches, was hard aground within sight of Sioux City the day after she was sent on a trip to Randall.[47]

Kountz was undaunted by his unprofitable year in the Sioux City trade. At the letting of the military contract for 1872, he once again submitted an unbelievably low bid. He may have been hoping to freeze out the Northwest Transportation Company by consistently taking the government trade away from them, but his attempts were unsuccessful. Kountz had to share the government business of 1871 with his rivals, and he lost both the military and Indian contracts to them in 1872.

The military contract for 1872 was let in Chicago the first part of

February. Grant Marsh represented the Northwest Transportation Company at the letting, and a Mr. Spiker of Pittsburgh represented the Kountz Line. Spiker's bid was the lowest, but he was not awarded the contract owing to irregularities in his bidding procedure. Spiker put in two bids, one high, the other extremely low. According to regulations, all bidders were required to provide $10,000 bond for each bid submitted, but Spiker posted only one bond. The Northwest

TABLE IX

RATES PAID DURFEE & PECK FOR

TRANSPORTATION OF FREIGHT TO UPPER MISSOURI INDIAN AGENCIES, 1872–1873*

| FROM SIOUX CITY, IOWA TO: | RATE PER 100 POUNDS | | |
	July & August 1872	Sept. & Oct. 1872	May & June 1873
Santee Agency	$ .10	$ .15	$ .08
Ponca Agency	.20	.15	.20
Yankton Agency	.20	.35	.21
Fort Randall	.30	.45	.25
Yellowstone Agency	.30	.53	.30
Upper Missouri Agency	.35	.45	.35
Fort Sully	.55	.75	.40
Cheyenne Agency	.65	.75	.65
Grand River Agency	.75	.90	.65
Fort Berthold	1.00	1.40	.85
Fort Buford	1.10	1.75	1.00
Fort Peck	1.75	2.00	1.60
Fort Benton	1.75	3.00	2.25

*Contract between Durfee & Peck and F. A. Walker, Commissioner of Indian Affairs, June 14, 1872, in Bureau of Indian Affairs, Interior Department, National Archives.

Transportation Company, upon learning of this omission, immediately sent a written protest to the Quartermaster General in Washington to forestall any possibility of the contract being awarded to Spiker.[48]

Spiker's low bid was 15 per cent lower than the contract rates of 1871 on which Kountz lost money. Grant Marsh's bid was approximately 30 per cent higher than Spiker's bid. Spiker's failure to file the second $10,000 bond cost both Kountz and the government money, but it was a profitable error as far as the Northwest Transportation Company was concerned. The contract for transportation of military supplies was awarded to them on February 28, 1872.[49]

The Indian contract, signed on June 14, 1872, and to remain in effect until July 1, 1873, went to Durfee & Peck, chief stockholders in the Northwest Transportation Company. Durfee & Peck's rates for transportation of Indian annuities for the year 1872 appear on Table IX.

The trading firm agreed to receive supplies at Sioux City, and also at St. Louis, Kansas City, and Omaha. For the transportation of supplies to Sioux City from these points, the firm was to receive the following: from St. Louis to Sioux City, forty cents per hundred pounds; from Kansas City to Sioux City, thirty-five cents per hundred pounds; from Omaha to Sioux City, eighteen cents per hundred pounds.[50]

Durfee & Peck anticipated such volume of freight on the Upper Missouri in 1872 that immediately after they signed the military contract, they announced their intentions of adding two new boats to their fleet. During the season, they operated nine boats on the Upper Missouri. The *Western*, one of the craft added to the fleet, was built during the winter at Allegheny City under the supervision of Sanford Coulson. The other boat added was the steamer *Sioux City*, which was purchased from the Arkansas River Packet Company.[51]

The Northwest Transportation Company became active early in April when the *Nellie Peck*, commanded by Grant Marsh, left for Whetstone Agency and intermediate points with three hundred tons of freight, most of it belonging to the government. The company was extremely rushed during the first two weeks in April; a reporter for the *Daily Journal* reported that railroad freight was coming into the transportation warehouse at the rate of four carloads a day. By the end of the month, the rush had fallen off, but trade began to revive early in June when the military shipped, by rail from Chicago to Sioux City, nearly two hundred tons of supplies destined for the Montana and Dakota posts.[52]

Throughout the remainder of the summer the Northwest Transportation Company was pressed to fulfill its military and Indian contracts. As late as August 1, the company had on hand the following amounts of freight yet to be shipped:[53]

> 71 ¼ tons for Grand River Agency
> 32 ¼ tons for Cheyenne River Agency
> 52 ¾ tons for Whetstone Agency
> 19 ¼ tons for Crow Creek Agency
> 1 ¾ tons for Lower Brule Agency
> 10 ½ tons for Yankton Agency
> 1 ½ tons for Ponca Agency
> 4 tons for Santee Agency
> 159 ¼ tons for Fort Peck

Because the Northwest Transportation Company's boats were the only ones that ran regularly to military posts and Indian agencies during the season of 1872 and stopped at all of them on each run, the company enjoyed a decided advantage in the transportation of civilian passengers. The company charged $7 passage from Sioux City to Yankton; $12 to Fort Randall; $18 to Brule Agency; $20 to Fort Thompson; $30 to Fort Sully; $30 to the Cheyenne Agency; $35 to Grand River Agency; $40 to Fort Rice; $50 to Fort Stevenson; $50 to Fort Berthold; $65 to Fort Buford; and $100 to Fort Benton.[54]

Some interesting facets of life on the Northwest Transportation Company boats were ably described by Dan Scott, correspondent for the *Sioux City Journal* and trader on the company's steamer *Western* in 1872. Most of the steamboats that plied the Missouri carried traders who had the concession to sell foodstuffs, tobacco products, and candy. The trader, despite the fact that his store was only a small cubicle, usually did a lively business, particularly with deck passengers, who had to provide their own food.

As trader, Scott was in a position to become well acquainted with both passengers and crew. In one of his communiques to the *Journal*, Scott described some of the travelers' reactions to the rattling noise of the "nigger." The low water and many crossings necessitated much sparring, which of course made necessary almost continuous use of the noisy little "nigger" engine. Scott related that Al Leighton, the post trader at Fort Buford, was so distraught by the engine noise that he overturned his breakfast plate, then began, "in the presence of a tableful of ladies and gentlemen, to whistle that familiar old tune, 'The Arkansas Traveler.'" Another passenger on the same trip, R. M. Whitney, succumbed to the noise of the nigger and left the boat to continue his trip on foot. The night before Whitney left the boat, Scott declared, he woke everyone in the vicinity of his stateroom by crying out loudly, and several times, "Stop that d——d nigger!" Said Scott, "It is fair to say that Mr. Whitney was asleep and dreaming when he made use of the mate's favorite expression, and in justice to that much abused machine, the 'nigger,' it was also quiet and the boat was moved to the shore."[55]

Scott noted that one of the commonest passenger solutions to the boredom of the steamboat trip was to drink whisky all night and sleep all day. Liquor was never difficult to obtain. Most boats had bars which were well stocked with a great variety of liquors. The barkeeper, like the trader, was not a regular crew member, but was instead an itinerant businessman. The bars not only provided a source of refreshment to those on board the steamer, but also to those at woodyards and posts where steamers stopped. Indian agents complained that it was impossible to keep liquor from the Indians as long as bar-equipped steamboats plied the river, since the barkeepers or boats' officers would sell intoxicants to the woodcutters, who in turn would trade it to their Indian neighbors. Boatmen many times found whisky to be a very popular form of payment for wood.

As a rule steamboat operators were very careful not to peddle liquor directly to military posts or Indian reservations, because of federal prohibitions. Steamboat men did transport, usually without their knowledge, liquor smugglers who had a nice trade with the "uniformed and blanketed sons of Uncle Sam." In 1872 a Dr. Walsh of Jackson, Michigan, a rather frequent excursionist on the Upper Missouri, was detected shipping a quantity of liquor, which he had disguised as a box of eggs and a barrel of dried apples.[56]

By early October of 1872, the Northwest Transportation Company was refusing to take private freight. Company boats were completely occupied with the transportation of supplies for the government and with the business of the trading firm of Durfee & Peck.

There was a considerable amount of business in carrying supplies to the Northern Pacific Railroad Crossing where Bismarck, North Dakota, is now located, but this trade was handled by the Kountz Line, and Dr. W. A. Burleigh. Burleigh was a prominent Yankton politician and former territorial delegate to Congress who entered steamboating in 1872 with the purchase of the *Miner* from A. F. Hawley.[57] The builders of the Northern Pacific intended to have track laid to the Missouri by the spring of 1873. In order to expedite construction, the managers of the road built from both east and west. The eastern part of the line was supplied by the railroad, but the western part was supplied by way of Sioux City and the Missouri River. During one week in June, Sioux City–based steamboats transported forty-eight carloads of lumber to the Crossing.[58] Burleigh's boat also carried ties for the Dakota Southern Railroad, which was being constructed from Sioux City to Yankton. The completion of this railroad in 1873 marked the beginning of the end of steam navigation domination on the Upper Missouri by Sioux City boating interests.

The extension of the railroad to Sioux City marked the beginning of a pattern which was thereafter repeated to a greater or lesser degree every time a railroad reached or crossed a higher point on the Missouri River. The first effect of these railroad extensions was to cut off the portion of the river below the extension, ending the domination of one steamboat center, but creating another dominant port at the new railroad terminus. Each time a new steamboat center was created, it depended heavily upon the railroad as its source of supply. Although boating concerns profited at each of the successive steamboat ports, the volume of freight as computed in ton-miles decreased. Profits also decreased because of rate reductions brought about by railroad competition and increased competition among steamboat companies owing to the decrease in the general volume of business. Steamboat men made their greatest profits on the longest hauls; the railroad to Sioux City virtually eliminated the 3,000-mile haul on the Missouri, and within a comparatively short period, the haul from Sioux City to Fort Benton, already diminished by the Union Pacific, was cut off by the completion of track to Yankton and Bismarck, both located above Sioux City.

VI

The Rise of Steamboat Ports
above Sioux City, 1873

DURING THE period 1870–1872, Sioux City steamboat men held a virtual monopoly over the trade of the Upper Missouri, but in 1873 the monopoly was broken when the Dakota Southern reached Yankton and the Northern Pacific was completed to Bismarck. When the railroads reached the Missouri above Sioux City, Sanford Coulson left the Northwest Transportation Company and moved to Yankton, where he and his associates set up the Missouri River Transportation Company. After Coulson was awarded the military contract for 1873, Yankton and Bismarck, instead of Sioux City, became the starting points for shipments of military supplies and personnel.

Yankton, the capital of Dakota Territory, was by 1870 an active frontier town. In that year the population of Yankton County was 2,097; of this number, 737 resided in the town. Yankton contained 180 buildings, and building expansion continued, made possible by five sawmills in the area, as well as local brick and lime kilns. Daily mail stages reached Yankton from Sioux City, and the telegraph line from Sioux City to Yankton was completed in 1870. The town had a good permanent river landing, and operated a steam ferry across the river, enabling it to tap a profitable Nebraska trade area.[1]

Promoters of Yankton and Dakota Territory believed that the agricultural potential of the area could not be realized until Dakota had railroad connections with the East. As early as 1864 the Dakota Legislature studied the possibility of routing a railroad through the territory, and three years later, when farmers intensified their demands for improved transportation, the legislature granted a charter to the Dakota and Northwestern Railroad.[2] The incorporators of the Dakota and Northwestern hoped to obtain a land grant from the federal government for the construction of a line from Sioux City to

Yankton. Congress, however, failed to make such a grant and the company never began construction work.

Sioux City businessmen initially opposed the extension of any railroad to the Dakota capital. Yankton promoters counteracted the opposition of Sioux City interests by attempting to connect with the Illinois Central at LeMars, Iowa, and thus bypass Sioux City. This attempt led Sioux City merchants to reverse their stand. Yankton businessmen were anxious to bypass Sioux City, but spokesmen for the farmers of Elk Point and Vermillion favored a railroad from Sioux City, because such a route would be laid through their towns.[3]

After the federal government refused to grant land to the Dakota and Northwestern in 1871, Dakotans decided to build a railroad with local funds. On March 17, 1871, Yankton businessmen organized the Dakota Southern Railroad. Yankton merchants were the principal purchasers of company stock, but they did not have sufficient funds to finance the entire project. This shortage of funds led to a very unique financing plan which was made possible by the Dakota Legislature.

In April, 1871, the Dakota legislators, in a special session, passed an act authorizing townships and counties to grant aid to railroad companies.[4] The Yankton businessmen next engineered an election in Yankton County in which the county agreed to sell $200,000 worth of bonds as a way of raising money to support the railroad. Farmers in Yankton, Clay, and Union counties were generally opposed to the idea of issuing bonds for this purpose but Yankton businessmen dominated the affair, and by late 1871 the Dakota Southern was sufficiently well financed so its promoters could go ahead with construction plans. In December of 1871, the Chicago construction firm of Wicker, Meckling and Company contracted to build the Dakota Southern. The company started work early in 1872, and the line from Sioux City to Yankton was opened to traffic on February 3, 1873.[5]

While the road was being built the Dakota Southern publicized its advantages to southeastern Dakota. John Brennan, a publicity agent of the railroad, wrote "we may approximate the carrying trade and travel of the Dakota Southern for the immediate future, but to reckon its trade and travel in years to come we must picture to ourselves the future of the great northwest whose inhabitants it is intended to accommodate."[6]

Brennan contended that the tonnage previously shipped upriver by steamboat from Sioux City would be transported to Yankton by rail after the Dakota Southern was completed, and that Yankton rather than Sioux City would serve as the great break-in-bulk point for the Upper Missouri trade. In an attempt to compute the amount of freight to be carried over the Dakota Southern, Brennan referred to the amount of steamboat freight shipped from Sioux City during the first three months of the 1872 season. He obtained his statistics from James Doud, superintendent of the forwarding and commission house of Milton Tootle & Co. of Sioux City, who had compiled a table which illustrated the amount of steamboat trade originating in Sioux City during the months of April, May, and June, 1872.

Doud recorded that during this three-month period Sioux City–based steamers made a total of twenty-eight trips to points on the Upper Missouri, carrying 6,683 tons of freight. Brennan claimed that the average tonnage per boat on its trip downstream was fifty tons, which would make a total downstream tonnage of 1,400, or a grand total of 8,083 carried by the Sioux City steamboats. In order to find the total freight for a season, wrote Brennan, simply double the amount of the first three months, and the prospective aggregate freight for an entire six-month boating season would be more than 16,000 tons.[7] Brennan's computation of the total prospective tonnage for a season was very generous, since he could not accurately assume that the tonnage of July, August, and September, normally rather slack months, would equal that of the first three months.

It was obvious in 1872 that the future of the Upper Missouri trade would be with Yankton because, logically, the federal government would start its contracts at the railhead closest to the posts and agencies. This realization led Sanford Coulson to break with Durfee and Peck and to establish his own steamboat company.

While the Dakota Southern was being completed, Coulson was organizing the Missouri River Transportation Company, also known as the Coulson Packet Line. Coulson was the chief organizer and general manager of the new company, but he had many important associates who also contributed to the success of the firm. When Coulson left the Northwest Transportation Company, his three older brothers, John, William, and Martin, who had also been associated with the company, accompanied him. Coulson, a native Pennsylvanian who had banking interests in Allegheny City, Pennsylvania, also brought his Allegheny City acquaintances J. C. McVay, D. S. H. Gilmore, John B. Dallas, and William Evans into the company with him. All of these men had considerable experience as steamboat entrepreneurs on the Ohio, Mississippi, and Missouri rivers. Coulson also persuaded Nicholas Buesen and Josephus Todd, two of the best-known steamboat captains on the Upper Missouri, to come with him. Throughout most of the eleven years of the Missouri River Transportation Company, Buesen and Todd were part owners of many of the company's boats.

Coulson planned to base his new company at Yankton, and also hoped to control the trade which originated at the Northern Pacific Railroad Crossing. During 1872 and early 1873 the small settlement located on the east bank of the river at the point where the Northern Pacific was to cross the Missouri was known as the Northern Pacific Railroad Crossing, or simply as the Crossing. In the spring of 1873 the settlement was named Edwinton. The name was changed to Bismarck in early summer by the town boosters who hoped thereby to encourage the Chancellor of Germany, Otto Von Bismarck, to buy land in the area. Coulson was interested in trade at the Crossing primarily because he believed that the government would name the Northern Pacific Railroad Crossing as starting point for part of its contract goods.

In order to make his shift from Sioux City profitable, Coulson had to get the military contract for transportation to the posts on the Upper Missouri. If the Northwest Transportation Company got the contract in 1873 as it had in previous years and continued to use Sioux City as the starting point, then both Coulson and the Dakota Southern would suffer. All of the interested parties in Yankton and Sioux City anxiously watched the contract proceedings during the early months of 1873.

The initial step in the letting of military contracts for the Upper Missouri was taken by the Quartermaster General of the Department of Dakota at St. Paul when he announced early each year that competitive sealed bids would be accepted by his office. The departmental quartermaster studied all bids, then made a recommendation to the Quartermaster General in Washington, D.C. The departmental quartermaster was not obliged to accept the lowest bid, but could use his own discretion in selecting the bidder who was most likely to carry out the contract efficiently. The selection of the contractor by the departmental quartermaster was usually seconded by the Quartermaster General, but it was possible for the Washington official to overrule the decision of his subordinate. Thus, the success of a would-be contractor many times depended upon good relations with the departmental quartermaster, the Quartermaster General, and even the Secretary of War.

Sanford Coulson consistently maintained cordial relations with the principal military officials and personally lobbied in Washington at contract time. Members of the Sioux City Chamber of Commerce followed the movements of Coulson and his associates with apprehension, fearing that Coulson, rather than the Northwest Transportation Company, would get the military contract. Their fears were well grounded; in the latter part of February, John B. Dallas, the bidder for the Missouri River Transportation Company, was awarded the contract.

In the contract signed by Dallas on February 21, 1873, the Missouri River Transportation Company was given all military business originating at points between Sioux City and Fort Benton for the period beginning March 20 and ending October 31, 1873.[8] Under the terms of the contract, Sioux City, Yankton, and the Northern Pacific Railroad Crossing were named as starting points for government freight, and Dallas agreed to keep an agent at both Sioux City and Yankton. The contract did not grant the company a monopoly of all government transportation business on the Upper Missouri, since the government reserved the right to hire St. Louis–based steamboats if it wished.

The Missouri River Transportation Company was to be paid for transporting freight during the months of March, April, and May, 1873, from Sioux City to the various destinations as shown on Table X.

During June and July the rates were to be slightly higher, and September and October rates were two to three times higher than the spring rates. An amendment was added to the contract which provided that Coulson was to ship freight which originated at Yankton for ten cents a hundred less than he shipped freight starting at Sioux City. This provision made it possible for the government to make a separate arrangement for transportation from Sioux City to Yankton with the Dakota Southern.

Sioux City businessmen, of course, had hoped that Durfee and Peck's Northwest Transportation Company would get the contract, but even after Coulson's bid was accepted, they still hoped Sioux City would be the starting point for the upriver military shipments. If government officials failed to reach an agreement with the Dakota

Southern for the transportation of freight from Sioux City to Yankton, they would have to fall back on Coulson's contract agreement on Sioux City to Yankton freight, and Coulson, in turn, would be forced to operate his steamers out of Sioux City.

TABLE X

RATES PAID MISSOURI RIVER TRANSPORTATION COMPANY
FOR TRANSPORTATION OF MILITARY FREIGHT TO UPPER MISSOURI POSTS, 1873*

From Sioux City to:	Rate per 100 Pounds.
Yankton Agency	$ .25
Fort Randall	.25
Whetstone Creek Agency	.75
Lower Brules Agency	.50
Crow Creek Agency	.75
Fort Sully	.60
Big Cheyenne Agency	.60
Grand River Agency	.90
Fort Rice	1.60
Fort Abraham Lincoln or Edwinton	1.75
Fort Stevenson	1.50
Fort Buford	1.60
Fort Benton	2.35

*Contract for Missouri River between Colonel D. H. Rucker, Assistant Quartermaster, U.S.A., and John B. Dallas, February 21, 1873, in Old Army Division, National Archives.

On March 6, a reporter for the *Journal* engaged in a bit of wishful thinking, speculating that perhaps there would be no agreement between the government and the Dakota Southern, because the government quartermaster officers in Sioux City had not been notified of any change of headquarters, and consignments of freight had already arrived for the Sioux City Quartermaster. Within three days, however, the *Journal* was forced to announce that the Dakota Southern and the government had reached an eleventh-hour agreement by which the railroad was to carry military supplies from Sioux City to Yankton for nine cents a hundred. The government could have made either Yankton or Sioux City the starting point, but the Dakota Southern had powerful lobbyists in Washington who were instrumental in securing the contract for the railroad. The foremost spokesman of the Dakota Southern in the nation's capital was Moses K. Armstrong, the delegate from Dakota Territory.[9]

According to the Dakota Southern contract, the railroad was to provide the government with free warehousing in Yankton. Property owners in Yankton promptly subscribed money to build a suitable warehouse, and Sanford Coulson; Joel A. Wicker, an official of the

Dakota Southern; and city officials selected a site at the foot of Walnut Street where a 46 by 200–foot building was erected.[10]

In December of 1872, the Sioux City Quartermaster posted a notice which opened bidding on contract goods to be shipped from Edwinton. Sioux City merchants hoped that they would be able to sell at least some of the contract goods which were to be carried by the Dakota Southern, but they knew absolutely that they would not have a chance to sell any of the supplies for contracts which started at Edwinton. Therefore, on December 31, the Sioux City Chamber of Commerce wrote to William Belknap, Secretary of War, protesting the naming of Edwinton as a shipping point. John C. Flint, Chairman of the Board of Directors of the Chamber of Commerce, wrote to Belknap that the Northern Pacific would not have its road ready by spring to meet the needs of the government, and that even if the road were ready, it would not be to the best interests of the government to use it. Flint wrote that the Sioux City Chamber of Commerce believed that "the great bulk of Government goods can be bought at this point, or delivered, here, and then transported to Edwinton by water at lower rates than can be delivered at that point."[11] Flint also argued that if Edwinton were made the starting point, New York and Philadelphia would be the purchasing points because all transportation would come via the northern route by way of the Great Lakes and Duluth. This, claimed Flint, would, mean that the government would be giving eastern capitalists virtual control over the Upper Missouri River business. Flint contended that eastern capitalists would supply all of the feed and forage for the military posts above Edwinton because the land between the Red and Missouri rivers in northern Dakota Territory was worthless. Flint further wrote that Sioux City was the best starting point because it "is surrounded by the best farming lands in the West, and offers the best market for the Government, for farming products on the entire Missouri River."[12] He also contended that it would be wasteful to use the Northern Pacific railhead because the government had already built two large warehouses at Sioux City, and it would be uneconomical to duplicate these facilities at Edwinton.

In order to emphasize further the demands of the Sioux City Chamber of Commerce, Flint wrote to Senator George Wright and Congressman J. Orr of Iowa and asked that they confer with the Secretary of War over the letting of the contract. Belknap, in answer to Orr's inquiry, assured the Congressman that Sioux City was not excluded from the competition for the contract, but that the government was merely interested in establishing a competitive situation. Orr also called on Chief Quartermaster General Meigs, and was assured by the General that the army had no intention of abandoning Sioux City as a shipping point for supplies. Despite the assurance that Orr received from Meigs, the Sioux City Chamber of Commerce was faced with the fact that the Dakota Southern had secured a government contract and also that the Northern Pacific had a contract to transport supplies to the end of its line at Edwinton.

When the steamboat season of 1873 opened, there were three major companies engaged in trade on the Upper Missouri. The Missouri River Transportation Company, based at Yankton, operated about fifteen boats during the season. Durfee and Peck announced that the Northwest Transportation Company would run between Sioux City and Fort Benton as they had during the two previous seasons, putting seven boats on the river. The third company to operate on the Upper Missouri was the Kountz Line, which transported the freight from Edwinton to Fort Benton for the Northern Pacific. Kountz announced in March that he intended to use four boats in his trade.[13]

When the steamboat season opened, the disposition of the Indian annuities business was still uncertain. The Indian contract was second only to the military contract in terms of financial reward to suppliers and transporters. Sioux City merchants had a good opportunity to salvage something from the contract business if the Northwest Transportation Company could put in a successful bid for carrying the Indian annuities.

The annuities contract for 1872 held by Durfee and Peck did not expire until June 15. On March 24, 1873, H. R. Clum, Acting Indian Commissioner, announced that sealed bids would be accepted for the next contract. The proposed contract called for the transporting of goods and supplies "from Sioux City, Iowa, or Yankton, Dakota, to the Yankton, Cheyenne, Upper Missouri (Crow Creek), and Grand River Agencies, and to Forts Randall, Berthold, Peck, and Benton, on the Missouri River. Also, by wagon from Fort Randall, Dakota to the Whetstone Agency, in Dakota."[14]

Bidding ended officially on April 28, and on May 2 this contract was awarded to Amherst H. Wilder of St. Paul, at special monthly rates per hundred pounds. Wilder did not own any steamboats, but bid for the contract with the intention of subletting the hauling to steamboat owners.

By June 12, twenty-one carloads of Indian goods had arrived in Sioux City for the various agencies, and Wilder had not yet made arrangements for their transportation upriver. Sanford Coulson, John Dallas, and E. H. Durfee all talked with Wilder about getting the business. Wilder decided to use both Sioux City and Edwinton as starting points for his contract goods. This way he could supply the agencies above Grand River from Edwinton, while Grand River and points below could be supplied from Sioux City. Wilder planned to send about 2,872 tons of Indian freight upriver from Sioux City; of this, 45 tons were for Santee Agency, 87½ tons for Yankton Agency, 921 tons for Whetstone Agency (at that time located approximately 175 miles west of Fort Randall), 422½ tons for Upper Missouri Agency, 475 tons for Cheyenne Agency, and 921 tons for Grand River Agency.[15]

In June Wilder announced that he would purchase his own boats to transport the goods, but this action was never completed. Instead, he dealt with various steamboat owners and made separate contracts every time he sent goods upriver. During the course of the season, Coulson, Kountz, and the Northwest Transportation Company all carried supplies for Wilder from both Sioux City and Bismarck.

Wilder's contract did not give him a monopoly of transportation of Indian supplies on the Upper Missouri. The Commissioner of Indian Affairs granted a second contract to the Northern Pacific Railroad for the shipment of freight from New York, Philadelphia, and Chicago to Fort Benton and Fort Peck. Goods from New York and Philadelphia were to be shipped for $2.70 per hundred and the Chicago supplies were to be carried for $2.30 per hundred.[16]

The navigation season of 1873 fully met the expectations of Yankton and Bismarck business interests. Tremendous amounts of trade were channeled through the two towns. The impact of the Dakota Southern was felt immediately by Sioux City steamboat men. During the month of April, the railroad transported 2,700 tons of freight from Sioux City to Yankton. The railroad also transported 843 civilian passengers and 767 military personnel.[17]

Missouri River steamboating showed a decided increase in 1873 as compared to the previous year. From the opening of navigation until June 30, 3,944½ tons had been shipped from Sioux City and Yankton combined. Of this total, over 3,000 tons had been shipped from Yankton, clearly indicating that Yankton had taken over much of Sioux City's trade. By late June, the supremacy of Yankton was apparent and the *Yankton Press* could afford to refer to Sioux City as "that ex-steamboat burg."[18]

While business at Yankton began auspiciously in the spring of 1873, the businessmen of Bismarck were at first frustrated because the Northern Pacific was not ready for operation at the start of the navigation season. The first boat loaded for the upriver trade at Bismarck, Kountz's *Peninah,* was not loaded until June 14.[19] The lack of activity at Bismarck led both Sioux City and Yankton interests to make disparaging remarks about the town. It was reported by C. C. Brookings of Yankton that Bismarck business was not good except with the hotel keepers and the saloon men. Brookings further asserted that

Bismarck mosquitoes are maintaining their national reputation, and make a residence there almost insupportable. With every evening a smudge is built in front of every house, and as the dense smoke arises it wraps all in a black pall which obscures sight, fills the lungs, waters the eyes, then begrims the flesh, until one begins to question his own mind which is the worst, the smudge or the mosquitoes.[20]

Business at Bismarck was not nearly as poor as the informants of the *Sioux City Journal* wanted the public to believe. Trade at Bismarck was quite lively once the Northern Pacific began delivering goods to the town. During the period June 9 to August 9 the railroad carried 4,653 tons of freight to Bismarck.[21] None of this freight was for railroad construction. The bulk of it was lumber for the construction of new buildings at Fort Abraham Lincoln. Most of the remainder of the freight was military and Indian supplies, which were transferred to steamboats and shipped upstream.

Colonel Clement A. Lounsberry, the editor of the *Bismarck Tribune,* claimed that the Northern Pacific contract had changed the channel of transportation and that in the future "this will be the route over which will pass all government supplies and freight." Lounsberry believed that Bismarck steamboat men would not only control the trade above Bismarck, but would also control a share of the trade to the forts and agencies below Bismarck, as Bismarck shippers would find it easier to navigate down the river to the agencies and forts than

Yankton navigators would find it to ascend the river. Lounsberry stated that shippers would find it extremely advantageous to ship to St. Paul and to take advantage of the forty-eight-hour train service to Bismarck rather than to ship to Yankton and risk possible loss in the hard-to-navigate portion of the river below Fort Rice.[22]

Bismarck's future as a navigation center was stimulated in August, 1873, when William J. Kountz, who had worked with Coulson earlier in the season, announced that he would cease cooperating with the Missouri River Transportation Company and in the future would operate exclusively from Bismarck in cooperation with the Northern Pacific Railroad. Kountz moved his boats to Bismarck and organized the Northern Pacific Railroad Line. He intended to winter all seven of the boats at Bismarck and to put the new line in full operation with the opening of navigation in 1874. In September, Kountz and the Northern Pacific completed their arrangements for the coming season through an agreement with the McClay Diamond Freight Line, which was to rendezvous with the steamboats at the mouth of the Musselshell and transport freight to Helena.[23]

Thus, by 1873, there were two co-existing centers of steam navigation on the Upper Missouri: Yankton, supplied by way of the Dakota Southern, and Bismarck, supplied by the Northern Pacific. Steamboat operators based at these two towns would control transportation on the Upper Missouri for some seven years before the pattern of trade was again modified by further railroad extensions.

VII

Yankton–Bismarck Steamboat Men

IF EVER boating on the Upper Missouri assumed unique characteristics, it was after 1873, when the activity was controlled by Yankton and Bismarck operators. For the first time in the history of Upper Missouri navigation the men who engaged in the business were men primarily concerned with transportation—not with the fur trade or gold mining. Unlike earlier navigators, they regarded the Upper Missouri as their home. Many of them became permanent residents and devoted their talents and capital to the development of the region. This small fraternity of boatmen came for the most part from the Ohio River region. Most of them were natives of Pennsylvania and Ohio who had worked on the Ohio, Mississippi, and Lower Missouri before moving upstream to one of the last lucrative steamboat frontiers in the nation. Since these men were dedicated to the Upper Missouri trade, they made a much more conscious effort to adjust to the river than any previous boatmen. These were not men with a "get rich quick" philosophy, as were many of the St. Louisians who engaged in the Fort Benton trade following the Civil War. These men knew that they had to live with the river during the entire boating season and that their business depended upon the successful delivery of goods from beginning to end of the season.

The Yankton–Bismarck steamboat men for the most part were organized as incorporated companies. Most of the boats were controlled by four major companies, the Missouri River Transportation Company, or the Coulson Line; the Kountz Line; the Peck Line; and the Fort Benton Transportation Company, or the Power Line. The largest and most successful of these companies was the Missouri River Transportation Company, which was headed by Sanford B. Coulson.

Coulson, the youngest of four steamboating brothers, was born at McKeesport, Pennsylvania, on August 29, 1839, and spent his youth in nearby Allegheny City.[1] These towns, located at the forks of the Ohio, were in one of the great trade centers of the country, since the Ohio led to the Mississippi and beyond. Coulson, like many of the boys in this area before the Civil War, was drawn into boating because it was one of the region's principal professions. While working on Allegheny River steamers as a youth, he also learned the blacksmith trade. He was an accomplished mechanic who loved to work with his hands. One of his favorite pastimes throughout life was carpentry work, especially boat construction.[2] He prided himself on being something more than a shore man who sat at a desk, and seems to have had the attitude that he could handle boat jobs as competently as anyone on the crew.

As a young man he entered the Ohio River and Mississippi River trade as an assistant engineer on a Davidson boat.[3] By the age of thirty, Coulson was working as first engineer on a Missouri River boat owned by William J. Kountz and several others from Allegheny City. Coulson left Kountz's employ after getting involved in an unpleasant dispute between the fiery Kountz and the other owners of the boat.[4] After this break the two men feuded intermittently throughout their careers on the Upper Missouri. Coulson regarded Kountz as not merely a rival, but as an enemy. The Coulson and Kountz families apparently knew each other quite well in Allegheny City. Both families were represented on the board of directors of an Allegheny City bank.

As Coulson matured, he displayed a talent for administration as well as for physical work. He was a strong-willed individual who preferred to lead rather than be led. He was extremely ambitious and was a master at evaluating a financial situation or business opportunity. Although he was never highly popular, he was widely respected and admired for his success in business. Coulson was not the type of individual who could win elections or overwhelm people with his winning smile or overpowering personality. He did have, however, an amazing ability for getting to know people. He spent a great deal of time cultivating acquaintances with people who could help him, such as generals, congressmen, and steamboat inspectors. His careful cultivation of important figures is one of the reasons why he was such an effective lobbyist in Washington. He realized full well that in many instances a contractor had to have more than the lowest bid to win contracts.

Coulson's first opportunity to use his administrative talents came when he was the general superintendent of the Northwest Transportation Company in Sioux City. His job was to line up freight, hire crews, load boats, and supervise all freighting activity. While in Sioux City, Coulson was also called upon to do some navigating, since the boat line was short of experienced officers. He commanded the *Far West* on the Sioux City to Fort Benton run in 1872 and gained the distinction of making the fastest recorded run from Sioux City to Benton, just over seventeen days, which was nearly six days faster than the record of the *Nellie Peck*, commanded by Grant Marsh. Coulson took pride in this feat for many years.[5]

Most of Coulson's career was spent in Yankton. During his first five years in the town, he and his family lived there only during the navigation season. They spent every winter back home in Allegheny City. In 1878 Coulson decided to become a permanent resident and constructed a $10,000 house which was regarded by his fellow townspeople as an elegant mansion.[6] He was reputed to be a millionaire and was so regarded in river towns from St. Louis to Fort Benton.

With deference to Coulson's position as commander of the biggest fleet on the Upper Missouri, he was almost universally known as "Commodore." His rather abrupt manner and aloofness also earned him a less kind appellation—"The Napoleon of the Big Muddy." Coulson's activities were continually followed by newspapers, and his appearance in a river town in the 1870's even in such a sizable city as St. Louis was enough to be considered a news item.

Coulson was very active in Yankton business affairs. He was one of the directors and vice-president of the First National Bank. Coulson had real estate interests in the town and also owned and maintained a 1,200-acre farm near Yankton. The farm was stocked with purebred sheep imported from Ohio. He also had financial interests in the Yankton Fire Insurance Company and in a brick factory.[7]

A Democrat, Coulson was quite active in local politics, serving at one time as a member of the school board and as a county commissioner. He was once named by a Democratic caucus to run for a seat in the territorial council, but this bid for election failed. Coulson was also a rather ardent civic booster. On one occasion he subscribed $5,000, about half of the amount required, to build a ferry boat and then did some of the carpentry work himself.[8]

Sanford B. Coulson's three older brothers, John, Martin, and William, worked with him in his steamboating ventures. These three, despite their seniority, deferred to Sanford's judgment in most business matters. John and William worked as boat officers on the Missouri, acting as pilots or masters on many of the Coulson boats. John moved to Yankton, but William resided in Allegheny City. Martin, who also remained in Allegheny City, spent most of his time supervising the construction of boats and managing the family's interest in an Allegheny City bank.

The Coulson brothers were assisted in the formation of the Missouri River Transportation Company by five Pennsylvania businessmen and two prominent steamboat men from Ohio. The five Pennsylvanians, all from the Allegheny City–Pittsburgh area, were James C. McVay, John B. Dallas, James Rees, William S. Evans, and D. S. H. Gilmore. The two Ohio navigators were Josephus Todd and Nicholas Buesen.

McVay moved from Allegheny City to Yankton, where he served as treasurer of the company. He was also manager and one of the directors of the First National Bank, and acted as treasurer of Dakota Territory for several years. John B. Dallas, who was not quite thirty when the Missouri River Transportation Company was formed, was the head of the boat chandlery firm of Evans, Dallas and Gilmore. Dallas infrequently visited the Missouri River, but he did work closely with Coulson in procuring military contracts. James Rees, who had run boats in the St. Louis–Fort Benton trade in the 1860's, had an interest in some of the Coulson boats. By profession he was a boat builder. Some of the Coulson Line boats were built in the Rees boatyards near Pittsburgh. William S. Evans, a brother-in-law of the Coulson boys, was born near Hagerstown, Maryland. After trying carpentry, he moved to the Pittsburgh area and took charge of a bar on a Monongahela River steamer. Afterward he commanded several steamers in the Ohio River–St. Louis–New Orleans trade. Evans seemed well known in steamboat circles. He habitually wore a cluster diamond pin and big gold watch chain. Steamboat men contended that it was very easy to spot a boat named by Evans—just look for a seven-letter name. Evans, it was reputed, was superstitious about naming boats and was even reluctant to buy boats that did not have seven-letter names. The frequency of seven-letter names in the Coulson boats would seem to support this claim. Some of the best known Coulson steamers were the *Far West, Key West, Rosebud, Western, Montana, Wyoming,* and *Dacotah.*[9]

Undoubtedly the three most highly regarded Coulson Line captains were Nick Buesen, Joe Todd, and Grant Marsh. These men were recognized in steamboat circles for their reliability, both in moving freight and handling men. Buesen was a native of Hamburg, Germany; from there he moved to Columbiana County, Ohio, where he met Todd. The two worked together on the Mississippi and Missouri rivers following the Civil War. They worked for the Northwest Transportation Company in 1872 and 1873 out of Sioux City. It was also at this time that they became well acquainted with the Coulsons. When Coulson moved to Yankton, Buesen and Todd went with him, subsequently becoming part owners of company boats as well as serving as captains. Buesen spent part of his time in Pennsylvania assisting in the construction of steamboats. He also held the distinction of having been granted the first pilot's license for the Yellowstone River.[10]

Grant Marsh, born in 1834, spent most of his youth in the river town of Rochester, Pennsylvania. He began his steamboat career as a cabin boy when he was twelve years old. His work on the river drew him ever farther west. Marsh first came to St. Louis as a deckhand in 1852 and later worked on boats in the St. Louis–Omaha trade. By 1858 he was a first mate on the *A. B. Chambers No. 2,* on which he was assisted by a then-unknown second mate, Samuel Clemens. During the Civil War, Marsh worked on boats in the Union Fleet on the Lower Mississippi and still later, in 1864, served on the *Marcella,* one of the boats in Sully's fleet on the Upper Missouri.[11]

During the five years after the war Marsh worked as a pilot and captain in the St. Louis–Fort Benton trade and then became associated with the Northwest Transportation Company at Sioux City.[12] Marsh moved to Yankton with Sanford Coulson in 1873 as a captain of one of the Coulson Line boats. Marsh worked with Coulson throughout most of the 1870's, although he was an independent operator for brief periods. Grant Marsh was a well-known and highly regarded figure in the Upper Missouri area years before he won national prominence by bringing out the wounded after the Battle of the Little Big Horn.

Sanford B. Coulson had numerous capable partners when he founded the Missouri River Transportation Company, yet the most vital man in the company next to Coulson was a latecomer—Daniel

Webster Maratta. Maratta, who ranked second only to Coulson as a policy maker and executive in the Coulson Line, eventually became even better known on the Upper Missouri than Coulson.

Maratta spent most of his early years on rivers. He was a native of Pennsylvania, from Bridgewater, in Beaver County, on the banks of the Ohio about forty miles below Pittsburgh. As a youth he was a cabin boy on an Ohio River steamer, where he became well acquainted with a fellow cabin boy, Grant Marsh, from nearby Rochester, Pennsylvania. By 1856 Maratta had earned his first administrative position—assistant clerk on a Mississippi River steamer. From that position he moved quickly to that of licensed pilot and licensed master. During the Civil War, Daniel and his four brothers, Frank, James, Hines, and Walter, all worked as officers on Union Army transports on the Lower Mississippi. Dan was a commander of an army transport during the Vicksburg campaign. Walter, the youngest of the four brothers, was killed at Island No. 35 above Memphis while serving on a boat commanded by Frank. Frank and James later worked on the Upper Missouri, operating out of Bismarck in 1878–1879.[13]

After the war Maratta continued to work on the Ohio and Lower Mississippi. Sometime in this postwar period he became associated with William J. Kountz. When Maratta entered the Upper Missouri business in 1873, he did so as captain of the Kountz Line steamer *May Lowry*, which was being used in the Bismarck–Fort Benton trade.[14] The next year he was back on the Upper Missouri as commander of the *Fontenelle*, which was reputed to be the fastest and most reliable of the Kountz boats. The *Bismarck Tribune* credited the success of the boat to Maratta, remarking that

The unvarying success which has attended the Fontenelle is mainly attributed to the ability and management of that model steamboat captain, D. W. Maratta. No man can successfully navigate the "Big Muddy" without both skill and experience combined, requirements which are indispensible and which Capt. Maratta possesses in an eminent degree. The passengers on the Fontenelle on the last trip from Bismarck to Carroll speak in the highest terms of Capt. Maratta's kindness, of his genial and happy disposition, and of his constant efforts to please and accomodate them in every way.[15]

It was while working for Kountz at Bismarck that Maratta met and became well acquainted with Sanford Coulson. Sometime before the opening of navigation in 1875 Maratta broke with Kountz and joined Coulson as his Bismarck agent.[16] The association of Maratta and Coulson was more than a convenient business arrangement. The two men became good friends. Maratta was the only man in the organization whose judgment Coulson seemed to respect consistently. The two worked together many times in their negotiations for government contracts. For two years Maratta handled the business of the company in Bismarck while Coulson supervised operations at Yankton. Then Maratta was promoted to general manager of the company. He spent most of his time in Bismarck, but did make occasional visits to Yankton and Sioux City. Maratta regarded himself as a resident of Bismarck and of Dakota Territory, but he always spent the winters in Beaver, Pennsylvania.

Maratta, in contrast to Coulson, was a man quick with a smile and a handshake. He continually played to the galleries. He relished his reputation for being friendly and accommodating. He aspired to know as many people as possible, and within a matter of months after moving to Bismarck he was as well known as anyone in the area. Extremely gregarious, he loved to talk, and was called "Slippery Dan" by his fellow boatmen because of his petroleum tongue. His business tactics were a combination of good will, fast talk, and bull-dozing. To most people who dealt with him, he appeared genial and easy going. To those that he had to push he must have seemed pugnacious. Maratta's personal reliability became a characteristic of the company, and he was very persuasive in advertising the efficiency of the Coulson Line, which he referred to as the "Old Reliable Line." He kept a tight control over the boat officers and managed to keep labor difficulties at a minimum, all of which contributed to his success in moving thousands of tons of freight upstream from Bismarck.

Maratta's thorough knowledge of steamboating combined with his popularity made him invaluable to the Coulson Line in negotiations with the government. He invariably attended the contract-lettings with Coulson and usually followed through by personally calling on congressmen to see that his company would be rewarded. He spent at least part of every winter in Washington, D.C., button-holing people who could aid in the final awarding of the contracts.

Like many ambitious men, Maratta was somewhat egotistical. After a few years in Bismarck, he presumed that everyone in the area knew who he was. Considering the amount of coverage he received from the *Bismarck Tribune*, everyone in the region should have known him. *Tribune* editor, M. H. Jewell seldom missed an opportunity to publicize Maratta's comings and goings, usually with tongue in cheek. Jewell made frequent references to Maratta's immaculate dress, his dignified and princely bearing, even going so far as to describe him as "the cynosure of all who have the good fortune of being thrown about him."[17]

On one occasion, Jewell recounted Maratta's encounter with a hotel clerk, a newcomer in town. Maratta, said Jewell, asked for a room at the Sheridan House, where he frequently stayed while in Bismarck, and the clerk asked him for a payment in advance because he had no baggage with him. Maratta huffed and puffed, and supposedly shouted at the clerk, "Everybody in the Missouri slope knows me, and you ought to know who I am, without any explanation or autobiographical sketch to assist you." The clerk continued to insist on the advance payment, and Maratta left the hotel with an oath never to enter its doors again. Jewell credited Maratta with consoling himself with the thought that "if Jesus of Nazareth had not where to lay his head, why should the 'little Jesus' of Dakota complain."[18] Whatever Jewell's motives were, for following Maratta's activities so closely, he did succeed in keeping the man in the public eye, which, in the long run, aided Maratta in his political career.

When he entered predominantly Republican Dakota Territory, Maratta was a confirmed and energetic Democrat. From the start he devoted much of his effort to selling his party and himself. He religiously attended political rallies, delivered speeches, and worked for the local and national Democratic organizations. He was soon regarded as the ranking Democrat in Bismarck and one of the foremost in the entire territory. In the early 1880's he was mentioned as a possible Democratic nominee for congressional delegate. In 1882 he did try for a seat in the territorial council and was narrowly defeated by his Republican opponent.[19]

The strongest competitor of the Missouri River Transportation Company during its first five years was William J. Kountz, principal owner and superintendent of the Kountz Line. Kountz operated his boats out of both Bismarck and Sioux City, but concentrated his efforts on the trade at Bismarck and above.

Kountz was born in May, 1817, at Wellsville, Ohio, where his father operated a pottery. At ten he became a cabin boy on an Ohio

River packet and then while still in his teens became commander of a keelboat. By the 1850's he was one of the best-known commanders on the Ohio and Lower Mississippi. He became particularly well known after he was given command of the *Crystal Palace*, a 300-foot-long "floating palace" complete with crystal chandeliers. This boat, which accommodated 173 passengers, became one of the outstanding steamboats on the river during the golden era of boating on the Mississippi.[20]

It was while boating that Kountz became acquainted with George B. McClellan of the Illinois Central and the Ohio & Mississippi railroads. Early in the Civil War McClellan was made a major general and placed in command of the Department of the Ohio. His principal task was to win western Virginia, which meant that he had to control the Ohio River in order to supply his forces. McClellan explicitly re-quested the War Department to enlist the services of Kountz and placed him in charge of the transports supplying his army. Kountz was only too happy to enter the military service, since he was a determined opponent of slavery and looked upon the war as a desirable way of exterminating the national evil. Kountz, who was commissioned a commodore, very quickly offended most of the army officers because of his impatience with military hierarchies and bureaucracy. He delivered supplies with a machine-like efficiency, but his sledge-hammer diplomacy was too much of a luxury for McClellan's command, and McClellan reluctantly consented to the removal of Kountz.[21]

It was while in federal service that Kountz had his famous brush with U. S. Grant. Kountz landed supplies for Grant's army at Pittsburgh Landing prior to the Battle of Shiloh. When Grant gave orders affecting the disposition of the transports, Kountz initially refused them and then was forced to submit. Kountz never forgave Grant for this affront. A militant teetotaler, Kountz was also bothered by Grant's imbibitions. It was commonly rumored that after the Battle of Belmont, in which Grant was repulsed, Kountz insinuated in a conversation with President Lincoln that Grant was drunk during the battle. To this Lincoln replied that if he knew where Grant got his liquor, he would send a barrel to each general in the Union Army.[22]

While primarily concerned with steamboating, Kountz did actively participate in politics in western Pennsylvania. In 1864 he was named the Democratic congressional nominee from the Twenty-third Pennsylvania District. He failed to win the election. In 1872 he failed again in this predominantly Republican district while running for Congress as a Greeleyite.[23]

The "Commodore," as he was styled after his war experience, never moved to the region of the Upper Missouri. He spent much of his time during the navigation season at Yankton, Sioux City, or Bismarck, but he maintained his residence in Allegheny City and spent an occasional winter in New Orleans. He was always regarded on the Upper Missouri as an absentee entrepreneur despite the fact that he did invest money in the region by buying land near Yankton.[24] His land purchases were evidently for speculative purposes. He also speculated in the cotton market and had other financial interests, including an interest in a bank, a newspaper, and a street railway company.

Kountz was never popular on the Upper Missouri. He made no effort to be. He was blunt and unforgiving. While he recognized the keen competition in steamboating, he could never accept a defeat graciously. His rivalry with Coulson was conducted in a bitter manner. Whatever the exact cause of the original break between the two, it was enough to leave Kountz in a most vitriolic mood. Kountz, with alarming frankness reprimanded John H. Charles for associating with Coulson by writing, "Now Charles, I have known men to select very singular bedfellows, but I never in my life have known a man that I have always regarded as a man of high sense of honor, to get right into bed with such a dirty dog as you have."[25]

Kountz used a variety of tactics in his unrelenting efforts to beat the Coulson Line. On at least one occasion he testified before a congressional committee which was investigating the supplying of Indian agencies that the Coulson boats were unseaworthy. By so doing, Kountz hoped to prevent the awarding of an Indian contract to Coulson. Coulson, however, had his backers, and was given the contract in spite of Kountz's testimony.[26]

Kountz's major weapon was his newspaper, the *Allegheny Mail*. He used the paper as a means to attack political and business enemies, especially Coulson. Coulson, Evans, and C. W. Meade, an official of the Northern Pacific, all brought libel suits against Kountz in the 1870's for articles about them published in the *Mail*. Once Kountz's association with the *Mail* became known, he was strongly attacked by editors in both Bismarck and Yankton. In 1877, according to the Yankton *Press and Dakotaian*, Kountz resorted to a diabolically clever scheme. Using the facilities of his newspaper office, Kountz supposedly printed items derogatory to Coulson. These items he then trimmed so as to give the appearance of having been cut from a newspaper. On the reverse side of the clippings, Kountz printed an advertisement for a drugstore purportedly located in Quincy, Illinois. He then sent a number of the clippings to government officials and insurance companies. The recipients of the clippings naturally assumed that they were taken from the Quincy *Herald* because of the advertisement.[27] These clippings caused Coulson some difficulty in securing insurance for his boats. Howe, Carroll and Powell, marine and fire insurance agents of St. Louis, advised Coulson that they managed to get insurance for him only after personally testifying to his reliability.[28] These agents, assuming that the attacks on Coulson were directed from the Quincy *Herald*, wrote to him, saying,

we think it is about time to make a little war from our side of the house: the eighth paragraph of the enclosed article is clearly libellous, and we recommend that you go to Quincy, Illinois as soon as practicable, or send a responsible representative, demand a complete and thorough retraction of the Quincy *Herald* and the name of their correspondent, so that we can proceed against him, or else institute suit for $25,000 damages. You have got to take these fellows by the throat and we are behind you.[29]

Kountz also used this technique on a St. Louis steamboat inspector and the Anchor Boat Line, a Mississippi River rival. He was finally arrested in St. Louis in 1880 because of action instigated by the Anchor Boat Line. Two years later he was found guilty of libel by a St. Louis court and was fined $100 and court costs.[30]

Kountz conducted his business on the Upper Missouri by forming temporary partnerships with such individuals as John Charles, Amherst Wilder, and C. K. Peck. At Bismarck, he regularly employed a general agent. During the time Kountz had boats on the Upper Missouri, he also ran boats in the St. Louis–St. Paul trade. He remained on the Upper Missouri until 1884, then retired to Allegheny City, where he was primarily concerned with the Pittsburgh & Allegheny Street Railway Company and a brickworks at Harmarville until his death in 1903.[31]

A second major rival of the Coulson Line was the Northwest Transportation Company, also known as the Peck Line. After the death of E. H. Durfee in 1874, C. K. Peck of Keokuk reorganized the company. The firm had headquarters at Sioux City, but Peck remained a resident of Keokuk. Peck's associates were George Durfee of Leavenworth, Kansas, a brother of E. H. Durfee; A. F. Brownell, a Keokuk banker; and Colonel H. C. Akin. In 1877 the Peck Line had the government contract to transport Indian annuities. Peck boats were used at the same time to haul contract goods for A. F. Terry of Sioux City, who had secured the military contract below Bismarck for that season. After Terry was awarded the contract, he and Peck formed the Contract Transportation Company for the purpose of handling the military shipments. Akin served as the Bismarck agent for both the Contract and Peck companies. Peck supervised the company operations on the Upper Missouri, but the most powerful man in the organization was Brownell, who controlled the company purse.[32]

Peck was beset by many troubles. His hardware business in Keokuk was failing. The firm of Durfee & Peck was also in difficulty with the U.S. Government. They had lost their licenses to trade at at least three major Indian agencies, Fort Berthold, Fort Peck, and Cheyenne River Agency, and the government was bringing suit against Durfee & Peck for alleged failure to deliver goods to Fort Berthold. Peck, in turn, was suing the government in the U.S. Court of Claims for failure to pay for military supplies. Peck must have spent as much time dealing with legal matters as with his transportation business. His claims against the government were still pending when he died in 1879.[33]

After his death the company operated for several more years, mostly out of Bismarck under the direction of Akin. Akin earned a considerable reputation in 1882 for stealing a steamboat from the U.S. Government. The previous year the *Peninah* was confiscated by the government because certain crewmen illegally sold liquor on a military reservation in Montana. The boat was not apprehended by federal authorities until she reached Bismarck. There she was tied up while the government dallied long and circuitously over the disposition of the craft. Meanwhile, Akin, quite bitter about losing the services of the boat, plotted to rescue her from the government. The possibilities of escaping by boat from the Upper Missouri were quite limited, as Akin realized. He apparently had the telegraph lines between Bismarck and Fort Yates cut, so the boat would have a fair chance of making a run past the garrison. This was done about an hour before some of Akin's men entertained the watchman who was guarding the *Peninah*. While the watchman was being appropriately lubricated, other men led by Captain Dave Campbell got up steam and started downstream. The boat proved to be considerably slower than the quickly repaired telegraph. All federal deputies along the river were alerted. The *Peninah* was finally apprehended by a deputy U.S. marshal just below Pierre.[34]

Of the men who served as officers on the Northwest Transportation Company boats, the most renowned was William H. Sims, better known as Captain Billy Sims. By the 1870's and 1880's Sims was one of the old hands on the Upper Missouri. He was born in Wheeling, Virginia, in 1842, but spent his youth in St. Louis, where he became a cub pilot at the age of fifteen under his uncle, Charles W. Blunt, Sr. This apprenticeship lasted from 1857 to 1860, during which time Sims worked in the St. Louis–Sioux City run. During the first three years of the Civil War he was a pilot on one of the transports supporting General Lyon's forces along the Missouri and Mississippi. After leaving the government service he worked on one of the steamers which transported Sully's troops up from Sioux City in 1864. After that he worked in the St. Louis–Fort Benton trade, then in the Sioux City–Fort Benton trade, and in the mid-1870's he moved to Bismarck, where he located permanently. Billy apparently had no interests other than boating, and long after he had retired from the business, he delighted in telling stories about the good old days on the river.[35]

The last important rival of the Coulson Line, and the company that ultimately succeeded it as the ranking steamboat concern on the Upper Missouri, was the Fort Benton Transportation Company, also known as the Power Line. The company was formed in 1875 by Thomas C. Power and his brother John Power, both of Fort Benton. Thomas C., the kingpin in the organization, was born in Dubuque, Iowa, on May 22, 1839. Before moving to Fort Benton as a merchant in 1867, he studied civil engineering, taught school, and did some surveying. In Benton he organized the merchandising firm of T. C. Power & Bro., which distributed supplies throughout Montana Territory and portions of Canada as well.[36] John W. Power, five years younger than T. C., joined his brother in all business activities. Besides merchandising, the Powers were financially interested in livestock, mining, banking, and freighting. Politically they were among the most active Republicans in Montana Territory.[37]

The Power brothers were so busy with their Montana affairs that they took very little direct part in the management of the steamboat line. They did, however, bring many experienced boatmen into the company. George Baker, of St. Louis, a steamboat salesman and wholesaler, was the first secretary of the company. Baker, who had worked in St. Louis steamboating most of his life, was a particularly valuable man in such matters as securing boats, obtaining insurance, and hiring personnel. The real center of company operations, however, was Bismarck, not St. Louis, so it was necessary for the company to have an agent in Bismarck. The first agent was James A. Emmons, who steamboated on the Upper Missouri from 1865 to 1872. He also operated a ferry between Bismarck and Fort Abraham Lincoln in 1876. Most of Emmons' activities in the mid-1870's were concerned with his extensive real estate holdings in Bismarck and the surrounding area, so his job as agent for Power was really only one of many interests. He did help the company get started in Bismarck, although he represented it for only two years.[38]

The Powers and Baker employed some very able navigators, men such as James McGarry, John Christie Barr, and Andy Johnson. McGarry was a boat captain in the Power Line for nearly five years until his death in 1879. He also supervised the construction of company boats and was one of the major stockholders. He was a man about whom little was known. He was in reality a river orphan. He had no family or known relatives. He was known by his contemporaries as a reserved bachelor who stayed at a Bismarck hotel and had very little to say about himself. It was known that he was born in Canada of Irish parents and that he entered Mississippi River steamboating in 1857 at about the age of eighteen. After 1864 he worked on the Missouri, either as a pilot or master. He had worked occasionally for the Northwest Transportation Company and also operated his own steamboat independently before joining the Power Line. McGarry died in a Bismarck hotel after a bout with mountain fever. Apparently the only person close to him was John Christie Barr, who came on the Missouri in 1876 as a clerk on a boat commanded by McGarry.[39]

Barr soon was a captain of one of the Power boats, and also acted as the general agent in Bismarck. For a four-year period, 1877–1880, Barr was the chief administrator of the Fort Benton Transportation Company. He was in charge of freight and passenger movement, attended contract-lettings, and generally supervised the movements of the boats.[40] He does not appear to have been too fond of his paper work, and when he got the opportunity to return to the river as a captain in 1881, he took it. Barr was replaced by Isaac Post Baker, who later became the dominant figure in the Bismarck navigation business.

Andy Johnson, who captained one of the Power boats, and acted as general superintendent of the boat line for a brief period while Barr was ill, was a native of South Carolina. His family moved to Missouri when he was only eight. In 1858, at the age of twenty-two, he began working on the Missouri River. He later served as a pilot and master for Durfee & Peck before joining Power. He quit steamboating in 1883 after the *Butte*, which he was commanding, burned near Fort Peck. After retiring from the river, Johnson started a shoe store in Bismarck.[41]

There were many men on the Upper Missouri who were not consistently affiliated with organized companies. These independents ranged from navigators who ran their own boats, to merchants, to absentee capitalists. Of the independents, those who had the greatest impact on the steamboat business were Ben Jewell, I. G. Baker, John H. Charles, and Amherst Wilder.

Ben Jewell was one of the best pilots on the Upper Missouri, and also one of the most interesting characters. Ben lived in Bismarck during the navigation season but maintained his residency in St. Louis. He was born in Kentucky in 1823 and raised in St. Louis, where his first business experience was with a dray line. He then bought a quarter interest in a steamer which soon sank. His next boat blew up. Undismayed, he stayed with steamboating as a mate, pilot, and part owner of boats in the St. Louis–Keokuk trade.[42]

Jewell entered the Upper Missouri as one of the pilots on the *Ida Fulton* in 1867. He soon established himself as the foremost Indian spotter on the river. He saw Indians behind every bush and at every woodyard. The mythical Indians soon became a joke with the crewmen. Jewell, who could laugh at himself, then started reporting to the alternate pilot who relieved him on watch that he had spotted fifteen Indians, but that they had just disappeared in the trees. Whenever he was relieved, he had the same report—fifteen Indians, but they had just disappeared. Besides his talent for locating Sioux, he was reputed to know the location of every woodyard on the river. Whenever the boat stopped for wood, Jewell ceremoniously instructed the captain to take on an extra large supply of wood, since it was a long way to the next yard.[43]

Jewell was a noted conversationalist—one who delighted in telling unlikely stories about himself. "Silent Ben," as many of his colleagues called him, was said to be the only man ever to swim the Missouri with $500,000 in silver coin in his pockets. This marvelous feat he accomplished while escaping from the James brothers. There were many stories of his wealth, most of them originated by himself. He claimed an interest in a gin distillery and a farm in Missouri, and on one occasion was said to have won $30,000 in the Louisiana state lottery.[44]

I. G. Baker of Fort Benton usually operated one or two boats between Bismarck and the head of navigation. Baker, who originally came to Benton as an employee of Pierre Chouteau Jr. & Co. stayed on after the company ceased operations and became one of the richest merchants in the town. During 1878 and 1879 Baker ran the steamer *Red Cloud* regularly between Bismarck and Fort Benton.[45] Baker's main interest was in transporting his own stores, but he did carry both military and private freight from time to time in order to fill out cargoes.

John H. Charles of Sioux City and Amherst H. Wilder of St. Paul were interested in steamboating as a financial investment. They also had to be concerned with steamboat transportation, since they were the largest government contractors on the Upper Missouri, and many of the places they served were on or near the river. Charles and Wilder sometimes worked together, and they also worked at various times with all of the steamboat companies. They never formed their own boat lines, but they did buy fractional interests in several vessels, and were continually hiring boats to transport their goods.

Charles was one of the first Sioux City pioneers. He moved there in 1856 at the age of thirty from his native Pennsylvania. By background a farmer, he engaged in the real estate business and worked for the merchandising firm headed by Milton Tootle.[46] Later Charles became a partner in a bank, operated his own wholesale grocery store, and entered government contracting on the Upper Missouri. Charles, for the most part, was a speculator in contracts. He would secure a contract to supply forage or grain to a post and would then sublet it, leaving himself a margin of profit. He did make some attempts to deliver his own contract goods, and for this reason he bought an interest in four of the Peck Line steamers.

Charles was an enterprising businessman who missed few opportunities for gain. As a merchant in the principal town that supplied the Upper Missouri he well realized the commercial worth of an expanding frontier. Charles was obviously not in sympathy with the Laramie Treaty of 1868 which left all land west of the Missouri in Dakota Territory as a massive Sioux reservation. The value of this land was dramatically publicized in 1874 when a military reconnaissance party under George A. Custer officially discovered gold in the Black Hills. Charles was one of a small group of prominent Sioux Citians who organized an expedition to open up gold mining in the Hills despite the fact that entry onto the reservation was illegal. Charles's part in the Collins and Russel party, as the group of twenty-six adventurers was called, was that of financier. He provided provisions and money for the outfitting of this group, which reached the Black Hills only to be arrested and removed by the military. Charles's part in the expedition contributed greatly to his reputation as a promoter and booster. Shortly after this he had one short fling in local politics. He was elected mayor of Sioux City in 1876.[47]

Amherst H. Wilder was a permanent resident of St. Paul. Moving there in 1859 at the age of thirty-one from his native New York, he became active in banking, railroading, the insurance business, and industry. He helped found the First National Bank of St. Paul and the Merchants National Bank. He was one of the financiers and promoters of the Sioux City & St. Paul Railroad. This railroad, completed in 1872, was designed to give St. Paul access to the Upper Missouri by a route other than the then still uncompleted Northern Pacific. He was one of the prominent stockholders in the St. Paul Fire & Marine Insurance Company and also was financially interested in the St. Paul Foundry & Manufacturing Company. Wilder's financial resources made it comparatively easy for him to speculate in government contracts. One of his first large contracts gave him the right to buy timber on the Leech Lake Indian Reservation of Minnesota in 1872.[48]

In 1873 Wilder, by virtue of winning numerous contracts, became the principal government contractor on the Upper Missouri. In that year he was awarded the transportation contract for Indian goods to be delivered by boat to Missouri River agencies, a transportation contract to deliver Indian goods by wagon from Fort Randall to Whet-

stone Agency, and three other contracts calling for the delivery of a
total of about ten thousand head of Texas cattle to the Indian agencies
of the Upper Missouri.[49] Wilder handled all of these contracts by
subletting parts of them to dozens of individuals. He continued contracting through the 1870's and expanded his activities by bidding on
military contracts as well as Indian contracts, by buying shares in
steamboats, and by securing post traderships. Wilder's large invest-
ments through contracting and speculating made him one of the
major financiers of the entire Upper Missouri region.

Steamboat owners and managers were responsible for the hiring
of a sizable labor force. They depended for the operation of their
boats on the roustabouts, or roosters, who made up the bulk of each
crew. From twenty to forty roustabouts were employed for each boat.
The roustabouts were on the lower end of both the salary and social
scales. Most of them were Negroes who were imported from St. Louis
or Leavenworth. Some were Irish and Scandinavian immigrants. Boat
officers were ordinarily intolerant of the poorly educated roosters, especially of the Negroes who were often referred to as "nigs," "Afri-
cans," and "Fourteenth Amendment Citizens." The roosters generally
carried knives, and knife fights were an expected and frequent oc-
currence among them. Most boat mates carried revolvers as a way of
insuring the obedience of the armed roosters. Every boat captain had
several sets of irons. The roosters constituted a problem to all of the
law enforcement officers of the river towns, since boat landings were
normally accompanied by drinking, carousing, and fighting.

In 1867, the Woodbury County sheriff had considerable difficulty
quelling a Sioux City brawl when some colored deckhands, encouraged by the mate, tried to restrain four white roustabouts who were
attempting to leave their jobs on the *Mountaineer*. In the fight which
took place at the foot of Pearl Street, the combatants first used brick-
bats, stones, and clubs. The fray took a more serious turn when some-
one fired a revolver down Pearl Street, narrowly missing some of the
spectators. The general fight ended with the capture of one of the
would-be deserters, who was overtaken, knocked down, and then, in
the words of the reporter, kicked "about the head and face from two
black and one white nigger."[50]

The wages of the roosters in the 1870's and early 1880's varied
from $20 to $75 per month. Most crews were paid in the neighbor-
hood of $35 to $45.[51] However, roustabouts were seldom given regular

employment. They were generally hired only by the trip, although their wages were quoted on a monthly basis. An individual would be hired for $30 a month. If he made a trip from Yankton to Pierre in ten days, he would be paid $10 and would then in all likelihood be dismissed. Five days later the boat might be ready to load for the return to Yankton. Then the roustabout would be rehired at the monthly rate, but again would be paid only for the period of time his services were required. It was very unusual for a roustabout to be guaranteed continuous employment throughout the navigation season.

The big advantage the roustabout had in his dealings with boat owners was the shortage of labor. The entire Upper Missouri as a frontier had a scarcity of available wage laborers. There were no urban concentrations which could provide labor, and all of the farm labor was needed on the land. In fact, during harvest seasons there was a severe labor shortage on the farms. This shortage tended to aggravate the shortage of steamboat labor. Each harvest season dozens of roustabouts would leave the boats for the better pay and working conditions on the farms.[52]

The labor shortage encouraged roosters to strike quite often for higher wages. Every season there were at least several strikes. Normally these strikes occurred during the harvest season, just before freeze-up, or near a contract deadline. They were so timed as to make it difficult for captains to hire replacement crews. In most situations the strikers were successful, since it was nearly impossible to hire substitute crews. If a substitute crew was hired, that frequently occasioned an incident. In one instance, a group of striking roosters who had been replaced raided the *Nellie Peck* at Bismarck armed with ropes and threatened to hang anyone who went to work for the Northwest Transportation Company. A company of soldiers was called in to restore order.[53]

Because Yankton–Bismarck steamboat men were almost completely devoted to the Upper Missouri trade, they made a much greater effort to adapt their boats to the river than did the St. Louisians who navigated to Benton in the late 1860's. Most of the boats used on the Upper Missouri in the 1870's and 1880's were constructed by either the Coulson Line or the Kountz Line. With but few exceptions, these boats were carefully designed to navigate the Upper Missouri. Most of them were built in the Pittsburgh area, usually at California or Brownsville, Pennsylvania. The Allegheny, Monongahela, and Ohio river ports near Pittsburgh were logical places to construct boats because of the availability of trained boat builders, a good lumber supply, steel manufacturers who could supply such heavy parts as engines and boilers, and boat chandlery firms which could supply accessories. Even after owners got their boats on the Upper Missouri they still depended on Pittsburgh contractors for machinery. Boat construction

TABLE XI

DIMENSIONS AND TONNAGES OF MOUNTAIN STEAMERS USED IN THE 1870's

Steamer	Length	Beam	Depth of Hold	Net Tonnage (Carrying Capacity)	Tonnage when Drawing 3 Feet	Tonnage when Drawing 2 Feet
Big Horn[a]	177'4"	31'3"	4'	293.86	192.1	85
Black Hills[b]	193'	32'6"	4'	370[c]	212.0	85
C. W. Meade[d]	193'	30'6"	4'	...	...	...
Daniel H. Rucker[e]	215'	35'	4'	...	...	...
E. H. Durfee[a]	206'	35'	5'5"	497.17	...	...
Far West[a]	189'	33'5"	5'	397.81	187.8	60
Frank Y. Batchelor[e]	180'	30'	3'	313.00[i]	195.6	90
Helena[f]	195'	32'	4'	352.31[i]	205.5	70
Josephine[a]	178'	31'	4'6"	300.51	180.7	70
Katie P. Kountz[g]	204'	34'	4'6"	550	...	...
Key West[a]	200'	33'	5'5"	422.60	182.3	50
Rosebud[a]	193'	33'	3'3"	286	182.1	75
Silver City[h]	190'	35'	...	550	...	...
Western[a]	208'	35'	5'5"	475.69	...	...

[a]Information taken from Mrs. R. E. Walpole's Notes. Mrs. Walpole, who resides in Yankton, South Dakota, is a granddaughter of John Coulson.
[b]*Press and Dakotaian*, March 14, 1877. (Source of length, beam, and hold.)
[c]*Ibid.*, May 26, 1877. (Source of tonnage.)   [d]*Bismarck Tribune*, April 14, 1875.
[e]*Press and Dakotaian*, March 12, 1878.   [f]*Ibid.*, April 19, 1878.   [g]*Ibid.*, October 22, 1879.
[h]*Bismarck Tribune*, May 30, 1877. [i]*Annual Engineer's Report, 1883*, pt. 2, pp. 1343–1344.

for the Upper Missouri was quite active until the late 1870's. There is no record of a boat being built for the Upper Missouri trade after 1879. The decline of steamboating in the 1880's caused steamboat owners to avoid new construction. Instead, the old craft were meticulously repaired. Thus there was a rather sharp deterioration in boat appearance in the 1880's.

The typical mountain steamer was actually quite small. Table XI shows the dimensions of some of the boats used in the 1870's. These boats were all stern-wheelers. The stern-wheeler was universally accepted by Upper Missouri navigators as being more practical in the snag-filled channels than was the side-wheeler. The paddle wheel was normally about twenty-four feet long and twenty feet in diameter. The boats were usually equipped with two or three boilers and two high-pressure engines which produced roughly 140 pounds of pressure per square inch.[54] The goal of all builders of mountain boats was to produce a boat with a light draft. This was achieved by building a flat-bottomed vessel which had great width and length in proportion to its depth. Care was also taken to use pine rather than oak in floor timbers, decking, and bulkheads because of its lightness. Most of the boats drew about twenty inches when empty. A rare boat such as the *Silver City* drew only fourteen inches light. A boat such as the *Far West*, which drew twenty inches light, would draw four feet, six inches if loaded to its capacity of 397.81 tons. Most of the boats, however, were not loaded to capacity, but only so as to draw two to three feet. The total construction cost of most mountain boats was from $20,000 to $25,000.[55]

Boat owners could not afford to insure a boat for its total value, since annual insurance rates commonly were more than 10 per cent of the boat's value. As a form of insurance, ownership was distributed among several individuals in a company. In the Coulson Line, for example, all of the boats were the property of at least four men. Sanford Coulson was the principal shareholder in the company, but he never held more than a half interest in any one boat. Most of the men in the Coulson Line held one-fifth or one-fourth shares in several boats. Sometimes partners owned as little at a one thirty-second share. Under this arrangement, it was impossible for a man to lose his total investment with the destruction of one boat.[56]

The navigators of the Upper Missouri undoubtedly envied their contemporaries of the Mississippi whose ornate luxury steamers carried more than twice the load of the ordinary boat used on the Upper Missouri. No one ventured to copy the Mississippi River boats until Sanford B. Coulson tried it in 1879 by constructing three large luxury-type boats—the *Montana*, the *Dacotah*, and the *Wyoming*. These were sister ships all built in the Pittsburgh area over the winter of 1878/79. The *Montana* and *Dacotah* were exactly the same length and breadth, 252 feet by 48 feet 8 inches. The *Montana* had a capacity of 959 tons, and the *Dacotah's* capacity was 957 tons. The *Wyoming*, the largest of the three, had a capacity of 1,034. The boats were all elaborately furnished. During the construction of the *Montana*, special contracts were let for the furnishing of upholstery, silverware, a piano, and custom-made furniture. The average construction cost of the boats was about $48,000. It seems strange that Coulson's company should

have invested money in these craft when others were no longer building mountain boats because of the declining business. Operating costs
of these big boats were also high, since each carried a crew of sixty,
about twenty more than a normal-sized boat.[57]

The large boats had the advantage of greater capacity over the
regular mountain steamers, but they also had the disadvantage of
increased draft. If loaded to capacity, each of the boats drew six feet.
Light, they drew two feet. During spring and early summer, the
traditional periods of high water, the boats could be loaded only to
half-capacity, drawing four feet. During most of the navigation season, however, steamboat men could not depend on any more than a
three-foot channel. The Dacotah, drawing three feet, could carry only
238 tons, the Wyoming 229 tons. In comparison, the Black Hills, a
193-foot mountain boat which cost less than half what one of the big
boats cost, could carry 212 tons drawing three feet and could be
operated for less. Only if the big boats could have counted on a
heavy passenger registration could they have been operated profitably
during the whole navigation season.[58]

In addition to limitations due to their size, the three boats encountered considerable ill-fortune. On June 30, 1879, after only a few
months of operation, the Montana was heavily damaged by a wind-
storm at Bismarck. It cost from two to three thousand dollars just to
get the boat to St. Louis to be repaired. After that time she was used
almost entirely in the St. Louis area. During her brief career on the
Upper Missouri, she did gain the distinction of carrying the largest
cargo on record from Bismarck to Fort Benton.[59] The Dacotah in her
first year struck a railroad bridge at Kansas City. Damages amounted
to $3,500. Three years later she snagged and sank near Providence,
Missouri.[60] The Wyoming hit the Kansas City bridge in 1882, suffering
extensive damages.[61]

Why did the men of the Coulson Line embark on such a venture
when they knew the boats could be used for the Upper Missouri in
only spring and early summer? There is a possibility that Coulson
and his associates envisaged a great tourist trade from St. Louis to
the Upper Missouri. Each boat had accommodations for about a hundred cabin passengers, which was considerably more than any regu-
lar-size mountain boat could carry. Then too, there is the possibility
that Coulson underestimated the rapidity of railroad construction
after 1879. The fact that railroad construction stood still for nearly

six years after the Panic of 1873 may have caused him to think that the slow recovery would continue for some years, thus extending the life of steamboating on the Upper Missouri. He may also have intended to use the boats on the Upper Missouri for a few years and then use them exclusively on the Lower Missouri or Mississippi. Whatever the reason for the venture, the experiment was a failure. The Upper Missouri never had a successful counterpart of the Mississippi's *Crystal Palace*.

Stephen H. Long led the Yellowstone Expedition up the Missouri in 1819. (Painting by Charles Wilson Peale, 1823. Courtesy of the Eastern National Park and Monument Association.)

Brigadier General Alfred Sully led punitive expeditions against the Sioux Indians of the Upper Missouri region during 1863–1865. (Courtesy of the Minnesota Historical Society.)

Kenneth McKenzie, the "King of the Missouri," dominated the fur trade during the 1830's through the American Fur Company.

Pierre Chouteau, Jr., headed the largest company engaged in trade on the Upper Missouri from 1838 until 1865.

The *Far West* and the *Nellie Peck* of the Coulson Line at Bismarck in the late 1870's. (Courtesy of the North Dakota Historical Society.)

I. G. Baker's steamer *Red Cloud* in the 1870's. (Courtesy of Captain Frederick Way, Jr.)

The Coulson Line steamers *E. H. Durfee* and *Western* in the 1870's. (Courtesy of Captain Frederick Way, Jr.)

Joseph LaBarge, a pioneer navigator on the Upper Missouri, commanded Pierre Chouteau Jr. & Co. steamboats and later organized LaBarge, Harkness & Co.

John J. Roe was a leading figure in the Montana and Idaho Transportation Line, the largest and most active company engaged in the Fort Benton trade during the mid-1860's.

Commodore William J. Kountz was one of the best-known captains on the Ohio and Mississippi rivers before the Civil War. He became a bitter rival of the Coulson Line.

Daniel W. Maratta commanded Kountz vessels on the Upper Missouri and afterward was general manager of the Coulson Line. (Courtesy of the North Dakota Historical Society.)

The dining saloon of the Coulson steamer *Far West*. (Courtesy of the North Dakota Historical Society.)

Isaac Gilbert Baker was a Fort Benton merchant who also operated steamboats in the Fort Benton to Bismarck trade. (Photograph, 1869. Courtesy of the Montana Historical Society.)

Amherst H. Wilder, a St. Paul financier, operated on the Upper Missouri as a transportation contractor in the 1870's. (Courtesy of the Minnesota Historical Society.)

John H. Charles, a Sioux City businessman, was active in river transportation from 1870 until 1900. (Courtesy of the Sioux City Public Museum.)

Captain Grant Marsh commanded the *Far West* on its historic run to Bismarck after the Battle of the Little Big Horn in 1876. (Courtesy of the North Dakota Historical Society.)

View of Main Street, Bismarck, Dakota Territory, in 1873. (Courtesy of the North Dakota Historical Society.)

The mackinaw *Montana* at Fort Benton in 1878. (Picture taken by photographer sent to the United States by Queen Victoria. Courtesy of the Montana Historical Society.)

The *Wyoming*, the largest of the three luxury steamers built by the Coulson Line in 1879, had a maximum cargo capacity of over one thousand tons. (Courtesy of Captain Frederick Way, Jr.)

The *Dacotah*, one of the luxury steamers added to the Coulson fleet in 1879, was 252 feet in length. (Courtesy of Captain Frederick Way, Jr.)

Thomas C. Power, a Fort Benton merchant, organized the Fort Benton Transportation Company in 1875. (Courtesy of the Montana Historical Society.)

Captain William F. Davidson was a famous Mississippi River steamboat owner whose Upper Missouri venture of 1877 resulted in failure.

John Christie Barr, a well-known pilot and captain of the Fort Benton Transportation Company. (Photograph, 1892. Courtesy of Mrs. Merrill Burlingame, Bozeman, Montana.)

Isaac P. Baker controlled commercial boating on the Upper Missouri from 1885 to the 1930's. (Photograph, 1919. Courtesy of the North Dakota Historical Society.)

The steamer *Rosebud* on the Missouri in the 1880's. This vessel was the last boat operated by the Coulson Line. (Courtesy of the North Dakota Historical Society.)

Fort Benton Transportation Company boats at Bismarck in the 1880's, with the Northern Pacific Railroad bridge in the background. (Courtesy of the North Dakota Historical Society.)

The *Helena* (foreground) and the *Western* at Yankton, caught in the ice jam that preceded the disastrous floods of 1881. (Courtesy of Captain Frederick Way, Jr.)

The Missouri River steamboat *Helena* transporting Sioux Indians. (Courtesy of the North Dakota Historical Society.)

Steamboat ways in Bismarck, 1886. (Courtesy of the North Dakota Historical Society.)

The *F. Y. Batchelor* on the Missouri River at Bismarck with troops from Fort Yates, probably in the early 1890's. (Courtesy of the North Dakota Historical Society.)

The *Jim Leighton* at Pierre, South Dakota, probably in the 1890's. (Courtesy of the South Dakota Historical Society.)

The steamboat *Benton* was wrecked near Sioux City on July 18, 1897. (Courtesy of the North Dakota Historical Society.)

VIII

Yankton and Bismarck as Steamboat Ports, 1873–1879

THE PERIOD during which Upper Missouri steamboating was dominated by Yankton- and Bismarck-based steamers was an active one. Steamboat men at these points benefited from the opening of the Black Hills, from increased government business along the river owing to the Indian Wars, and the movement of settlers into the Upper Missouri and Yellowstone River regions. The success of steamboat companies headquartered at Yankton and Bismarck during this time can perhaps be partly attributed to the Panic of 1873. The Panic stalemated railroad construction, and although track reached these two towns, it did not extend beyond them for several years.

Military shipments were vital to the transportation business; steamboat entrepreneurs vigorously denied the common charge that government contract shipments were the sole support of the steamboat business, but in spite of the fact that private freight shipments on the Upper Missouri showed a definite increase in the years after 1874, the government freight shipments remained the backbone of the transportation business. The history of steamboating on the Upper Missouri reveals a constant struggle among the major companies for control of the shipment of military stores and Indian annuities.

Government freight shipments on the Upper Missouri increased considerably during the 1870's. Much of this increase can be related to another war with the Sioux in 1876. This war was a direct outcome of the miners' invasion of the Black Hills. The army, which had anticipated an easy victory over the Sioux, was defeated at the Battle of the Little Big Horn. The events leading up to the battle, and the military campaigns after it, immediately intensified military demands for river transportation. After the Battle of the Little Big Horn, the

MAP 2. YANKTON-BISMARCK TRADE AREA, 1873–1879

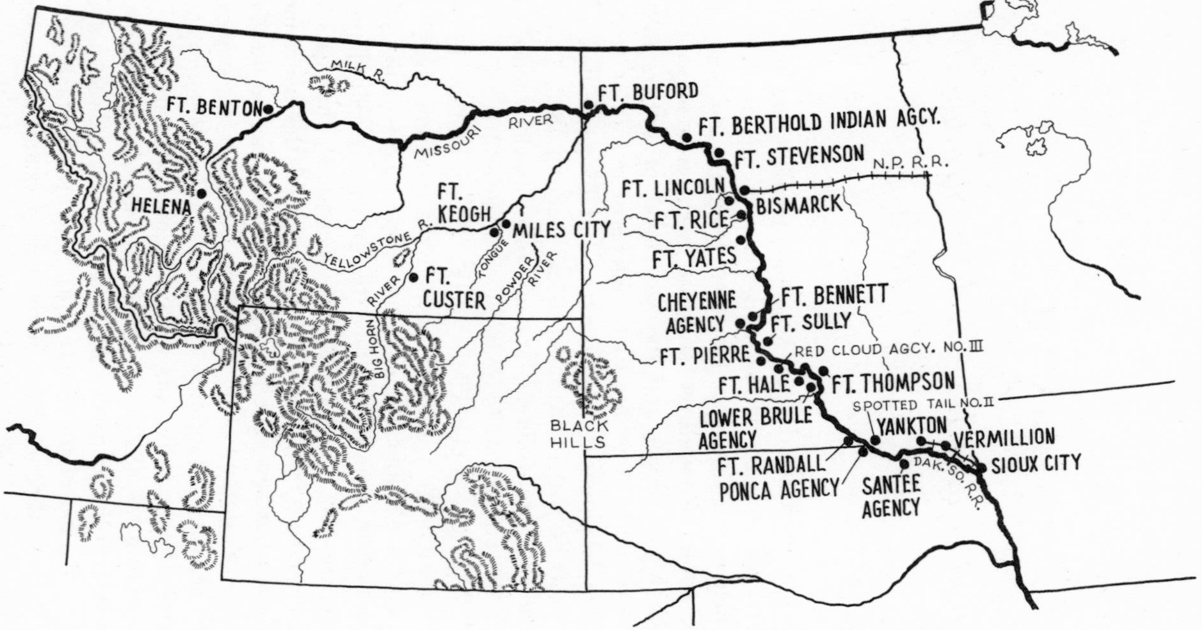

DISTANCES FROM YANKTON BY RIVER

Sioux City .... 70 miles   Ft. Buford .... 1,200 miles
Bismarck .... 800 miles   Ft. Benton .... 1,900 miles

War Department strengthened the military defense of Montana Territory by adding three new posts, Fort Keogh, Fort Custer, and Fort
Assiniboine. Construction materials and supplies for these posts were
transported by steamers.

The maintenance of the military frontier in the 1870's was a tremendous task, since the army had hundreds of troops, dependents,
and civilian government employees stationed at the posts stretching
from Fort Randall to Fort Benton. Military supplies were transported from Yankton and Bismarck. Although Sioux City was actually
named as the starting point in the contracts of 1873, 1874, and 1875,
the army made separate contracts with the Dakota Southern to transport men and supplies from Sioux City to Yankton.

It was this government agreement with the railroad that made
Yankton the actual starting point for most military shipments. The
goods that started at Yankton were ordinarily shipped to the posts in
Dakota Territory, although on occasion Yankton-based steamboats
delivered government supplies to Carroll and Fort Benton. The government used Bismarck as its principal starting point for military
shipments to Fort Stevenson, Fort Buford, Fort Benton, and to Carroll. The army, as a policy, did not send Bismarck-based steamboats
downstream. Bismarck steamboat operators and writers for the *Bismarck Tribune* contended that the government would actually save
money by sending government supplies downstream from Bismarck
rather than upstream from Yankton. Their basic assumption was that it
was much cheaper to transport downstream than upstream. The army
however, seldom made a great distinction between upstream and
downstream rates. In most contracts there was no difference in the
rates, and when a distinction was made, it never amounted to more
than a 10 per cent reduction in the downstream rates. One basic
premise that the Bismarck spokesmen continually ignored was that
government supplies destined for both Bismarck and Yankton came
primarily by rail from Chicago. In 1877 freight charges per hundred
pounds from Chicago to Yankton were 52½ cents while freight charges
from Chicago to Bismarck were $1.00.[1] Thus it was to the govern-
ment's advantage to use Yankton steamers to supply the military
garrisons at Fort Randall, Lower Brule Agency, Fort Sully, and
Cheyenne River Agency. The government, if it had been interested
in strict economy, would have found it cheaper to send most of the
supplies to Standing Rock Agency and Fort Rice downstream from

Bismarck rather than upstream from Yankton as they did. Many times, however, there was a definite shortage of boats at Bismarck. During 1876 and 1877 there was marked urgency in the government transportation demands at Bismarck because of the need for efficient, consistent support of the military forces on the Yellowstone River. The army, therefore, used Yankton steamboats to carry supplies to the forts below Bismarck rather than take a steamer out of the trade above Bismarck. Table XII presents a comparison of the government

TABLE XII

COMPARISON OF THROUGH-RATES ON GOVERNMENT FREIGHT FROM CHICAGO
TO UPPER MISSOURI DESTINATIONS BY WAY OF YANKTON AND BISMARCK, 1877*

| FROM CHICAGO TO: | PER 100 POUNDS | |
	Via Yankton	Via Bismarck
Fort Randall	$ .91½	$2.03
Brule Agency	.96	1.78
Fort Sully	1.23	1.50
Cheyenne Agency	1.26	1.48
Standing Rock Agency	1.59	1.15
Fort Rice	1.65	1.08
Fort Lincoln	1.73	1.01
Bismarck	1.74	. . .
Fort Stevenson	1.91	1.06
Fort Buford	2.35	1.60
Fort Peck	2.71	1.97
Carroll	3.02	2.27
Cow Island	3.11	2.36
Fort Benton	3.55	2.61

*Press and Dakotaian, April 4, 1877.

freight rates in 1877 from Chicago through Yankton and Bismarck to the various destinations on the river.

The success of Yankton as a steamboat port was due primarily to the business acumen of Sanford B. Coulson. Coulson, by establishing a cooperative relationship with the Dakota Southern Railroad, managed to control most of the military freight shipments on the Upper Missouri from 1874 through 1879. In 1874 and 1875, despite considerable competition, Coulson got the government contracts for supplying the military posts in the upriver area. In 1876, too, Coulson was awarded the major portion of the government work, although Walter Burleigh, an independent operator, was given the contract for carrying men and supplies above Bismarck. The rates for the Coulson contracts for 1874, 1875, and 1876 are shown in Table XIII.

The Coulson contract for 1874 was sizable; by May 23, the Coulson Line had already carried the following freight shipments:[2]

Destination	Tons
Fort Benton	35½
Fort Buford	191¾
Fort Stevenson	40½
Fort Lincoln	257¾
Fort Hancock	1¼
Fort Rice	125¾
Grand River Agency	32½
Cheyenne Agency	32½
Fort Sully	103¾
Brule Agency	41¼
Fort Randall	64¾

The Sioux City *Journal* also reported that the government had 27 tons of freight at Yankton awaiting shipment to Fort Rice, Grand River, Fort Brule, and Fort Randall, and that 100 tons were expected shortly for the military posts in Montana. According to the Yankton *Press and Dakotaian,* 3,500 tons of government provisions were shipped upriver from Yankton in 1875 and 6,500 tons in 1876.[3]

After four profitable years, the Missouri River Transportation Company lost the military contract in 1877. Coulson put in one of the lowest bids at the St. Paul contract-letting, but the contract was awarded to Dr. A. F. Terry of Sioux City.[4] Terry joined with C. K. Peck to form the Contract Transportation Company, which operated out of both Yankton and Bismarck in 1877. Members of the Coulson Line were convinced that they failed to get the contract because of duplicity on the part of John Charles and Amherst Wilder. William Evans wrote to Sanford Coulson on April 11, 1877, that

The Wilder and Charles part have been bulldozing us and it has been my opinion all the time they was not acting square ever since the bidding in St. Paul in January. For just as sure as the sun rose this morning . . . he Charles the unprincipled scoundrel stole the copy of the bid made out by you for Coulson and Wilder and gave it to Woolworth and he shaded it. There is no doubt in my mind of the fact. . . .

Evans concluded his letter by advising Coulson that it would be best to have no further dealings with Charles.[5]

At any rate, the contract for 1877 was awarded to Terry and his partners in the Contract Line. The Contract Line, which was using

TABLE XIII

RATES SHOWN ON MILITARY CONTRACTS AWARDED TO S. B. COULSON,
1874, 1875, AND 1876*

From Yankton to:[a]	Officers	Soldiers	Pound Freight, per 100 lbs.	Horses, Cattle, per head	Wagons, Carts, Ambulances
1874[b]					
Ft. Randall	$ 5.00	$ 3.00	$ .25	$ 8.00	$ 7.00
Whetstone Agency	5.00	3.00	.25	8.00	7.00
Lower Brules Agency	8.00	3.00	.25	10.00	13.00
Crow Creek Agency	8.00	4.00	.25	10.00	13.00
Ft. Sully	11.00	4.00	.50	18.00	20.00
Big Cheyenne Agency	11.00	6.00	.60	18.00	20.00
Grand River Agency	14.00	9.00	.60	20.00	22.00
Ft. Rice	15.00	9.00	.65	20.00	22.00
Ft. Abraham Lincoln (or Bismarck)	17.00	10.00	.70	22.00	25.00
Ft. Stevenson	22.00	14.00	.95	25.00	25.00
Ft. Buford	25.00	14.00	1.15	35.00	35.00
Ft. Benton	40.00	18.00	2.40	40.00	40.00
1875					
Ft. Randall	5.10	3.40	.42½	5.95	5.95
Whetstone Agency	5.10	3.40	.42½	5.95	5.95
Lower Brules Agency	6.80	4.25	.55¼	5.95	10.20
Crow Creek Agency	6.80	4.25	.55¼	5.95	10.20
Ft. Sully	8.50	5.10	.68	11.90	12.75
Big Cheyenne Agency	10.20	5.10	.76	11.90	12.75
Grand River Agency	10.20	6.80	.97	14.45	12.75
Ft. Rice	13.60	7.65	.97	14.45	15.30
Ft. Abraham Lincoln (or Bismarck)	15.30	9.35	.97	14.45	17.00
Ft. Stevenson	17.00	10.20	1.06	18.15	17.00
Ft. Buford	25.50	12.75	1.35	23.80	21.25
Ft. Benton	38.25	15.30	2.05	29.75	34.00
1876					
Ft. Randall	5.00	3.50	.24	5.00	6.00
Whetstone Agency	5.00	3.50	.24	5.00	6.00
Lower Brules Agency	8.00	4.50	.34	6.00	8.00
Crow Creek Agency	8.00	4.50	.34	6.00	8.00
Ft. Sully	9.00	6.00	.44	10.00	12.00
Big Cheyenne Agency	9.00	6.00	.44	12.00	13.00
Grand River Agency	12.00	7.00	.64	13.00	15.00
Ft. Rice	15.00	7.50	.64	14.00	16.00
Ft. Abraham Lincoln (or Bismarck)	15.00	10.00	.74	15.00	17.00
Ft. Stevenson	18.00	[c]	.74	16.00	18.00
Ft. Buford	20.00	14.00	1.14	25.00	19.00
Carroll	35.00	16.00	1.54	28.00	25.00
Ft. Benton	40.00	18.00	1.74	30.00	30.00

*Old Army Division, National Archives, "Tabular Statement," from *Contract between Col. D. H. Rucker, Asst. QM, USA and Sanford B. Coulson, Chicago, March 14, 1874;* "Schedule of Rates," from *Contract between Col. D. H. Rucker and Sanford B. Coulson, Chicago, March 18, 1875;* "Tabular Statement," from *Contract between Lt. Col. S. B. Holabird, Dep. QM, USA and Sanford B. Coulson, Chicago, March 20, 1876.*

[a]The contract of 1874 named both Sioux City and Yankton as starting points. Yankton is

Peck boats to deliver the military goods, finally had to sublet portions of the contract to Coulson in order to meet the demands of the government. Terry's greatest difficulty was that military goods were delivered sporadically and there were rush periods during which the Peck fleet was inadequate. Terry was virtually swamped during the first few weeks of the season. He estimated that by May 1 the boats would have to ship 1,500 tons from Yankton to the upriver posts.[6]

The chaos of 1877 caused by the inability of the Contract Line to fulfill its original agreement with the government led Maratta to suggest the pooling of the Coulson interests with the Fort Benton Transportation Company headed by T. C. Power. This action would have formed a combination large enough to outbid any other company, freezing out the small companies and the independently operated boats. In December, 1877, Power mentioned to Martin Coulson and Evans that he would be receptive to a cooperative venture with the Coulson Line, whereby Coulson would handle the military contract and Power the private freight business.[7] Power and Coulson occasionally worked together in 1878 carrying each other's freight, but there is no evidence that the two companies ever achieved a systematic working arrangement.

Coulson was seriously disturbed by the loss of the contract in 1877 and was determined to secure the contract for 1878. At the annual bidding in St. Paul, Coulson submitted the lowest bid for government transportation on the Missouri River. He was awarded the contract by the Quartermaster General at St. Paul, who then transmitted the bid to the Quartermaster General of the Division of the Missouri in Chicago. From there the bid went to the Secretary of War. After getting the award at St. Paul, Coulson and Maratta went to Washington, D.C., to exert personal influence in behalf of their bid. They turned to their acquaintances in Congress, who were asked to help influence Secretary of War G. W. McCrary. On February 4, 1878, Maratta wrote to McVay that "Wallace of Pennsylvania, Matthews Thurmond of Ohio, and several members of the house will render us assistance when called."[8] The contract was approved by the Secretary of War and formally signed on March 12, 1878.

---

used in the table because most of the goods actually started at that point. The difference in charges on 100 pounds of freight from Sioux City and Yankton was ten cents.

[b]The contract of 1874 was set up on a schedule which was geared to the probable river stages. The rates on freight for 1874 on the table are for the months of June and July.

[c]This rate was illegible on the contract.

This contract provided that Coulson would ship from either Yankton or Bismarck to all points on the Missouri River, but did not include forts on the Yellowstone. Kountz was given a special contract for the Yellowstone River trade. Coulson agreed to transport army officers at three cents a mile, enlisted men and government employees at two and one-half cents a mile, and horses and livestock at four cents a mile. The rate on military stores and supplies ranged from forty-five cents per 100 pounds per 100 miles up to a distance of fifty miles, to nine cents per 100 pounds per 100 miles on distances of eight hundred miles or more.[9]

Military shipments from Yankton increased in 1878; by mid-June approximately nine thousand tons had been forwarded.[10] In addition to transporting military supplies and provisions as specified by the annual contract, Coulson's boats also carried large shipments of grain as a result of supplementary grain contracts which had been let to his associates.

In 1877, when the Coulson Line did not have the military contract business, various members of the company secured government grain contracts. These contracts sometimes called for the delivery of grain to Yankton, with the responsibility of shipping it upstream left to the government. Other contracts specified that grain be delivered to a particular fort with the responsibility of river shipment resting on the contractor. Whether the grain was to be delivered to Yankton or a fort, the Coulson Line was usually given the transportation contract, since it had the boats available.

Coulson's partners continued their practice of bidding for grain contracts in 1878 and secured several lucrative contracts. In April, 1878, the Quartermaster of the Department of Dakota let contracts for 4,231 tons of corn and 5,545½ tons of oats to be delivered to military posts on the Missouri and Yellowstone rivers. Contracts were awarded to J. C. McVay for the delivery of 500 tons of the corn and 1,000 tons of the oats to Yankton. This grain was then relayed upstream by Coulson's boats. Maratta was awarded a contract for 1,221 tons of oats, also.[11] The practice of transportation men bidding for grain contracts was continued throughout the 1880's and 1890's. By the mid-1880's speculating on fulfilling grain contracts had become so profitable that transportation companies made more money buying and selling grain to the army than they did in transporting it.

The year 1879 was the last big year in the military contract business for Coulson and the town of Yankton. By the spring of 1880 the

Milwaukee Railroad had been extended to a point some seventy miles above Yankton. Coulson received a contract covering all military transportation on the Missouri and Yellowstone rivers for 1879. Although the government began letting special contracts for the Yellowstone River transportation business in 1877, this was the first time Coulson had ever received both contracts. In the contract of 1879 he agreed to transport officers on the Missouri River for three cents per mile, enlisted men and government employees for two cents, and livestock for three cents. Coulson was given ten cents per 100 pounds per 100 miles on all freight originating at Yankton and delivered to points between Yankton and Fort Benton.[12]

For stores and supplies originating at Bismarck, Coulson was given twelve cents per 100 pounds per 100 miles. The Yellowstone River rates on the contract were four cents per mile for officers, three cents for enlisted men, and three cents for livestock. The rates on supplies while the boats were actually navigating the Yellowstone River was twenty-five cents per 100 pounds per 100 miles.[13]

The military contracts for 1873 through 1879 named both Yankton and Bismarck as starting points for shipments. Yankton-based steamers primarily carried goods for posts in Dakota Territory while the Bismarck-based boats handled most of the freight for the posts above Bismarck and all of the Yellowstone freight. Coulson kept boats at both Bismarck and Yankton. While he dominated the trade from Yankton, he had considerable competition at Bismarck because Kountz, Peck, and Power also kept boats there.

In Bismarck's first year as a port, steamboat trade above the town was controlled by William J. Kountz, who worked in cooperation with the Northern Pacific Railroad. Kountz had elaborate plans for the future of his business above Bismarck after 1873, but his schemes were thwarted almost immediately when the military contract for 1874 was awarded to Coulson. This contract specified transportation of officers, enlisted men, freight, livestock, wagons, ambulances, and carts from Bismarck to Fort Abraham Lincoln, Fort Stevenson, Fort Buford, and Fort Benton. Coulson must have been aware when he bid for the military contract for Bismarck and points above that he was faced with more determined competition than that which he encountered in the Yankton bidding; the rates for freight shipped under the Coulson contract from Bismarck were substantially lower than rates for comparable distances and classes of goods transported under terms of his Yankton contract. The contract was set up according to a schedule by which Coulson would be paid more during the periods when the river was low and navigation more difficult. Coulson was to be paid fifteen cents per 100 pounds on freight from Bismarck to Fort Abraham Lincoln, thirty-five cents to Fort Stevenson, fifty cents to Fort Buford, and $1.25 to Fort Benton during the months of March, April, and May. Rates for June were decreased slightly because of the annual June rise, while the August, September, and October rates were approximately double the spring rates.[14]

Coulson controlled military shipments from both Yankton and Bismarck in 1875, but in 1876 the contract for transportation above Bismarck was awarded to Walter A. Burleigh of Yankton.[15] Burleigh and his son operated steamers from Yankton as early as 1872 but never had any more than one or two boats in the trade. The government apparently gave Burleigh the contract solely on the basis of his being the lowest bidder, although most commonly the army quartermaster considered the ability of the company to transport the goods as well as the rate at which they were willing to carry them. It should have been apparent to the military when they awarded the contract to Burleigh in the latter part of March that he would not be capable of filling it in light of the military program for 1876.

In 1876 the army planned the biggest offensive against the Sioux since the Sully Expeditions of the 1860's. This move was prompted by hostile actions of the Sioux, who were alarmed over the miners' invasions of the Black Hills. Many of the hostile Sioux, including renegades from the reservations, concentrated in southeastern Montana during the winter of 1875/76. General Phil Sheridan, Commander of the Division of the Missouri, planned to subdue the Sioux through the use of three armies which were to converge in the Big Horn and Powder River area. He ordered Crook to march from the south, Gibbon from the west, and Terry from the east. The eastern army based at Fort Abraham Lincoln was to be supplied by steamboats operating on the Missouri and Yellowstone rivers.

Burleigh's inadequacies were apparent by late April. The army could have forced him to sublet portions of his contract, thereby making him directly responsible for delivering all military men and supplies. Such a procedure, however, would have incurred great delays and the military undoubtedly considered it much more expedient to take over the business themselves.

While the military campaigns were underway the Bismarck Quartermaster virtually worked around the clock chartering boats, contracting for special trips, and even pressing into service boats that under normal conditions would not have been considered seaworthy. In late April, the quartermaster called on Coulson to furnish two steamboats to carry supplies from Bismarck to the mouth of Glendive Creek on the Yellowstone. Coulson eagerly complied, as he was to receive approximately $300 per day for the services of each of the boats. Steamboat operators considered the chartering of boats much more satisfactory than a contract calling for the specific delivery of goods because the charter relieved them of the responsibility of guaranteeing delivery. Charter rates were set very high because of the possibility of damage or loss of the boat during military operations.

By mid-June, 1876, the military needs for steamboats on the Yellowstone increased further because General Terry began moving his supply depot from the mouth of Glendive Creek upstream eighty-two miles to the mouth of the Powder River. Steamboats were also used for moving troops up and down the Yellowstone.[16] The most pressing military need for steamboat transportation in 1876, and perhaps in the whole history of Missouri River navigation, occurred after the Little Big Horn disaster.

One of the great heroes of the Indian campaign was Grant Marsh, captain of the steamer *Far West*, who succeeded in steaming up the previously unnavigated Big Horn sixty-four miles to the mouth of the Little Big Horn and evacuating the wounded from the battlefield. Marsh could very easily have kept his boat safely back on the Yellowstone, well away from the battlefield, but he chose instead to push up the shallow Big Horn, facing the possibility of stranding the boat and being annihilated by the Sioux. In spite of these dangers, he moved the *Far West* to within fifteen miles of the battlefield where he thought he could render the most assistance. The wounded men of Reno's command were carried from the battlefield on a night so dark that General Terry had fires built to light the way for the litter bearers over rough places. The men were loaded on the *Far West* at about two o'clock on the morning of June 28, and Marsh immediately started for Bismarck. Perhaps Marsh's greatest feat of navigation was not in ascending the Big Horn, but rather in steaming from the mouth of the Little Big Horn to Bismarck, approximately nine hundred miles, in fifty-four hours, an exploit unrivaled in the history of Missouri River navigation.[17]

It was ironic that Marsh, in his desperate race to save the lives of the wounded on board his steamer, should also have been the one to bring news of the Custer disaster to the world. Marsh quickly returned to the Yellowstone and brought down more wounded and then made yet another trip with supplies for Terry's expedition.[18] The urgency of the Marsh trips was indicative of the drastic needs of the military by July, 1876. The entire problem of the Yellowstone River military frontier was taken up by Congress, and $200,000 was immediately appropriated for the construction of two posts on the Yellowstone River.[19] Post Number One, later named Fort Keogh, was located near the mouth of Tongue River, and Post Number Two, later named Fort Custer, was located at the mouth of the Little Big Horn. In 1876 Fort Keogh was usually referred to simply as the Tongue River Post.

On July 24, the Quartermaster General, Department of Dakota, advised Second Lieutenant Drubb, the Bismarck Quartermaster, that the two new posts had been authorized and gave instructions in regard to the shipping of supplies. Drubb was then confronted with a major problem: the contracting of boats to carry construction supplies to Tongue River. Five days after Drubb was advised that the posts were to be built, he was instructed to load Coulson's *Key West* with lumber and shingles and then send the boat to Fort Buford to take on a military guard. The Chief Quartermaster, to add to Drubb's problems, advised him "that as we do not know where the new post will be located direct steamers to see General Forsyth and ascertain the site—but if they should not see him not to go above Tongue River until advised of the site selected."[20] During the next month, Drubb employed more of the Coulson boats, and also Wilder's *Silver Lake* and Peck's *Nellie Peck*. His most urgent problem was forwarding all of the Tongue River supplies, but he also had to make arrangements for transporting portions of the Fifth Infantry Regiment upstream. Throughout this period the military relied most heavily upon the Coulson steamers. A writer for the *Bismarck Tribune* reported that the Coulson Line had so much business in 1876, its six steamers could not handle the freight and Coulson chartered six other boats from rival lines.[21]

Many companies profited from the military campaigns in 1876, and the government transportation needs promised to be even greater in 1877. Twenty bidders were attracted to the St. Paul letting. The prime contenders for the contract were Coulson, Kountz, Burleigh,

Wilder, Terry, and William F. Davidson of St. Paul. All of the major bidders except Davidson were experienced in Missouri River steamboating. Davidson, president of the Keokuk Northern Packet Line, had long been a power in Mississippi River steamboating. John B. Davis represented the Davidson interests at the contract-letting. Davis estimated that 5,000 tons of freight were to be carried from Bismarck to Buford and figured that it could be carried profitably at fifteen cents per 100 pounds per 100 miles for the 300-mile distance, which would amount to $45,000. He figured there would also be 4,000 tons at Buford for Tongue River and 4,000 for the Little Big Horn, and that a bid of fifty-seven and one-half cents per 100 per 100 miles would gross $108,000 for the delivery of the Tongue River goods and $184,000 for the Little Big Horn goods. The total estimated gross receipts for the delivery of those supplies would be $337,800. Davis also believed that, in addition to the supplies, there would be extensive transportation of troops and civilian laborers and that this might run from $50,000 to $100,000 above the contract.[22] Davis computed that the contract business alone would net about $100,000, since it would cost the company approximately $228,000 to operate ten boats and twelve barges.

Bidding was opened on March 15 by General Card, Chief Quartermaster, Department of Dakota. Davis' successful bid, and those of his competitors, are shown on Table XIV.

Davis' bid for the Missouri River and Yellowstone River freight contract was lower than those of the leading Missouri River steamboat companies, perhaps owing to Davis' lack of familiarity with the problems of navigation on the Missouri and Yellowstone rivers. The bid submitted by E. Fenton and Levi Wilson of Leavenworth was still lower than Davis'; Fenton and Wilson, however, feared that transportation of the freight could not be completed by steamboat, so they incorporated in their bid a provision that if freight had to be carried by wagon, the rate would be $1.43 per 100 pounds per 100 miles. Because of this rider, B. C. Card rejected their bid in favor of Davis'.[23]

To carry out the contract, Davis, William F. Davidson and his brother Peyton, and John Reaney, an agent and partner in the Keokuk Northern Packet Line, organized the Yellowstone Transportation Company. This company was based at Bismarck during the season of 1877 with Reaney as the general manager.

The Yellowstone Transportation Company's venture on the Missouri and Yellowstone rivers seemed ill-fated from the beginning. Originally, Reaney tried to purchase some Missouri River steamers; first, because they were designed for the shallow river, and second, to avoid having to remove too many of Davidson's boats from the

TABLE XIV
BIDS FOR MILITARY CONTRACT—1877*

BIDDER	RATES PER 100 LBS. PER 100 MILES	
	Missouri River	Yellowstone River
E. Fenton and Levi Wilson	$ .14	$ .57
John B. Davis, St. Paul	.15	.57½
Simon Reineman	.19	.90
Oliver Townsend	.20	.85
W. A. Burleigh, all to Buford	.18¾	.95
Warren Robinson	.19½	.64
F. Williams	.19¼	.41
John H. Dunton	.17½	.61
Vincent N. York	.30	2.00
John Baker	.18	.57
Reuben Barrett	.19	.52
John Healey	.18¼	.46¼
Jas. Kinney, Dan Silver, A. F. Terry	.20	.90
James Hamilton	.24	.90
John LaBarge	.15	. . .
John W. Barlow	.19½	.93
Jos. Leach, 2,000 tons	. . .	.80
S. B. Coulson and A. H. Wilder	.19½	.74½

*Press and Dakotaian, March 20, 1877.

Mississippi River trade. He tried to purchase boats through Amherst Wilder and John Charles, and Charles said he could provide four boats for $53,000. Reaney refused to buy. He believed this price was extremely high and that Wilder and Charles were merely plotting with Coulson to squeeze the Yellowstone Transportation Company out.[24] Davidson and his associates then decided to use Mississippi River steamboats. At St. Louis, these boats were loaded with coal— which the company intended to use for fuel because of the difficulty in procuring wood along the Yellowstone—and then proceeded up-river. Some of the boats towed barges up the Missouri. Davis intended to use them on the Upper Missouri and on the Yellowstone River, if possible.[25] Reaney also supervised the construction of several other barges at Bismarck. Construction costs at Bismarck were extremely high, and Reaney complained constantly about the scarcity of lumber and carpenters. The barge experiment proved to be an expensive mistake and within a short time was abandoned.

The Yellowstone Transportation Company was "Yellowstone River" in name only. The company tried to use Mississippi River boats, Mississippi River men, and Mississippi River methods on the Missouri and the Yellowstone. Reaney was plagued by a succession of minor misfortunes which, totaled up, amounted to the inability of the company to transport supplies as fast as the army needed them. The army felt a particular urgency in the shipment of Yellowstone River freight because of the construction of Fort Keogh and because of General Nelson Miles's campaign against the Nez Perces. Reaney claimed the company could not keep up with the freight because it took boats longer to reach their destinations than he had expected, which he attributed to the inexperience of the officers and crews.[26] Other misfortunes followed; the company lost one boat and all of its stores when the *Osceola*, captained by Mark D. Flower, was wrecked by a tornado at the mouth of the Powder River.[27]

Meanwhile, Sanford Coulson and Daniel Maratta were prepared to capitalize upon the misfortune of the Yellowstone Transportation Company. They realized that the army would have to call on other steamboats if the contractors failed to deliver goods rapidly.[28] Coulson's hopes to corner a share of the military freight were realized by mid-June when the army called upon him to help transport the rapidly accumulating Tongue River freight at Bismarck.

Throughout the rest of the season Coulson's boats carried considerable freight to the Yellowstone River post. Whenever a Davidson boat was not available, Second Lieutenant Drubb loaded Coulson boats. By fall, there were very few Davidson boats on the Missouri and Maratta wrote to Coulson that if the Davidson boats were completely out of the way, the Missouri River Transportation Company could fix their own prices.[29]

Reaney claimed that the Yellowstone Transportation Company had delivered eight thousand tons by late August, thereby completing its contract with the government. The company was apparently anxious to get off the Missouri River and the fall trade was left almost entirely to Coulson. The late fall trade was sizable; on October 10, the *Bismarck Tribune* reported that over six hundred tons of military freight still awaited shipment.[30]

Despite his poor showing in 1877, Davidson fought vigorously for the contract in 1878. When General Charles Tompkins, the Department of Dakota Quartermaster, accepted Coulson's Missouri River bid and Kountz's Yellowstone bid, Davidson tried to get General Holabird, Quartermaster of the Division of the Missouri, to reverse the decision.[31] When this move failed, Davidson went on to Washington, where he made a final, futile attempt to have his bid accepted. After Davidson failed to secure the business in 1878, the Yellowstone River Transportation Company went out of existence.

The bidding for the Yellowstone River freight in 1878 was evidently very brisk. Kountz got the Yellowstone contract at twenty-nine cents per 100 pounds per 100 miles, or barely half of what Davidson had received the previous year. Kountz had difficulty with Yellowstone River deliveries and failed to deliver 750 tons within the specified contract time. The Yellowstone was so low in October that steamboats could not reach Fort Keogh and the freight had to be delivered by wagon. Wagon transportation from Buford cost as much as $2.00 and possibly $4.00 or $5.00 per 100 pounds; consequently Kountz must have lost a great deal on his contract.[32] The successive poor performances by Davidson and Kountz were partially responsible for the government's awarding of the military contract to Coulson in 1879.

Bismarck and Yankton interests competed as actively for the profitable Indian annuity transportation contracts from 1874 to 1879 as they did for the military contracts. Competition amounted principally to a struggle between the Northern Pacific, Bismarck steamboat men, and Bismarck contractors on one hand and the Dakota Southern, Yankton steamboat men, and Yankton contractors on the other. Most of the time the Dakota Southern and Yankton group were successful. In 1874 all of the annuity goods with the exception of about a hundred tons for the Crow and Blackfeet agencies was forwarded by way of the Dakota Southern and Coulson's boats.[33] During 1875, the Indian goods were delivered to Bismarck by way of the Northern Pacific Railroad, but in 1877, 1878, and 1879, the goods were again delivered to Yankton via the Dakota Southern.

Kountz was always bitter about his failure to get the Indian contracts; he lost the bid in 1873 to Coulson and later charged in the *Allegheny Mail* that one of Coulson's associates, William Evans, failed to deliver some of the annuities; Evans promptly sued Kountz for libel. In 1876, Kountz testified before a House subcommittee in Washington that he had been denied the contract many times in favor of individuals who had actually bid higher than he.[34]

Kountz did not benefit from the contract of 1875 either, even though the Indian annuities were carried to Bismarck by the Northern Pacific Railroad, because Coulson's steamers moved the freight upstream. Coulson delivered some of this freight to Carroll, where it was transferred to McClay's Diamond R Freight Line and forwarded by wagon to Fort Belknap and the Blackfeet and Crow agencies.[35]

When the Indian Service held the 1877 contract-letting in New York, most of the men interested in Missouri River steamboating attended. Coulson, McVay, and Charles went to New York, accompanied by George Merchant, superintendent of the Dakota Southern, and two prominent merchants, James E. Booge of Yankton and Charles E. Hedges of Sioux City. Coulson lost the bid to C. K. Peck. Peck got a contract to transport supplies from Bismarck to Berthold Agency, Standing Rock Agency, and any new agencies created, and also to carry annuities from either Yankton or Bismarck to Red Cloud and Spotted Tail agencies. An associate of Peck, C. M. Primeau of Keokuk, secured the contracts from Sioux City to Crow Creek Agency, Cheyenne Agency, Lower Brule, Yankton Agency, Santee Agency, and the Fort Berthold Agency. He also had a contract to ship annuities from Bismarck to the Cheyenne Agency. Goods to be moved by Primeau and Peck totaled approximately 2,500 tons.[36] Most of the Primeau and Peck supplies were shipped by way of the Dakota Southern and Yankton. Peck's agent, H. C. Akin, set up an office in Yankton and managed the operations of five steamers which carried the Indian annuities, as well as Terry's military freight.

The following year Peck got only a part of the Indian contract. He was to transport annuities to Crow Creek, Cheyenne, and Red Cloud agencies. Coulson got the contract to carry supplies to all other agencies. As in 1877, most of the annuities were shipped by way of the Dakota Southern and Yankton. Quantities of goods to be shipped under the contracts of 1878 promised to be large; a writer for the *Press and Dakotaian* estimated that the Red Cloud and Spotted Tail agencies would need nine hundred carloads of supplies during the year.[37]

In 1879 Coulson beat all competitors and obtained the entire contract to supply all agencies. Coulson and McVay had worked closely with George Merchant in drawing up their bids. Merchant bid five cents per 100 pounds by rail from Sioux City to Yankton and McVay bid eight cents per 100 pounds per 100 miles from Yankton to all of the agencies except Standing Rock, Fort Berthold, and Fort Peck. He bid less than eight cents on freight for these three agencies. The annuities for 1879 amounted to three thousand tons to be delivered between July 1, 1879, and July 1, 1880. An editorialist for the *Bismarck Tribune* attributed Yankton's success in 1879 to high freight rates charged by the Northern Pacific. He accused the railroad of driving thousands of tons of freight away from Bismarck during the season because of high rates.[38]

During the period 1874–1879, the major business of the various steamboat companies was the shipment of government supplies. However, much of their success also has to be attributed to the increased shipments of private freight. The two major destinations for private freight shipments from Bismarck and Yankton were Fort Benton and the Black Hills. Bismarck interests dominated the Fort Benton trade, while Yankton concerns controlled most of the Black Hills trade.

Fort Benton trade declined in the early 1870's, but began to increase again in 1875. This increase can be credited to a number of significant factors. Many shippers to Montana found it more convenient to transport goods by way of the Missouri River than by the Union Pacific and the overland wagon route. Moreover, Fort Benton merchants acted as suppliers for a great hinterland that stretched northward into Canada. Another important reason for the increase in the Benton trade was the settlement of northern Montana, an area which could not be effectively supplied by the Union Pacific. Then too, Montana miners and fur traders continued their activities throughout the 1870's, and some of them still relied upon the steamboat for the transportation of their goods.

During the revival of the Montana steamboat trade, Fort Benton was challenged by a new town, Carroll. This center, located near the mouth of the Musselshell River in 1874, was meant to serve as a freight landing for steamboats and as the beginning of a wagon trail across the Judith Basin to Helena. The town backers, notably the Diamond R Transportation Company, enjoyed a fairly lively business in 1874 and 1875. Low water in the Rocky River made Carroll an attractive landing, and twenty-one steamboats unloaded at the village during this period. The Diamond R worked with both the Kountz and

Coulson lines, whose boats carried freight from the railhead at Bismarck. In 1875 Coulson commenced weekly packet service to Carroll and by June 2 about one thousand tons of freight had been shipped from Bismarck to Carroll, and about five hundred tons from Carroll to Bismarck. This Carroll route was more practical than the Fort Benton route, claimed a *Tribune* reporter, because Carroll freight was reaching Helena ten days earlier than freight routed through Fort Benton.[39]

Carroll's activities were short-lived. Sioux war parties harassed the town, and with the return of high water in 1876 steamboat operators passed the village by on their way to Benton. Carroll remained in existence a few years after 1876, but never again attained importance as a trade center.[40] After 1876, if boats could not reach Benton they usually stopped at Cow Island, about sixty miles above Carroll and just short of the rapids portion of the river.

The Bismarck-based steamboat men who worked in the Fort Benton run maintained a lively competition for the speed record from Bismarck to Benton. The nature of the river prohibited actual races, so the competition was against the clock. The prize was a set of large elk horns which were tacked to the pilot house of the fastest boat. The custom of passing the elk horns was transferred to the Upper Missouri from St. Louis, where it had been in practice as early as the 1850's. The Bismarck trophy passed from boat to boat as new records were set. The average trip from Bismarck to Benton took approximately fourteen days, but in 1877 I. G. Baker's *Red Cloud* made the run in fifteen minutes less than ten days, which was nearly a day better than the previous record.[41] The next year the time was lowered to nine days and one hour, and the triumphant Captain McGarry claimed the horns.[42]

In 1875, six boats reached Fort Benton. In 1876 the number increased to sixteen and then to twenty-five in 1877.[43] The trade for the year 1877 was extensive. Lieutenant Edward Maguire of the Corps of Engineers, who was in charge of river improvement above the mouth of the Yellowstone in 1877, reported that during the year twenty-five steamers delivered 5,283 tons of freight and about 1,500 passengers to Benton and took down 3,200 tons of freight and about 500 passengers. Maguire's figures included both military and private freight. The Montana exports were mainly private freight, including 1,225 tons of gold ore and silver bullion in addition to over 200,000 pounds of wool and 50,000 buffalo robes. Maguire placed the total value of Fort Benton river commerce at $3,458,536.60, an increase of roughly 50 per cent over the trade of 1870.[44] Maguire used I. G. Baker as the authority for most of his information.

In 1878, forty-six steamers reached Fort Benton, and Maguire reported that upriver shipments amounted to 8,764 tons. Of this amount, 200 tons were military supplies shipped from Yankton and Bismarck, 200 to 300 tons were Indian freight, and the remainder was private freight. Maguire was unable, in 1878, to determine exactly the amount of Montana exports, but he did report that wool shipments totaled 696,000 pounds, a considerable increase over the previous year.[45]

A writer for the *Bismarck Tribune* summarized the private freight shipments from Bismarck to points in Montana for the year 1879. According to this reporter, a total of 4,675 tons of freight—almost equally divided among the Coulson Line, Benton Line, and the Baker Line—was transported to all points on the Missouri and Yellowstone rivers. Private freight shipped upriver from points below Bismarck amounted to approximately 2,750 tons, making a total of nearly 7,500 tons of private freight shipped into Montana.[46]

In 1877 freight rates from Bismarck to Fort Benton or Carroll ranged from $1.50 to $2.50 per 100 pounds. The Coulson Line never operated for long periods of time on a fixed rate schedule. Maratta, as company agent, worked out rates for individual shipments. Rates always depended upon the condition of the river, crew's wages, the size of each shipment, and the sender of the goods. In April, 1877, Maratta set private freight rates from Bismarck to Benton at $1.50 per 100 pounds; within three weeks he had increased the rate to $2.50. In September of the same year Maratta's rates ranged from $1.25 to $2.50 per 100 pounds. He set the lower rates on supplies for McClay and Power, both of whom did much business with Coulson. The high rate was set on a small consignment of miscellaneous private freight.[47]

In 1876 Yankton business was stimulated by the rush of miners into the Black Hills. Gold was discovered in the Hills by members of the Custer Expedition in 1874 and the next year miners illegally entered the area, which had been set aside as a permanent Indian reservation. The thousands of miners who entered the Black Hills were supplied by four principal routes: the wagon route from Bismarck, wagon routes from Fort Laramie on the Union Pacific, the Sidney, Nebraska, wagon route, and the Yankton to Fort Pierre route. Of these, the Yankton—Fort Pierre route was the most direct and efficient. This route consisted of three types of transportation—railroad to Yankton, steamboats from Yankton to Fort Pierre, and freight wagon from Fort Pierre to the Black Hills. By 1879, three-fourths of all Black Hills freight was shipped by this railroad-steamboat-wagon combination.[48]

This combination was first formed in 1876 when George E. Merchant, superintendent of the Dakota Southern, and Sanford B. Coulson made an agreement to ship Black Hills freight to Fort Pierre. This agreement was essential to Merchant, since he had to assure shippers that Black Hills freight would not be stranded at the terminus of the Dakota Southern, but would be quickly forwarded by a reliable steamboat company. The agreement was obviously advantageous to Coulson's company, also.

Once the freight reached Fort Pierre, it was transferred to wagons. There were two major wagon lines engaged in the Fort Pierre—Black Hills trade, the Merchants Line, owned by Downer T. Bramble of Yankton, and the Evans Line, formed in 1876 by Fred Evans of Sioux City. Evans' first wagon outfit was destroyed by the army because of illegal entry into Indian land. After Evans' initial setback, the government was forced to close its eyes to illegal entry into the Black Hills because of the uncontrollable rush of miners and the breakdown of relations with the Indians. The next year the Black Hills were legally opened by a government treaty with various bands of the Sioux. Black Hills traffic expanded rapidly; during 1879, Evans delivered 5,000 tons of freight to the Hills, using approximately 200 wagon teams.[49]

It was logical that Downer T. Bramble and his junior partner, William Miner, would enter the wagon freighting business. Bramble and Miner were wholesale merchants, operators of the Yankton steam elevator and owners of the Excelsior Mills, which produced thousands of pounds of flour annually. Bramble and Miner found it advantageous to enter the Black Hills trade if for no other reason than to distribute their own goods. Imports of the Black Hills miners consisted principally of foodstuffs, clothing, and mining supplies and other hardware. Bramble and Miner handled all of these items. Much of Bramble and Miner's wholesale goods came into Yankton via the Dakota Southern and was then shipped to Fort Pierre on Coulson's steamers.

The Dakota Southern, Coulson's Missouri River Transportation Company, and Bramble and Miner worked out coordinated schedules which insured speedy transfers and deliveries of Black Hills freight. Bramble and Miner in 1879 shipped approximately five thousand tons of Black Hills freight from Fort Pierre. A *Bismarck Tribune* reporter claimed that Black Hills freight over the Yankton—Fort Pierre route showed an increase in 1879 because of shipments of heavy mining equipment such as quartz mills which had previously been sent overland through Sidney, Nebraska.[50]

By 1880 Bramble and Miner's freight line was employing three hundred men and using two thousand head of oxen. The capacity of each wagon train was estimated at 700 tons, which would mean that three to four steamboat loads were needed to complete one full wagon train. By August, 1880, the Bramble and Miner wagons had forwarded 4,000 tons, with expectations of doing a business of over 5,000 tons for the entire season.[51]

During the period 1876–1880, Coulson ran semiweekly steamers in the Yankton to Fort Pierre trade. Coulson's company carried most of the Yankton to Pierre freight, but his Yankton competitor, Burleigh, also entered the trade in 1877. Burleigh's Yankton and Black Hills Line, however, never operated more than two steamers on the Yankton to Fort Pierre run.[52]

The Yankton steamers were vital to the prosperous opening of the Black Hills because they provided rapid transportation between the Yankton railhead and the wagon route. While the boats operated from April to November, they speeded the delivery of essential imports into the Hills. They also brought down from the Hills gold quartz, furs, and buffalo hides. These exports were transferred to the Dakota Southern and some of the gold quartz was forwarded to the Omaha smelting works.

Yankton steamboat operators made most of their money in the Black Hills trade on upriver shipments, since imports always exceeded exports and much higher rates were charged for upstream shipments. In 1876 Coulson charged seventy-five cents per 100 pounds on freight from Yankton to Fort Pierre while the river was high, and in early October he advanced the rates to $1.50 per 100. Still later in the season, he boosted the rates to $2.00 per 100, giving as reasons low water, high wages, and a scarcity of wood.[53] These upstream rates for 1876 were the only rates found in available newspaper and manuscript sources pertaining to the Yankton and Fort Pierre trade. They obviously do not give the total picture of upstream charges during the period 1876 to 1879, but they are an indication of the profits reaped in the Black Hills trade.

In 1877 the steamer *Black Hills* carried freight downstream from Sully, Cheyenne, and Fort Pierre to Yankton for twenty cents per 100 pounds per 100 miles. These rates were taken from an isolated statement in the I. P. Baker Papers and once again can only be used as an indication of rates.[54]

During the late 1870's when Yankton and Bismarck dominated Upper Missouri River steamboating, approximately thirty-five boats operated from each of these two ports. Steamboat activity can be roughly calculated in terms of the number of steamers on the river and the total number of arrivals and departures at each of the two ports.[55] In 1877, thirty-six steamers operated out of Yankton, and thirty-six out of Bismarck. Bismarck steamers made 145 arrivals and 144 departures. Three years later, Bismarck recorded 172 arrivals and 172 departures. Yankton, in 1878, had 132 arrivals and 126 departures. Steamboat arrivals and departures were significant to these ports because local labor many times was used in loading and unloading. Steamboats were also repaired, outfitted, and wintered in both Yankton and Bismarck, benefiting local carpenters, machinists, and calkers. Yankton was the major wintering port because it was Coulson's home base and he had the largest fleet on the Upper Missouri.

The many steamers on the Upper Missouri attested to the profitableness of the trade. Obviously steamboat operators made money or they would not have remained in the business. Unfortunately, a complete record of steamboat profits is not available. This type of information was not usually published in the newspapers; however, some statements for individual steamers are located in the Baker Papers.

Table XV represents profits of some of the Coulson steamers for the year 1877. This table is not intended to give the total profits of the Missouri River Transportation Company, but merely represents what statistical information was available. These figures should serve as tangible evidence of the amount of business, calculated in dollars and cents, that individual steamers were capable of doing.

Both Yankton- and Bismarck-based steamboat companies found the years 1874 to 1879 profitable ones. Railheads at these points gave them primacy over Sioux City as shipping points for both government and private freight for the Upper Missouri. But in 1880, the Milwaukee Road built track to Running Water above Yankton, and the trade pattern once again changed. Many boats were loaded at

TABLE XV
SAMPLES OF NET PROFITS
MADE BY MISSOURI RIVER TRANSPORTATION COMPANY STEAMERS, 1877

Name of Steamer	Profits	
Western	$24,679.19[a]	(profits for year)
Black Hills	15,416.49[b]	(profits for year)
Far West	26,956.60[c]	(profits for year)
Custer	8,000.00[d]	(profits for year)
Peninah	17,000.00[d]	(profits for year)
Rose Bud	10,000.00[e]	(profits for three trips)
Big Horn	13,000.00[f]	(net gain to August 31)

[a]Statement of Steamer *Western*—1877, in Baker Papers.
[b]Statement of Steamer *Black Hills*—1877, in Baker Papers.
[c]Statement of Steamer *Far West*—1877, in Baker Papers.
[d]Martin Coulson to S. B. Coulson, dated Allegheny, December 1, 1877.
[e]Martin Coulson to J. C. McVay, dated Allegheny, October 31, 1877.
[f]Joe Todd to J. C. McVay, dated Bismarck, September 6, 1877.

Running Water in 1880, and within a year or two more, railroads were completed to Chamberlain and Pierre, practically removing Yankton from contention as a major steamboat port, and leaving Bismarck the one major port on the Upper Missouri with access to a large trade area.

IX

Bismarck as the Last Important Steamboat Port on the Upper Missouri River, 1880–1885

THE FIRST half of the decade of the 1880's was a period of significant transition in the history of Upper Missouri River steamboating: a period in which river transportation assumed a minor role compared to the part it played in the economic development of the previous decade. The extension of railroads to points on the Missouri between Bismarck and Yankton forced steamboat operators to make shorter and less profitable hauls. When the Milwaukee Road reached the Missouri at Running Water in 1880 and Chamberlain in 1881, and the Chicago & North Western reached Pierre in 1880, wagon operators could compete with steamboat owners, particularly in the area between Yankton and Bismarck. Moreover, by 1880 military campaigns in the Upper Missouri region were history. Because the Indians in the area had been subdued and placed on reservations, the garrison strength at most posts was decreased. Thus there were no more lucrative military contracts with the government. However, the business of carrying annuities to the Indian agencies remained sizable. After 1880, Bismarck was the only port which had access to a large trade area, so steamboating was concentrated at that place. The Coulson and Power companies competed fiercely for the declining business until Coulson finally retired from the river in 1885. After that, Thomas Power and Isaac P. Baker, operating exclusively out of Bismarck, enjoyed a virtual monopoly of the river carrying trade.

In bypassing Yankton and Sioux City the railroads eliminated them as important steamboat ports. The railroad termini at Running Water, Chamberlain, and Pierre became the new ports on the Upper Missouri and broke up the long haul that had previously existed between Yankton and Bismarck. But, for the time being, no railroad was extended to a point on the Missouri above Bismarck, and Bismarck

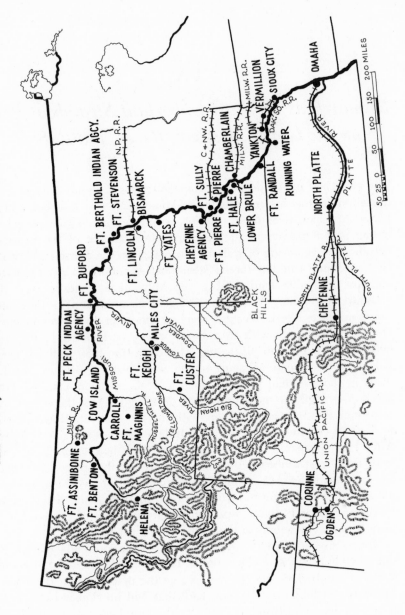

Map 3. Major River Points and Railheads, 1880–1885

businessmen could retain much of the trade upriver from that point.

The first blow to Yankton trade occurred in 1880 with the completion of the Milwaukee Road to Running Water. Yankton had been named the starting point for government shipments in the contract of 1880, but after the railroad reached Running Water, the government signed another contract with the Milwaukee Road naming Running Water the shipping point for Upper Missouri supplies. There were no warehouse or landing facilities at Running Water, and goods delivered there were piled on a sandbar to await pickup by steamboats.[1] Yankton operators often had to run nearly empty steamers the seventy miles to Running Water to take on the military freight. In the spring of 1880, no government freight was shipped to Yankton by way of the Dakota Southern. The only substantial freight shipments originating at Yankton were government grain and flour procured locally under separate contracts by Coulson and his associates.

Yankton business interests felt the impact immediately. Goods for Fort Randall and the nearby Indian agencies which had formerly been shipped to Yankton were now sent directly to Running Water. The Peck Line abandoned both Sioux City and Yankton to operate out of Running Water during the navigation season. From Running Water, the Peck Line boats controlled a large portion of the Black Hills trade. Most of the freight destined for the Black Hills in 1880 was carried by the Milwaukee Road to Running Water, then by Peck boats to Fort Pierre, where it was transferred to freight wagons for the final lap of the haul. One of the Peck boats, the *Fontenelle*, was used regularly in the Running Water to Pierre trade and transported 3,696 tons of freight during the season of 1880.[2]

With the completion of the Chicago & North Western to Pierre in November of 1880, private freight shipments tended to shift to Pierre. Coulson, the Peck Line, and Fred T. Evans all operated boats out of Pierre beginning in the spring of 1881. The principal destinations for the Pierre boats after the completion of the railroad were the town of Chamberlain and the Lower Brule and Cheyenne River Indian agencies.

The railroad to Pierre was especially damaging to steamboat operators engaged in the Black Hills trade. Black Hills freight which had previously been carried from Running Water to Fort Pierre by steamboat now reached Pierre via the railroad, and had only to be transported across the river from Pierre to Fort Pierre, the starting point for Black Hills wagon lines.

In September, 1881, yet another change took place in the Missouri River trade. The completion of the Milwaukee Road to Chamberlain enabled that town to vie with Pierre for the Black Hills trade. The competition between Pierre and Chamberlain was actually a competition between the Milwaukee Road and the Chicago & North Western. In order to attract Black Hills shippers, the Milwaukee Road had to match or undercut the Chicago & North Western rates, and provide as good, or better, service. This problem was complicated because Chamberlain, the terminus for the Milwaukee Road, was forty miles downriver from Fort Pierre. Thus, to compete successfully with the Chicago & North Western, the Milwaukee Road needed a steamboat ally at Chamberlain in order to assure shippers prompt delivery to Fort Pierre.

William J. Kountz provided the connecting link between Chamberlain and Fort Pierre for the Milwaukee Road when he moved two of his boats from Sioux City to Chamberlain. Kountz's boats could make the round trip to Fort Pierre in as little as two and one-half days.[3] This boat service was fast enough to enable the Milwaukee Road to compete with the Chicago & North Western, since wagon trains were not scheduled for daily departures from Fort Pierre.

Most of the freight transported from Chamberlain was mining machinery, railroad iron, general merchandise, and beer for the Black Hills, and provisions, including coal, for Fort Randall and Fort Sully. Coal became a major trade item after the completion of the railroads to Pierre and Chamberlain because the military posts could then afford to import it for fuel. The Kountz boats also did a big business ferrying cattle across the Missouri, sometimes transporting as many as 2,400 head in a single day.[4] Many of the cattle were used on the agencies and others were being driven to the Black Hills.

The Chamberlain trade, though never requiring more than two full-time steamers, was quite large by 1884. In that year the steamers *General Terry* and *D. H. Rucker* transported 4,000 tons of Black Hills freight to Fort Pierre, and 14,000 tons of coal and general provisions to Cheyenne River Agency and Fort Sully.[5] The coal trade was brisk again in 1885. The *Democrat* of June 18 reported 1,300 tons of coal piled at Chamberlain awaiting shipment to military posts.

Yankton spokesmen were never willing to admit that the extension of the railroads to Running Water, Pierre, and Chamberlain was responsible for the decline of Yankton as a steamboat port. A *Press and*

Dakotaian reporter attributed the decline to the ruinous spring breakup and flood of 1881, in which the Coulson boats and steamboat ways were severely damaged. In actuality, Yankton's decline was apparent to many businessmen even before the flood. As early as 1880, Sanford Coulson and his associates sold nearly half of their boats, mostly to operators on the lower Missouri and Mississippi rivers. Coulson, after 1880, operated primarily out of Bismarck.

Because no railroads touched the river above that point, Bismarck in the early 1880's was the only remaining starting point for a long haul on the Upper Missouri. Although volume of trade originating at Bismarck declined in comparison to that of the previous decade, Bismarck steamboat operators still had a trade area extending nearly 1,100 miles to Fort Benton. Fort Benton, in turn, gave access to a large trade area in northern Montana and Canada. In 1880, there were twenty-three steamboat arrivals at Fort Benton; in 1881, eleven; in 1882, twenty-nine; in 1883, twenty-three; in 1884, fifteen; and in 1885, fifteen arrivals.[6]

Table XVI is a compilation, for the navigation seasons 1881 through 1885, of the most common destinations of Bismarck-based steamers, general kinds of freight they carried, and rates at which it was carried. This information was taken from letters, financial statements, and portage books in the Baker Papers, and from the files of the *Bismarck Tribune*.

During the navigation season of 1880, about two-thirds of all government freight shipped on the Upper Missouri was started at Bismarck. These government shipments amounted to 8,232 tons. Of this total, 6,128 tons were shipped from Bismarck and only 1,536 from Yankton. Government freight started at Bismarck in 1880 was distributed as follows:[7]

Destination	Tons
Yankton	19¼
Fort Randall	1
Fort Hale	⅙
Fort Sully	2¼
Fort Bennett	42
Fort Yates	557
Fort Lincoln	675
Fort Stevenson	275
Fort Buford	1,810
Poplar Creek	114½

Carroll 40
Cow Island 40
Coal Banks 2,369¼
Fort Benton 184

Government freight shipments were sizable again in 1881 because of the enlargement of Fort Maginnis and the enlargement of the Canadian military post, Fort Walsh. Large quantities of provisions and construction materials for western Canadian posts were shipped by way of the Northern Pacific and the Missouri River steamers. By 1881 the Northern Pacific controlled nearly all of the government freight consigned to points above Bismarck, and the government discontinued shipping freight for posts above Bismarck from Yankton or Running Water. A writer for the *Bismarck Tribune* estimated that the government could save $2.00 per hundred pounds by shipping Montana freight through Bismarck rather than from any point below Bismarck. The Northern Pacific was also interested in attracting private freight shipments for Montana. The railroad joined with the Fort Benton Transportation Company in publishing joint tariffs to Fort Benton, Helena, and all points in Montana. This agreement greatly facilitated the transfer of goods from the railroad to steamboat at Bismarck.[8]

Bismarck trade was important enough by 1881 to cause the two major steamboat companies, the Fort Benton Transportation Company controlled by T. C. Power and Isaac Baker, and Coulson's Missouri River Transportation Company, to construct new warehouses on the Bismarck levee.[9] The government and the Northern Pacific also constructed warehouses on the levee that year.

The large Bismarck trade area was seriously curtailed in 1882 by the extension of the Utah and Northern Railroad into southwestern Montana and the construction of the Northern Pacific into the Yellowstone River Valley. Major E. B. Kirk, U.S. Army Quartermaster at Bismarck, estimated that government freight shipments to points in Montana during 1882 would be less than half the amount shipped in 1881 because of these two railroads. In 1881 steamboat freights to points on the Yellowstone River amounted to 4,210 tons, but in 1882 they declined to only 695 tons. Some shippers apparently found it advantageous to ship by rail to points such as Miles City and Billings and then by wagons to the final destinations rather than to use the

TABLE XVI
EXAMPLES OF FREIGHT CARRIED ABOVE BISMARCK, 1881 THROUGH 1885

Year	Destination (from Bismarck)[a]	Kind of Freight	Rate per 100 lbs.	Month of Shipment
1881	Fort Berthold	groceries	$ .25	Oct.
	Fort Buford	groceries	.30	June
	Fort Buford	oats	.30	Oct.
	Fort Buford	flour	.50	Oct.
	Fort Buford	furniture, dry goods	.75	Oct.
	Miles City	lumber, grain	.75	May
	Miles City	dry goods	1.00	May, June
	Fort Keogh	lumber, grain	.75	May
	Fort Keogh	misc. goods	1.00	June
	Glendive	lumber, grain	.75	May
	Glendive	?	1.00	May
	Fort Custer	misc. goods	1.50	June
	Poplar River	furniture, dry goods	1.50	Oct.
1882	Little Muddy	hardware	.60	Apr.
	Fort Buford	hardware, groc's, oats	.60	Apr.
	Fort Buford	hardware, groc's, oats	.40[b]	Apr., June
	Miles City	beer	.70	Apr.
	Poplar River	?	.60[b]	Apr., June
	Poplar River	groc's, dry goods, beer	1.00[b]	Apr.
	Wolf Point	?	.75	June
1883	Washburn	tobacco, dry goods	.30	Oct.
	Fort Stevenson	groc's, tobacco, dry g'ds	.30	Oct.
	Fort Stevenson	?	.50	Aug.
	Fort Berthold	dry goods	.60	Oct.
	Little Muddy	groceries	.65	Oct.
	Fort Buford	hardware, groceries	.50[b]	June
	Fort Buford	groceries	.75[b]	Oct.
	Fort Buford	groceries	1.00	Aug.
	Poplar River	beer, sacked corn	.65[b]	June
	Rocky Point	groceries	1.50	Aug.
1884	Washburn	?	.35	May
	Stanton	coal, hardware, groc's	1.00	Apr.
	Stanton	?	.40	May
	Fort Stevenson	?	.40	May
	Fort Buford	groc's, medicine, beer	.40	Aug.
	Fort Buford	groceries	.65	Oct.
	Poplar River	groceries, liquor	.90	Oct.
	Rocky Point	groceries	.50	Aug.
	Rocky Point	?	.75	May
	Coal Banks	?	.90	May
	Fort Benton	groceries, hardware	1.00	May, June
	Fort Benton	?	.75[c]	May, June
	Fort Benton	?	.85[c]	May, July
	Fort Benton	flour, lumber	.75[c]	July
	Fort Benton	?	1.00	May

TABLE XVI (CON'T.)

Year	Destination (from Bismarck)[a]	Kind of Freight	Rate per 100 lbs.	Month of Shipment
1885	Washburn	?	$ .35	May, June
	Stanton	?	.35	May, June
	Fort Stevenson	?	.40	May, June
	Fort Berthold	?	.40	May, June
	Fort Berthold	groceries	.50	Sept., Oct., Nov.
	Fort Buford	?	.40[b]	July, Aug.
	Fort Buford	?	.60	May, June
	Fort Buford	misc. frt., small pkgs.	.75	May
	Poplar River	?	.75[c]	Apr.
	Poplar River	?	.80	May, June
	Wolf Point	?	.75[c]	Apr.
	Wolf Point	?	.80	Apr., May, June
	Wolf Point	?	1.00	May, June
	Rocky Point	?	.80	Apr., May, June
	Rocky Point	?	1.00	May, June, Sept., Oct., Nov.
	Coal Banks	?	1.25	May, June
	Coal Banks	?	.90	July, Aug.
	Fort Benton	?	.90[c]	May, June
	Fort Benton	?	1.00[c]	July, Aug.
	Fort Benton	?	1.25	May, June

[a] Following is a list of distances from Bismarck to various points on the river. These distances are as given by a Missouri River pilot and are estimated "according to the sinuosities of the stream." (*Bismarck Tribune*, May 9, 1882.)

Fort Stevenson .... 100 miles		Wolf Point (Ft. Peck) .... 615 miles
Fort Berthold .... 125 miles		Rocky Point .... 925 miles
Fort Buford .... 400 miles		Coal Banks .... 1,025 miles
Poplar River .... 580 miles		Fort Benton .... 1,085 miles

[b] Special rates given to Leighton & Jordan, a St. Paul wholesale concern that did extensive business with the Fort Benton Transportation Company.

[c] Special rates given to Fort Benton merchandising firm belonging to T. C. Power and John W. Power.

steamboat route to Fort Benton. The Northern Pacific route was used by T. C. Power to supply his Billings and Benton stage line. By 1882, the railroad–wagon line trade had grown so profitable that Power moved warehouses into Billings to provide storage facilities.[10]

The influence of the Northern Pacific was further extended in 1883 when, on March 4, the railroad signed an agreement with the Fort Benton Transportation Company and the Missouri River Transportation Company which assured the railroad and these two cooperating steamboat companies a virtual monopoly of the river trade above Bismarck for the navigation season of 1883. The contract provided—

1. that any imports or exports of points on the Missouri above Bismarck carried by the agreeing company's steamers, which also had to be

handled by railroad, would be channeled through the Northern Pacific,

2. that the two steamboat companies could not carry freight which was delivered to the Missouri below Bismarck,

3. that the steamboat companies could not carry freight destined for points on the line of the NPRR,

4. that no steamboats would trade on the Yellowstone River, and,

5. that the railroad would give the steamboat companies the benefits of reduced rates and rebates.[11]

The first provision of the contract gave the Northern Pacific control over all of the trade into or out of the Missouri area above Bismarck carried by the two steamboat companies, essentially making the companies adjuncts of the railroad.

The monopolistic intentions of the Northern Pacific were further revealed in the second provision, by which the steamboat lines agreed not to go below Bismarck to pick up freight of other railroads for delivery to points above Bismarck. The only products that the boats below Bismarck could bring to Bismarck or points above were pork and hog products or other freight produced locally in Sioux City or Yankton. This provision of the agreement removed a shipper's bargaining power because there was only one route by which freight could be delivered above Bismarck. The railroads that touched the Missouri at Pierre, Chamberlain, and Running Water were too far downstream to make it profitable for them to compete with the Northern Pacific for the trade above Bismarck. The Northern Pacific, in turn, agreed that any of its freight destined for points on the Missouri above Bismarck would be carried by a Coulson or Power boat.

The Northern Pacific was further protected by the third provision, which forbade the steamboat lines to transport any freight destined for points on the railroad line. This assured the railroad that no freight from the east could reach such points as Miles City, Billings, Bozeman, or Helena except by rail.

The fourth provision of the contract removed the steamboat challenge to the Northern Pacific in Montana Territory by forbidding the two steamboat companies to trade on the Yellowstone River. Since the Power and Coulson companies were the two largest on the Upper Missouri, the result of this agreement was almost to eliminate steamboat competition to the railroad in the Yellowstone River Valley.

The Northern Pacific made only minor concessions to the steamboat companies. The railroad agreed to carry freight consigned to the steamboat companies at reduced rates and also to give special reduced rates on flour and grain in carload lots. The reduced rates were handled as rebates. If, however, the steamboat lines violated their agreement with the railroad in any respect, the rebates were to be retained by the railroad. There was no provision penalizing the Northern Pacific in the event it violated the agreement.

TABLE XVII
FREIGHT SHIPPED FROM BISMARCK 1880-1883

Year	Tons of Private Freight	Tons of Military Freight
1880[a]	8,457	4,518
1881[b]	13,780	3,600
1882[c]	13,547	2,550
1883[d]	10,125	1,686

[a]Annual Report of Chief of Engineers, 1881, pt. 2, p. 1673
[b]Annual Report of Chief of Engineers, 1882, p. 1742.
[c]Annual Report of Chief of Engineers, 1883, pt. 2, p. 1362.
[d]Bismarck and Mandan Directory, 1884, (St. Paul: R. L. Polk & Co. and A. C. Danser, 1884), p. 11.

Although the railroad dictated the terms of the contract of 1883, the agreement proved highly profitable to Coulson and Power. Nearly all of the small operators were forced off the upper end of the Missouri River, leaving the entire commerce to the two larger companies. Although there is no evidence as to whether or not this contract was renewed after 1883, Coulson and Power were still left in control of the Upper Missouri business until Coulson withdrew in 1885.

Although the military trade fell off rapidly after 1880, private freight shipments from Bismarck increased because of settlers moving into western Canada, northern Montana, and regions near the Missouri in Dakota. These newly occupied areas could best be supplied by way of the Missouri from Bismarck. Table XVII shows the volume of trade during the first four years in which Bismarck transportation companies controlled the Upper Missouri business.

Downriver freight to Bismarck during this period consisted mainly of wool, buffalo hides, and bullion. Captain Edward Maguire, Corps of Engineers, estimated the value of these exports in 1882 at $612,930.[12]

Despite the amount of steamboat freight in the early 1880's, the importance of steamboating in the economy of the Upper Missouri region had very definitely declined. In the 1860's, nearly all settlers in the Missouri Valley depended solely on the steamboat; in the

1880's railroads and wagons carried the bulk of the freight. The volume of freight shipped in the early 1880's compared favorably to that of the 1870's, but it did not net the profits of the previous decade because of the break in the long hauls caused by railroads and reduced rates brought about by the sharp competition between steamboat lines.

The completion of railroads to Running Water, Chamberlain, Pierre, and points on the Yellowstone River put the railroads within reach of all of the principal trade areas on the Upper Missouri, thus enabling wagon lines to compete with the steamboat operators and forcing steamboat owners to reduce their rates. Also, by 1880 there was no Indian threat and virtually any storekeeper at a river point near a railhead could carry his own freight.

The "short-haul" nature of the business led boat owners into cutthroat competition. Operators had great difficulty keeping all of their boats busy because once the river route was broken into a series of short sections, a steamboat could make many short trips in the time that boats formerly operating out of Sioux City or Yankton took to make one longer trip. This meant that the transportation business actually supported fewer men and boats than the business of the 1870's.

The short-haul business was particularly concentrated between Bismarck and Yankton. Boat owners who could not keep all of their boats busy in that area removed their surplus boats to Bismarck, where they hoped to engage in the long-haul business to Benton. In 1880 Coulson had six boats at Bismarck and Power had three.[13] Even this small number of boats proved to be an oversupply for the Bismarck trade, since much of that trade was actually to nearby Fort Yates and Fort Berthold. The inability of the two companies to keep all of their boats busy caused a rate war which ended only with the dissolution of the Coulson Line.

Coulson's company, the "Old Reliable Line," was the oldest company on the upper river. After the railroads reached points above Yankton, Coulson conducted most of his business out of Bismarck, where he was faced with the competition of the Fort Benton Transportation Company. The Fort Benton Transportation Company was organized in 1875 by Thomas C. Power, a Fort Benton merchant. Power operated his boats out of Bismarck after 1875 mainly because of his cooperation with the Northern Pacific. During 1879 and 1880

John Christie Barr was Power's agent at Bismarck. In 1881, Power replaced Barr with Isaac Post Baker, twenty-six-year-old nephew of George Baker. Baker, despite his comparative youth, was an experienced businessman. After attending Central College at Fayette, Missouri, he worked with his father, John F. Baker, a wholesale merchant, steamboat agent, and government contractor in St. Louis. Before coming to Bismarck, Baker had served in St. Louis as an agent for several boat lines.[14] He became an active partner in the Fort Benton Transportation Company in 1883 with the purchase of an interest in the company's boats.

Power and Coulson had cooperated in moving freight from Bismarck in 1877 and 1878 and enjoyed good relations up to the 1880's. The first indication of enmity came in 1880 when Barr reported to Power that Coulson was desperate for business and had lowered his rates sharply in an attempt to beat all competition. Barr went on to say that he could not understand Coulson's actions because of the friendship between Coulson and Power.[15] This action on the part of Coulson would indicate that by February of 1880 he had decided to make an attempt to corner the Bismarck trade because of the impending collapse of the Yankton business.

In the spring of 1881, Coulson and Power reached a truce in the form of a pooling arrangement wherein they would split the private freight shipments from Bismarck. Isaac Baker was appointed pool agent with instructions to load each company's boats according to the agreement made between the companies.

Baker had some difficult times as pool agent, especially when Coulson and Maratta accused him of unfairness in distributing freight. Another piece of Coulson's "dirty underhand work" as Baker labeled it, was to damage the Benton Line's reputation with the Northern Pacific Railroad by carrying these tales to Hannaford, the general agent of the railroad. By August, 1881, Baker was convinced that Coulson and Maratta would leave "no stone unturned if they could underhandedly crush out. . . ." the Benton Line.[16] Despite the trouble within the pool, the unfriendly allies continued such arrangements in 1882 and 1883, but they also continued their efforts to freeze out each other.

In 1882 Coulson made a desperate attempt to maintain his position in the transportation business and in so doing incurred the enmity of John H. Charles, an agent with whom Coulson had occasionally worked during the 1870's. Charles of Sioux City put in a low bid for the military freight between Yankton and Bismarck in 1882, as did Coulson, who had been beaten out of the military contract by the Peck Line in 1880 and 1881. Charles did not own any boats and was bidding in the interest of Power, to whom he had agreed to turn over the freight if he was awarded the contract. The Charles bid was slightly lower than Coulson's, and Charles was awarded the contract by the Quartermaster General of the Department of Dakota in St. Paul.[17]

Coulson was not content with the St. Paul ruling and sent Maratta to Washington to talk to the Chief Quartermaster. On March 31, 1882, Maratta wired the *Bismarck Tribune* "Coulson gets the contract from Yankton to Bismarck." The Chief Quartermaster had disallowed the decision of his subordinate; in this instance Coulson proved that a good political connection was worth more than a low bid. The reversal brought immediate outcries from writers for the *Bismarck Tribune* and the Sioux City *Journal*, who were sympathetic to Power and Charles. The writer for the *Tribune* charged that Coulson had constantly used his political connections in Washington to obtain government transportation contracts.[18] The *Journal* reporter mentioned that the action in Washington had caused "considerable sensation in steamboat circles," since it was clear to all in attendance at St. Paul that Charles deserved the contract.[19]

During April the contract was reviewed by Secretary of War R. T. Lincoln, who reversed the decision of the Chief Quartermaster and returned the contract to Charles. Lincoln's decision was technically based on the fact that Coulson's rates were graduated, which was not permitted under the terms of the contract advertisement, which called for a straight bid of so much per 100 pounds per 100 miles.[20] Coulson's manipulation in 1882 brought him much criticism from the *Bismarck Tribune*, the organ of steamboat interests on the Upper Missouri. Coulson, however, probably cared less about the loss of prestige than he did about the loss of the contract which was almost vital to his business.

In 1883 the military freight was again an issue between the competitors, but the contract was initially granted to Charles Wright, who bid for W. J. Kountz. In late April, however, the army announced that the contract would have to be relet because Wright was not of age and consequently was not eligible to bid. In May the contract was

awarded to T. C. Jones of St. Paul.[21] Jones owned no steamboats but
had to deliver freight along the Missouri from Bismarck to Benton,
which meant that he would have to rely on either the Coulson Line
or the Benton Line. Jones chose to deal with Coulson. Although Coulson's boats carried the military contract freight, Coulson still entered
a pooling arrangement with Power and Baker for private freight.

The real issue between the two rivals developed over government
freight that was not included in the Jones contract. The pool called
for a "fair divide" of the private freight and this government freight.
There was difficulty within the pool on the government freight because Sparks, the quartermaster agent at Bismarck, was instructed
by the army to give preference to Coulson boats. Sparks informed
Baker that he could only ship on a Benton Line boat when there was
no Coulson boat in port. Sparks and Major Kirk, according to Baker,
were deliberately working things for Coulson, and Baker was convinced that Coulson had engaged in some "underhand" work to influence Kirk and Sparks in violation of the pool.[22]

In the meantime Baker was encouraging Charles to undercut
Coulson in what trade there was out of Sioux City, Yankton, and
Running Water. In 1884 Power was awarded the military contracts for
the Upper Missouri[23] and his company continued to provide stiff
competition for Coulson. On May 31, 1884, Baker wired Charles:
"Business dead dull on the Upper End—Coulson is played out on the
Upper End—hope you will freeze him out below."[24]

Coulson and Maratta continued to operate from Bismarck in 1884,
but ran only two boats. In April of 1885, Coulson denied that he was
through on the Upper Missouri, claiming that he had plenty of
private freight to deliver. However, by that time the once large Coulson Line was reduced to one boat, the *Rosebud*. There is no evidence
that Coulson even operated the *Rosebud* in 1885, and by the spring
of 1886 the boat had been purchased by Baker. In the fall of 1885,
Coulson ran the *Wyoming* on the Lower Missouri, but never again
did he enter the Upper Missouri trade. From 1885 until his death in
1896, Coulson was active in farming and banking ventures at Yankton.[25]

Daniel Maratta, Coulson's partner, also retired from steamboating
and devoted full time to political affairs. Maratta, who had actively
campaigned for Democratic presidential hopefuls, was finally rewarded for his efforts after the election of Cleveland in 1884. During

his first term, Cleveland appointed Maratta U.S. Marshal of Dakota Territory and during his second term appointed him as consul general to Melbourne, Australia.[26]

The withdrawal of Coulson and Maratta from the Upper Missouri left river transportation almost completely in the control of the Benton Transportation Company. By 1885, little steamboating business was coming from the army, and steamboating was restricted to a comparatively small portion of the river. This area became even more restricted when railroads reached points on the river above Bismarck. In spite of the limited area of operations, I. P. Baker remained in the transportation business for fifty more years.

X

The Last Years of Commercial Navigation on the Upper Missouri, 1885-1936

FROM 1885 until the 1930's commercial boating on the Upper Missouri was controlled almost entirely by Isaac P. Baker, who was associated first with the Benton Transportation Company and later with the Benton Packet Company. During this period, boating on the Upper Missouri was reduced to a local-haul business from Bismarck. The Benton Transportation Company operated from 1885 until 1904 and was succeeded by the Benton Packet Company, which existed until 1924. From 1924 until 1936 the business was primarily controlled by two of Baker's sons, who organized the Benton Transportation Company.

In 1885, the Fort Benton Transportation Company, which had been founded by T. C. Power in 1875, was reorganized and chartered by the state of Iowa for a twenty-year period as the Benton Transportation Company. This company, with a capital of $6,000, was formed by Baker, T. C. Power of Helena, John H. Charles of Sioux City, and Joseph H. McKnight of Great Falls.[1]

When Baker and his associates organized the Benton Transportation Company, they also formed several other boat lines, including the Helena Transportation Company, the Judith Transportation Company, and the Montana Transportation Company. All of these companies were small, some operating only one boat. The intent of this arrangement apparently was to distribute the assets in such a way as to limit the liability of all companies in the event of a law suit. In 1887 and 1888, Baker began selling the boats which constituted the assets of the smaller companies, and by 1892, all remaining property was consolidated into the Benton Transportation Company.

The actual management of the Benton Transportation Company

153

was in the hands of Baker, who was the general agent and one-sixth owner of the firm. The principal stockholder, T. C. Power, had little time for company affairs because of his preoccupation with politics in Montana.[2] Power's efforts were rewarded by his election to the U.S. Senate in 1890.

Charles, as secretary, worked out of Sioux City. His main responsibilities were to bid for Indian and military contracts for agencies and posts on the Upper Missouri and to buy grain in the Sioux City area in order to fill the contracts. In 1895 Baker and Charles began expanding their contract business by bidding for contracts for posts and Indian agencies as far off as Arizona Territory. This contract business was a speculative venture, pursued under the name of the Benton Transportation Company.

A Great Falls merchant who held a one-eighth interest, J. H. McKnight, was really an owner *in absentia*.[3] He seldom visited the scene of the company's operations. McKnight died a few years before the expiration of the company's charter.

The annual stockholders' meeting of the Benton Transportation Company was held at Fort Benton until 1888, and after that time at Helena. At the meetings, Baker reported to the owners on the financial status of the line and made the company's books available to the stockholders for examination.[4]

The only competitors of the Benton Transportation Company were the Missouri River Transportation Company, H. J. King of Chamberlain, South Dakota, and a boat line organized by the Bismarck, Washburn & Great Falls Railroad. The Missouri River Transportation Company was formed in 1890 by John M. Turner, president of the Mandan Roller Mill Company. The company operated only one boat for two years, and it was used primarily for picking up wheat at the river landings near Bismarck and transporting it to the mills. The line operated by the Bismarck, Washburn, & Great Falls Railroad, formed in 1901, also collected wheat at river points. There is no evidence that the company operated more than one season.[5]

Most of the Benton Transportation Company's business in its early years was in the Fort Benton trade. The company operated five boats in 1886 and nine in 1887.[6] The trade above Bismarck increased in 1887 because steamboats were used to carry construction supplies to the Great Falls extension of the St. Paul, Minneapolis & Manitoba Railroad (later known as the Great Northern). In 1887 there were

TABLE XVIII

TONNAGE CARRIED ON THE UPPER MISSOURI RIVER, 1886–1934

YEAR	TRAFFIC BY RIVER REACHES BETWEEN:						
	Sioux City and Bismarck (tons)	Bismarck and Ft. Benton (tons)	Bismarck and Ft. Buford (tons)	Sioux City and Pierre (tons)	Pierre and Bismarck (tons)	Great Falls and Stubbs Ferry (tons)	Total above Sioux City (tons)
1886[a]	5,000	7,070					
1887[b]	6,064	7,897					
1888[b]	6,075	6,820					
1889[b]	16,622	2,102					
1890[b]	9,735	3,591					
1891[c]	10,410		2,645				
1892[c]			5,301	2,634	7,247		
1893[c]			2,125	5,436	6,256		
1894[c]			4,461	1,491	19,171	28	
1895[c]			5,591	10,485	5,136	50	

After 1895, *Annual Engineer's Reports* give only total tonnage of freight shipped above Sioux City.

Year	Total above Sioux City (tons)	Year	Total above Sioux City (tons)	Year	Total above Sioux City (tons)	Year	Total above Sioux City (tons)
1896[d]	10,368	1906[d]	43,987	1916[g]	22,151	1926[h]	3,350
1897[d]	17,105	1907[d]	45,123	1917[g]	6,285	1927[h]	9,205
1898[d]	26,896	1908[d]	17,517	1918[g]	3,986	1928[h]	5,431
1899[d]	23,041	1909[d]	41,203	1919[g]	1,572	1929[i]	5,268
1900[d]	27,179	1910[d]	25,037	1920[g]	3,261	1930[i]	6,825
1901[d]	37,340	1911[d]	11,290	1921[g]	9,164	1931[i]	273
1902[d]	31,070	1912[e]	15,823	1922[h]	5,843	1932[i]	3,205
1903[f]	37,994	1913[f]	40,081	1923[h]	5,941	1933[i]	1,939
1904[h]	28,951	1914[f]	20,913	1924[h]	6,022	1934[i]	837
1905[h]	52,956	1915[h]	17,976	1925[h]	12,223		

[a] *Annual Engineer's Report, 1887*, pt. 2, p. 1600. [b] *Annual Engineer's Report, 1891*, pt. 4, p. 2236.
[c] *Annual Engineer's Report, 1896*, pt. 3, Appendix Z, p. 1894. [d] *Annual Engineer's Report, 1912*, p. 845.
[e] *Annual Engineer's Report, 1913*, p. 941. [f] *Annual Engineer's Report, 1916*, p. 1147.
[g] *Annual Engineer's Report*, Extract, "Commercial Statistics, 1921," p. 830.
[h] *Annual Engineer's Report*, Extract entitled "Commercial Statistics, Water-borne Commerce of the United States for the Calendar Year 1928," p. 616.
[i] *Annual Engineer's Report, 1934*, p. 703.

thirty steamboat arrivals at Fort Benton.[7] The demands of the rail-road created a short-lived, atypical situation which boomed steam-boating for the one season. The size of the trade above Bismarck is indicated on Table XVIII, which shows the amount of freight carried on the Upper Missouri from 1886 to 1934.

Although the extension of the railroad increased upriver steam-boating for a time, downriver business showed a steady decline. In 1886, 1,320 tons of freight came downstream to Bismarck; in 1887, the tonnage was 928. In 1888, only 860 tons of freight were shipped downstream. Wool, fur, hides, ore, and grain made up the bulk of downriver cargoes.[8]

Although construction of the Manitoba Road stimulated steam-boating in 1887, its completion to Great Falls in 1888 dealt another blow to steamboating. The new railroad center at Great Falls replaced the old river port of Fort Benton as the distributing point for northern Montana and portions of Canada. Baker anticipated the end of the Fort Benton trade in July of 1887 when he sent three steamers, the *Benton*, the *Judith*, and the *Eclipse*, to St. Louis, where they were to be sold for service on the Lower Missouri and Mississippi rivers.[9] The *Eclipse* was wrecked on a snag on the downstream trip.

In 1888 there were only four steamboat arrivals at Fort Benton. In 1890, Baker's *F. Y. Batchelor* carried the last sizable commercial cargo up the river to Fort Benton. There is no evidence of any long-haul business to Fort Benton after that time. In 1907, Baker sent the little, fifty-nine-ton steam packet, the *O.K.*, to Benton, primarily for publicity purposes. The boat never made the return trip to Bismarck. It was used in the Fort Benton area as an excursion boat and burned at the levee in the summer of 1908.[10]

The Benton Transportation Company showed sizable profits in 1887. In fact, seven of the company's nine boats showed profits that year totaling $47,330.28. The other two company boats, the *Missouri* and the *Tompkins*, had a combined loss of $3,984.36. The *Missouri* had shown a slight profit before the cost of purchase and rebuilding was charged to the account of the boat.[11]

After 1887 the Benton Transportation Company's books showed but small profits. In 1888 the company stayed out of the red, but only because of a slight increase in the trade below Bismarck, the sale of two boats, and the favorable settlement of the suit involving the steamer *Terry*, which was wrecked on a pier of the Union Pacific bridge at Omaha while on the way to St. Louis to be sold. Baker had brought suit against the Union Pacific, charging negligence because the piers of the railroad bridge were so close together that they were an obstruction to navigation. The United States District Court in Omaha found the Union Pacific guilty and ordered them to pay for the loss of the boat. This settlement helped the company "out of a bad hole," according to Baker.[12]

In 1889 the company's fleet of six boats was reduced to three. Two boats were sold and the services of the steamer *Batchelor* were lost for the season when the boat snagged and was extensively damaged. In spite of the fact that the proceeds from the sale of the two boats were entered on the books as profits, the company lost money in 1889. Baker claimed, however, that the sale of the boats prevented the losses from being large. Baker attributed the financial difficulties of 1888 and 1889 not to the railroads, but to hard luck and extremely low water, which kept the boats from moving fast enough to handle available freight.[13]

Another factor which contributed to the economic distress of boatmen was the sharp increase in insurance rates in 1889. Rates were as high as 18 per cent on hulls during a portion of the navigation season. Insurance rates on cargoes were also raised by the underwriters in 1888 and 1889. The Missouri River Commission reported that the steamboat tonnage enrolled on the Missouri in 1889 was the lowest since 1850, placing the blame for this on the "almost prohibitory insurance rates."[14]

After the loss of the Fort Benton trade, Baker sent boats only as far upstream as Judith Landing, Montana, which was about 727 miles from Bismarck. Baker thought he could still service this point because the Manitoba Railroad ran about 50 miles back from the Missouri, for a distance of about 250 miles between the Milk and Marias rivers.[15] For that reason, Baker believed that settlers in the area could be better supplied by boat than by rail. However, steamboating into this area was never important because the region was sparsely populated and actually could be supplied by wagon lines operating from points on the railroad.

The freight shipments from Bismarck to points above Buford were never large after 1888. Of the 3,591 tons transported above Bismarck in 1890 only 1,124 tons were shipped above Fort Buford.[16] This amount of freight was probably handled in only four or five boat trips.

The shrinking business above Buford led Baker to concentrate his boats in a still smaller trade area. In the spring of 1892 Baker advised Captain Charles W. Powell, U.S. Army Engineer, that in the future most of his boats on the Upper Missouri would run between Pierre and Fort Berthold Indian Agency during the navigation season.[17] After this time, Baker seldom sent a boat to any place above Fort Buford.

TABLE XIX

MAJOR LANDINGS USED BY BENTON TRANSPORTATION COMPANY—1896*

Landings Upstream from Bismarck	Landings Downstream from Bismarck	Distance
Washburn, N.D.		40 miles
Conkling, N.D.		45
Stanton, N.D.		55
Mannhaven, N.D.		65
Hancock, N.D.		68
Coal Harbor, N.D.		70
Benton, N.D.		82
Stevenson, N.D.		84
	Cannon Ball, N.D.	42
	Gayton, N.D.	48
	Winona, N.D.	76
	Fort Yates, N.D.	78

*Baker to the Mercantile Guide and Bureau Company, Indianapolis, Indiana, September 4, 1899, in Baker Papers, Letter Press Book, June 13–September 13, 1899, p. 426.

Baker continued participating in the downriver trade to Pierre through the navigation season of 1895. In this trade Baker usually sent boats out from Bismarck with cargoes of general merchandise and coal for the various settlements, army posts, and Indian agencies. The boats then picked up cargoes of grain, hides, buffalo bones, potatoes, and wool which were consigned to the railhead at Pierre.[18] At Pierre, the Benton Transportation Company boats would again be loaded with merchandise and coal for points as far downstream as Fort Randall. The boats would then be worked back to Pierre, where they would unload such cargoes as they had and pick up freight for points between Pierre and Bismarck. During the first half of the 1890's the bulk of the steamboat commerce on the Upper Missouri was carried on the Bismarck–Pierre section of the river. (See Table XVIII.) Baker

MAP 4.   TRADE AREA SERVICED BY BISMARCK BOATS AFTER 1895

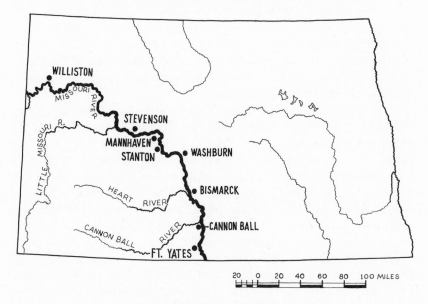

DISTANCES FROM BISMARCK

	Upstream			
Williston	....	190 miles	Washburn	40 miles
Stevenson	....	84 miles		Downstream
Mannhaven	....	65 miles	Cannon Ball	42 miles
Stanton	....	55 miles	Fort Yates	78 miles

met considerable competition in the Pierre trade because the railroad operated its own ferries, and both King and Turner operated boats. In most instances, shippers gave priority to the locally owned boats. In the year 1892 Baker operated only two steamers, the *Rosebud* and the *F. Y. Batchelor,* and in 1894 he attempted to sell one of these, indicating that the company's business could be handled by only one boat.[19]

The competition from boat operators at Pierre and Chamberlain finally caused Baker to confine operations after 1895 to a very small area near Bismarck which was not affected by rival boats or railheads. In 1896 Baker announced that as a matter of policy the company boats would not go below Fort Yates, which is about eighty miles downstream from Bismarck.[20] After 1896 Baker's business was confined primarily to the landings which are given in Table XIX.

In 1896 and 1897 freight shipments reached an all-time low and there seemed to be little prospect of reviving trade. Baker noted in the spring of 1896 "we have work for one boat only at present, and that only occasional trips."[21] The lack of business in 1896 and 1897 led the Benton Transportation Company to concentrate on the development of the grain trade between Bismarck and nearby river points which were still dependent on boats.

One of the difficulties Baker encountered in converting to the short-haul grain business lay in the fact that, while the nature of the transportation business had changed considerably during past decades, the steamboat basically had changed not at all. The large awkward boats designed for long hauls proved more and more cumbersome as boats began making shorter and more frequent trips. When Baker got into the short-haul grain business, the steamers proved to be extremely uneconomical and inefficient, and he, and other navigators, realized that a smaller, faster vessel was needed.

In the summer of 1900, John C. Bloodgood of New Salem, North Dakota, constructed a boat powered by an internal combustion engine. The paddle wheel of the boat was connected to the engine with an iron chain. Bloodgood immediately entered into competition with the Benton Transportation Company, but high rates and faulty equipment put him out of business within a year. Bloodgood's innovation proved to have a serious flaw; the chain connecting to the paddle wheel was of soft, malleable iron, and broke and fell into the river about every five miles.[22] Although Bloodgood failed in his transportation business, he did construct the first of a new type of boat, the gasoline packet, which revolutionized river transportation near Bismarck.

Bloodgood sold his boat to the Benton Transportation Company in the fall of 1900, and through the winter months, Baker made improvements on the boat, most important of which was the replacing of the soft iron chain with a steel chain. The impressive performance of the improved boat during the following season convinced Baker of the economy of the gasoline packet. All boats added to the Benton Transportation Company's fleet after that time were gasoline powered. Only one steamer was retained by the company.

The specially constructed gasoline packets were stern-wheelers with a forty- to eighty-horsepower engine and a carrying capacity of 100 to 200 tons. The boats were usually something less than 100 feet long, had a hold about 70 feet long and 20 feet wide, and could carry two to three thousand bushels of grain. The depth of the hold was usually about three feet, and the draft of the boats when loaded was close to three feet. The cabins were extremely small and located near the stern, leaving about seven-eighths of the deck space clear for cargo storage.[23]

The primary advantage of the packets was that they were cheaper to operate than steamboats. This economy was effected by cheaper fuel and a smaller crew. The average daily cost of fuel for a packet was only $6.00 compared to $30.00 for a steamboat. Gasoline was also easier to handle than wood or coal, which contributed to the economical operation. The packets needed no firemen, and the captain was usually the engineer. In addition to the captain-engineer the crew of a packet consisted of five or six deckhands, a cook, a pilot, and a watchman.[24]

The owners of the Benton Transportation Company stimulated the river grain trade by organizing elevator companies at such places as Mannhaven, Expansion, and Deapolis. During the late 1890's Baker and Power organized at least six such companies, which constructed elevators at river points near Bismarck, bought grain, shipped it to Bismarck on boats of the Benton Transportation Company, and then sold it to Minneapolis and Duluth firms. After 1896 it is impossible to separate the business of the elevator companies from the boating business. The major reason for running the Benton Line seems to have been to provide transportation for grain which was bought and sold by the owners of the boats. The grain business accounted for the increase in river freight on the Upper Missouri after 1897. The success of the grain business depended upon the cooperation of the Northern Pacific Railroad, which moved the grain east from Bismarck. Baker worked very closely with the railroad and negotiated several through tariffs to river points, which assured the boat line of reduced rail rates and also routed the eastbound wheat by way of the Northern Pacific.

Most of the wheat originated within a hundred miles of Bismarck and had to be moved quickly during the harvest season. Some of the wheat was picked up at shallow landings that did not have elevators or docks. Since the wheat was shipped short distances, there was no need to store it in the holds of boats, as it could just as well be stacked in sacks on the deck. All of these considerations made it feasible for the Benton Transportation Company to abandon the steamboat in favor of the gasoline packet. After 1900 the gas packets were much more common on the Upper Missouri than steamboats. Of the twenty-six commercial boats on the Upper Missouri in 1901, fifteen were gasoline packets.[25]

The business of the Benton Transportation Company increased rapidly after 1897 and by 1900 the company was operating four boats on the river near Bismarck. Despite the increased business and the expansion of the company, Baker and his colleagues had financial problems with the boat line, mostly a result of the cost of constructing the gas packets. In April, 1900, Baker wrote to McKnight that the loss balance of the transportation company was $13,166.25. However, the company had an interest in some cattle which returned a profit of $10,200, so the total loss of the company to April, 1900, was only $2,966.25.[26]

The company also incurred losses on government contracts to Indian agencies. Charles and Baker often contracted to supply Indian agencies with provisions that originated at New York, Chicago, or Detroit, obligating the company to pay rail charges from these points to the river. In 1898 the company lost approximately $1,000 on the contract business to Poplar Station, in Montana, and nearly that much on the business to Harlem, Montana, because the purchasing and shipping of contract goods by rail from eastern points to Bismarck actually exceeded the government contract payments.[27]

In 1903, its last year of existence, the Benton Transportation Company was indebted to the Bismarck Bank for $34,395.85.[28] There is no record of how or when this debt was liquidated, or whether it was assumed by the Benton Packet Company, which was formed in 1904.

When the charter of the Benton Transportation Company expired in 1904, Baker, Thomas C. Power, Charles P. Power, Thomas's son, and Charles W. Blunt organized the Benton Packet Company. The new company, organized on May 14, 1904, had a capital stock of $40,000, which was divided into four hundred shares at par value of $100 each.[29] Thomas C. Power was a partner in the company until his death in 1923, and his son was associated with the company throughout its history.

Charles W. Blunt, the new partner, was a native of St. Louis who had moved to Bismarck in 1878 at the age of twenty. Blunt worked independently as a steamboat captain a number of years before going to work for Baker in the late 1890's. Blunt continued to work with Baker and Baker's sons until his death in 1926.[30]

The business of the Benton Packet Line, like that of the Benton Transportation Company, was based primarily on the grain trade. After 1911 most of the grain was carried to the Soo Railroad at Washburn and then forwarded by rail to Duluth.[31] The company's boats during slack periods moved quantities of building materials, especially lumber and sand, and coal, agricultural implements, and general merchandise. The boats were loaded with this freight at Bismarck or Washburn, and then sent to destinations between Williston, North Dakota, and LeBeau, South Dakota. On the return trip the boats brought back livestock, hides, and miscellaneous freight. During the harvest season, Baker was so rushed to move the grain that the miscellaneous freight such as lumber and coal merely delayed company operations.[32]

Freight shipments increased rapidly during the first few years the Benton Packet Company operated; by 1911 Baker operated eight boats in the grain trade, all but one of them gas powered. The company also had two grain barges, which were towed whenever the wind and water were favorable.[33]

Of the 15,823 tons of boat freight moved above Sioux City in 1912, 11,005 tons, mostly grain, were moved by the Benton Packet Company.[34] The productive harvests in the early 1900's caused Baker and his associates to build additional elevators at Williston, Baker's Ferry, Senechal, Crowsheart, Ree, and Sanger.

Freight shipments fluctuated a great deal from year to year, as they depended upon the size and time of the grain harvest. The shipments in the years 1904–1906 were heavy because of an early harvest, a good market which encouraged rapid sale of grain, and favorable weather, which enabled farmers to get their wheat to the elevators. The small shipments of 1914 and 1915 were a direct result of an extremely late harvest, which prevented the marketing of much grain before the close of navigation.[35]

In 1910 Baker extended his boating business up as far as the Milk River in Montana and to Glendive on the Yellowstone. Baker claimed the trade above the mouth of the Yellowstone was practical by 1910 because of the increased population and agriculture in the immediate river valley, which could not be serviced by railroads. Baker also claimed in 1910 that he was entertaining plans of reviving the Fort

Benton run.[36] There is no indication that Baker ever re-entered the Fort Benton trade, though he did increase the activities of the Benton Packet Line above the mouth of the Yellowstone in 1914, probably because of the lack of business near Bismarck.

In May, 1914, Baker announced that the company would operate one or more boats on the Missouri between Rip-Rap Spur (three miles south of Snowden, Montana) and Judith. Baker believed that there would be westbound freight, such as machinery and miscellaneous merchandise, and that the exports would consist of wool, hides, and possibly grain. Baker's attempt to develop this section of the river was not successful. The *Gros Ventre* made two trips from Snowden to Cow Island, Montana, in 1914 loaded with brick and iron for the Rocky Gulch Mining Company and then went downriver, spending the rest of the season in the Washburn grain trade. There is no evidence that the company did any business above the mouth of the Yellowstone after 1914.[37]

During the last decade in which the Benton Packet Company operated, Baker saw a disastrous blow dealt to the grain trade which he had methodically developed during the company's first ten years. Drought caused wheat production in the Bismarck area to fall off sharply in 1916 and 1917. In 1919 and the early 1920's, crop failures forced the closing of some of the elevators along the river, and the drought led to extremely low water during the fall months, forcing navigation to an early halt. (For a summary of grain production in the five river counties serviced by Baker, see Table XX.)

In 1916, the freight carried above Sioux City dropped to 6,285 tons. Freight shipments continued to fall off, reaching a low of 1,572 tons in 1919. In 1919, the grain trade was practically nonexistent, as only thirty tons of grain were shipped on the Upper Missouri, and in 1920 only 315 tons of grain, the equivalent of but two or three packet loads, were moved on the Missouri.[38]

In 1916 Baker operated seven packets and four barges, but in 1917, he started selling the company's floating property. In 1918 the company operated only three boats. By 1921 the Chief of Engineers reported only three registered gasoline vessels with a total capacity of 224 tons operating above Sioux City.[39]

The Benton Packet Company lost money during every year from 1917 through 1924. Despite the losses, the company continued to operate. Baker, Power, and the Bismarck Elevator and Investment Com-

TABLE XX

Average Harvested Yields per Acre in Bushels of All Spring Wheat in the Five North Dakota River Counties, 1911–1947*

| YEAR | YIELDS IN BUSHELS PER ACRE | | | | |
	Burleigh County	McLean County	Mercer County	Morton County	Oliver County
1911	6.1	5.8	8.0	4.8	4.1
1912	16.0	17.3	17.7	17.1	17.8
1913	7.7	8.4	11.6	8.8	14.5
1914	13.4	15.4	17.2	14.2	15.0
1915	21.0	18.0	18.0	16.0	18.5
1916	6.0	8.0	7.0	5.0	6.0
1917	6.0	4.5	5.5	8.5	5.5
1918	10.0	8.0	11.0	9.0	12.0
1919	4.9	5.8	5.3	4.9	5.8
1920	8.8	9.4	9.6	7.3	9.8
1921	5.8	7.7	9.6	3.4	7.2
1922	12.7	14.7	13.7	13.7	12.6
1923	6.6	6.6	8.9	7.8	6.6
1924	15.1	15.1	16.1	15.6	15.6
1925	9.5	12.7	12.7	14.8	10.6
1926	4.3	4.8	5.4	5.4	4.8
1927	14.8	14.7	16.1	15.6	16.1
1928	14.2	13.5	12.1	13.2	11.4
1929	6.5	9.3	10.5	7.6	8.7
1930	9.5	9.9	9.9	10.1	9.7
1931	4.2	3.1	2.9	5.7	4.4
1932	9.8	10.0	12.2	12.4	10.6
1933	5.6	6.4	4.3	4.1	5.8
1934	2.2	2.7	3.1	2.6	3.3
1935	5.3	6.3	7.4	6.3	6.9
1936	2.0	2.1	2.2	2.0	2.5
1937	4.3	3.2	3.3	3.9	3.9
1938	6.7	5.9	5.5	4.1	5.6
1939	11.6	11.2	9.1	9.7	12.1
1940	8.2	12.3	11.7	10.8	11.4
1941	14.5	17.5	19.5	20.0	18.4
1942	16.4	19.4	19.5	17.5	18.5
1943	14.4	20.8	19.0	19.0	18.3
1944	14.9	18.0	18.0	18.0	18.5
1945	15.1	15.0	15.5	16.5	16.0
1946	11.4	10.5	8.5	12.0	12.0
1947[a]	11.9	13.0	15.0	10.0	12.5

*The table contains only figures for the five river counties, selected from a complete tabulation for the entire state of North Dakota in H. L. Walster and P. A. Nystuen, *North Dakota Wheat Yields*, (Bulletin 350 [May, 1948]), Agricultural Experiment Station, North Dakota Agricultural College, Fargo, pp. 26–31, *passim*.

[a]Preliminary estimates.

pany, a Baker and Power concern, subsidized the boat line. In 1917, $22,626.21 were poured into the faltering transportation company, $11,703.44 in 1918, $19,413.02 in 1919, $8,335.91 in 1920, $10,078.40 in 1921, $6,561.04 in 1922, $6,566.39 in 1923, and $5,730.97 in 1924.[40]

Baker and his partners pumped money into the boat line with expectations that the grain business would again become profitable. They had no way of knowing that the grain business near Bismarck would be poor for nearly two decades or that once production revived, motor trucks and improved roads would replace the gasoline packets and the river route. Baker, after having worked in river navigation for over forty years, found it difficult to realize that it had become an antiquated business and should be abandoned. He was probably victimized by memories of the "good old days," and this, as well as hopes for a bright future, lured him into sending good money after bad in a final attempt to save the dying transportation business.

Baker's last years with the Benton Packet Company were disappointing, and after the expiration of the company's charter in 1924, he did little. He and his son Finley reorganized the company in 1924, but they operated only until 1928.[41] Baker also served occasionally as a director of the boating company organized by his sons Frayne and Benton. Baker's main concern after 1924 was with the Bank of Bismarck, of which he was part owner. During the decade prior to his death in 1938, he lived in semiretirement.

The last company to operate boats on the Upper Missouri was the Benton Transportation Company, formed in 1924 by two of Baker's sons, Frayne and Benton, and Charles Blunt. The company had a capital stock of $25,000 and was chartered for twenty years. Several years after incorporation, Willard Leach, Baker's son-in-law, and S. W. Corwin and N. O. Churchill, North Dakota businessmen, bought into the line. This company existed until 1937, the last year that a company report was filed with the North Dakota Secretary of State.[42]

Benton Baker was only associated with the company until 1926, when he left Bismarck. In the 1930's, Sam W. Corwin of Fargo was one of the principal owners of the company. He held 120 of the 250 shares of stock. According to Leach, Corwin never actively operated any of the boats but merely held stock in the company. Leach, secretary of the company, stated that Corwin, who bought in at a time when the company was nearly through, lost money in the line. In 1933 the Benton Transportation Company reported net losses of $5,853.97. The next year the company reported a net loss of $5,753.07. In 1934 the company's gross income from river transportation was only $460.74.[43]

Business conducted by the company after 1934 was meager. No grain was carried on the Upper Missouri after the crop failures of the 1930's.[44] In the report to the Interstate Commerce Commission, the company stated that it had two boats, the *Frayne* and the *R.J.B.*, and two barges, the *Bill* and the *Betty*. Leach could not recall when these boats were sold, but he believed that most of the property was disposed of in 1935 and 1936.[45] In spite of the fact that the company claimed to be active in 1937, there is no evidence that they ran boats.

When the Benton Transportation Company ceased operating, commercial boating on the Upper Missouri ended. For many years, however, navigators using the natural river route had dominated commerce in the Upper Missouri area and made invaluable contributions to the development of the region. The economy of the Upper Missouri area, like that of any other, was directly related to the quality of available transportation. By 1860, steamboats were traversing nearly the entire course of the Missouri River, providing the transportation essential to the development of the area. But by that time, Easterners were enjoying the advantages of rail transportation. The speed, efficiency, and economy of the railroad made it superior to slow-moving steamboats following the sinuous course of the shallow Missouri. Although the steamboat was indispensable in the development of the Upper Missouri area, it was only a matter of time until it was replaced by railroads.

After 1868, steamboating was directly related to the extension of railroads into the Upper Missouri region. Railroads reached Sioux City, Corinne, Yankton, Bismarck, and ultimately Fort Benton. Every time a railroad touched the river, the pattern of steamboating changed. By 1880, Bismarck was the only remaining important steamboat port. Commercial boating on the Missouri lingered on in the Bismarck area until 1936, but was important only in a local sense.

The advance of the railroad into the Upper Missouri area made settlers less dependent upon river towns. New inland trade centers developed. The area along the banks of the Upper Missouri was never densely settled; not one major population center ever developed there. If the region along the upper river had been highly productive and heavily settled, commercial boating might still exist.

Since 1937, the use of boats on the Upper Missouri has been primarily confined to river improvement projects—the construction of dikes at Sioux City; the Fort Peck Dam in Montana; the Garrison, Oahe, Fort Randall, and Gavin's Point dams in the Dakotas. The great course of the Missouri River, its natural obstructions once cursed by navigators, is now forever obstructed by man-made devices. The dams are without locks; the gigantic reservoirs have been planted with game fish. If there is a future in boating on the Upper Missouri, it lies in the hands of those who are developing the reservoirs for recreational purposes.

XI

The Role of the Federal Government in Upper Missouri Steamboating

THE FEDERAL government played an active role in the development and conduct of navigation on the Upper Missouri. Steamboating on the Upper Missouri throughout most of its history was carried on in a frontier area far removed from population centers. One might easily reach the conclusion that there were no government controls on these frontiersmen who plied the Upper Missouri. Yet this was not the case. Steamboat men were controlled by various federal services; it was quite apparent to them that their interests and those of the federal government were closely related. The government regulations for the frontier enterprise were imposed and enforced by a complex of federal agencies and officers—judges, marshals, attorneys, revenue agents, and inspectors—all of whom thrust the arm of government into the Upper Missouri River frontier.

Federal government controls were principally manifested through three services: the Customs Service, the Steamboat Inspection Service, and river improvement. The first two were looked upon as impositions by the steamboat operators, but the third was eagerly solicited by navigators, military men, farmers, and merchants of the Upper Missouri.

The first control established by the federal government, the Customs Service, was a subordinate branch of the Treasury Department from 1789 until 1903, when it was transferred to the Department of Labor and Commerce.[1] The four major duties of the customs service were "documentation of boats," the administration of the marine hospitals, the registration of boat titles, and the collection of miscellaneous fees.

Documentation of boats was required by the law which made the

169

Customs Service part of the Treasury Department in 1789. In the process of documentation, customs officials measured a boat, determining the length, breadth, depth, draft, and tonnage of the vessel, and then assigned it an official number.[2]

The most difficult part of documentation was the determination of the tonnage, or capacity, of the boat. Each ton was equal to one hundred cubic feet, and the boat was measured in a series of cross-sections. This was necessary because of the narrowness of the boat at the bow and stern. Officials determined both gross and net tonnage. Gross tonnage was the measurement of the entire internal capacity, whereas the net tonnage was the capacity after allowances had been made for machinery, boat stores, and crew. The net tonnage of a vessel was always the register, or official, tonnage.[3] Any changes made on a boat which altered its specifications had to be reported to the nearest customs office.

Perhaps the most controversial function of the Customs Service on the Upper Missouri was the administration of the Marine Hospital Fund. A congressional act of 1798 provided that all seamen and boatmen were to pay a monthly fee to a marine hospital fund, the fund to be used for building hospitals at ports to provide care for injured and sick sailors and boatmen.[4] While St. Louis was the headquarters for Upper Missouri steamboat men, the hospital fund was no issue. After 1869, however, when steamboating on the Upper Missouri became a regional business with virtually no connection to the Mississippi River, it was inconvenient and sometimes impossible for Missouri River steamboat men to go to the marine hospitals located at St. Louis and Galena, Illinois, for treatment.

In 1877, the crews of nine boats paid a total of $749.54 in hospital dues to the customs officer at Bismarck, yet the only medical service available to the steamboat men was emergency treatment provided by the post surgeon at Fort Abraham Lincoln, which probably would have been available anyhow. Even though the Customs Service had made arrangements with the post officials to provide medical care for steamboat men, marine patients were often prematurely discharged to make room for military personnel. The *Bismarck Tribune* led a campaign throughout most of the 1870's and 1880's for the establishment of a marine hospital at Bismarck, but without success. The problem of administering the marine hospital fund on the Upper Missouri was never satisfactorily solved.[5]

The third major duty of the Customs Service was to register all papers pertaining to the title of boats and to renew boat licenses. The customs houses, by a law passed in 1850, were made the recording offices for all papers affecting titles of marine property. Prior to that time, if marine titles were recorded at all, they were recorded with the county register of deeds. According to this law, steamboat owners had to inform customs houses of even such minor transactions as the sale of steamer parts. The usual procedure was for the owner to simply send a copy of a receipt or bill of sale to the customs house.[6]

The recording requirements of the federal government were no great burden to Upper Missouri steamboat businesses as long as a collector of customs was located in Bismarck. In 1886, however, the position of collector of customs at Bismarck was discontinued and was never renewed despite efforts by Isaac Baker. Baker sought to have the office re-established, arguing that a customs collector was necessary at Bismarck because boat officers had to take out annual licenses, which could be done only in the presence of a customs official. With no customs office at Bismarck, Upper Missouri captains, pilots, and engineers had to travel either to Omaha or St. Paul in order to complete the license requirements.[7] Baker was very active in 1886 and 1887 in trying to have the port of Bismarck re-established, and he carried on an intensive letter campaign to Assistant Secretary of the Treasury W. E. Smith and Secretary of the Treasury Fairchild. Baker's main argument was that it was an unfair expense for steamboat officers to have to travel to St. Paul or Omaha simply to be relicensed. Baker, of course, was looking at the matter from the viewpoint of personal inconvenience and expense. The action of the Customs Service in discontinuing the office at Bismarck was certainly justified in light of the rapidly declining trade on the Upper Missouri.

The fourth function of the Customs Service was the collection of fees. The government charged fees for the documentation of vessels, the recording of changes in title, for boat licenses and licenses for boat officers, and also collected fines which were assessed for violations of the customs or steamboat inspection laws.[8] The Customs Service and Steamboat Inspection Service were separate bureaus, but the former nevertheless collected fines assessed because of violations of steamboat inspection laws.

The second regulatory arm of the federal government over water transportation was the Steamboat Inspection Service. This service was a direct result of the steamboat wrecks of the 1820's and 1830's, which were usually charged to faulty equipment or to negligence on the part of officers. The early steamboat explosions led to public demands for investigations. Since most boats were active in interstate commerce, the federal government was the logical source of control. Investigations by congressional subcommittees resulted in the recommendation of federal regulations, the first of which was passed in 1838.

The steamboat inspection law of 1838 established a new federal bureau, the Steamboat Inspection Service, in the Treasury Department. The law of 1838, in addition to founding the service, required the owners of steamboats to apply for inspection of hulls every twelve months and boilers every six months.[9] According to this law steamboat owners would request inspection of the United States District judge, and the judge would appoint appropriate inspectors. The inspectors were not employees of the federal government, but received their compensation from the boat owners. There was no provision that the inspectors had to be experienced steamboat men; thus this initial law left room for political favoritism on the part of the district judges. The law had another great shortcoming in that it did not provide for the inspection or licensing of boat personnel, but only applied to the boat itself.

The Steamboat Inspection Service was improved by the passage of the Steamboat Act of 1852, by which the United States was divided into nine steamboat inspection districts, with a supervisor at the head of each district. Each of the supervisors had to be experienced in the construction and operation of steam vessels. The supervisors were to meet every year, work out rules and regulations, and also redefine their districts, if necessary. A tenth supervisor was added to the group by an act of 1864.[10] Although the annual meetings of the supervisors were always attended by an agent or representative of the Secretary of the Treasury, there was no one individual who was considered the head of the Steamboat Inspection Service.

The act of 1852 required the annual licensing of pilots and engineers, as the pilot and engineer were believed to be the officers most closely connected with the safety of the boat. Promotions, such as from second engineer to first engineer, could not be made until the individual had passed a written examination.

The one obvious shortcoming of the act of 1852 was that it did not require the licensing of captains and mates; the supervising inspectors believed that these officers should be licensed also. As a result of the annual meeting of the supervisors in 1870, N. Broughton Devereau, the Treasury Department agent, and George S. Boutwell, Secretary of the Treasury, recommended that Congress pass legislation which would require the examination and licensing of captains and mates.[11]

This recommendation was made a law in 1871. The act of 1871 also improved the administrative machinery of the Steamboat Inspection Service by providing for a Supervising Inspector-General, who was responsible to the Secretary of the Treasury and who would administer the entire service and preside at the annual meetings of the ten district supervisors.[12]

The region of the Upper Missouri was, until 1884, under the jurisdiction of the supervising inspector of the fourth district at St. Louis. In 1884, the control of the Upper Missouri region was transferred to the fifth district office at St. Paul.[13] This fifth district office was later moved to Dubuque, Iowa.

The supervising inspector of the fourth district was assisted by two local inspectors, one of whom was an inspector of hulls and the other an inspector of boilers. Most of the inspection work done on the Upper Missouri during the active trade period of the 1870's was performed by Peter Vandervoort and John Schaffer. These two men and their supervisor, Frank Burnett, were the only steamboat inspectors in the fourth district, which included the Mississippi and its tributaries from the mouth of the Ohio to Quincy, Illinois. Vandervoort and Schaffer not only inspected hulls and boilers, but also granted licenses to boat officers. The inspection of boats alone was a tremendous job. During 1876 the inspectors of the fourth district checked 169 steamers. During the same year they licensed 278 masters, 114 pilots, 104 mates, and 224 engineers.[14]

The usual inspection of boat hulls consisted of boring small holes into the timbers and planking to determine the soundness of the vessel. The recommended procedure for testing boilers was to apply hydrostatic pressure in an attempt to detect weak places. About one-fourth of all boilers inspected in 1876 were found to be defective. Boats were also inspected to determine whether or not they met safety requirements. Safety requirements for passenger boats were more exacting than requirements for freight boats, and in some instances owners would not apply for passenger licenses because of the strict requirements.

The licensing of boat officers was done on the basis of a written examination designed to determine their familiarity with the river. Pilots, especially, were given tests over the navigation rules. The Steamboat Inspection Service had a standard set of regulations for navigation on the western rivers, but also had regulations applying to particular rivers. These specific regulations usually pertained to the signaling procedure and the right of way in difficult navigation spots.

In addition to inspecting boats and officers, the inspectors had to see that each boat had a complete set of navigation rules. They also had to grant special permits for such things as the transportation of gunpowder and combustible material. Inspectors were charged with the duty of reporting all violators of the steamboat inspection laws to the nearest U.S. attorney. Any violation which called for a fine was reported to the collector of customs. Local steamboat inspectors sometimes illegally collected fines. This practice was singled out as a violation of official duties by John Sherman, Secretary of the Treasury, in 1877. Sherman's action came as a direct result of complaints from steamboat owners.[15]

The work of the inspectors of Upper Missouri River boats was fairly easy as long as St. Louis was the headquarters for the Upper Missouri trade. After the boats were headquartered at Sioux City, Yankton, and Bismarck, it was necessary for Vandervoort and Schaffer to make annual trips to these ports to inspect boats before the commencement of navigation each spring. The most common complaint against inspectors was that they were often late in the spring, keeping boats in port after the opening of navigation. In 1877, Walter Burleigh had one hundred passengers booked for Pierre and had to detain his boats until the inspectors could arrive and complete their work. Other boat owners at Yankton were also disturbed and were reported to be "indulging in about as much profanity as river men are permitted to use in this portion of the world." Boat owners were usually careful not to start an uninspected boat, because this violation could result in a fine of as much as $10,000.[16]

Isaac P. Baker, a consistent denouncer of the "interfering" government, believed that steamboat regulations were so petty and numerous that operators did not have any freedom. Baker complained in 1892 that "under present regulations a Steam Boat can scarcely blow a whistle, make a landing or kick a Roustabout without reporting to either Custom House, Inspector or Treasury Department. . . ."[17] By 1906 Baker had relinquished all of his passenger licenses except one because he felt government requirements were unreasonable.[18]

There was some sentiment on the part of steamboat owners that the Steamboat Inspection Service was more burdensome than beneficial. Boat owners believed that federal licenses of boats and officers should be testimony as to their reliability. Courts would not recognize federal licenses as adequate evidence of a qualified boat or officer. In any case involving a boat or a boat officer, the owners were required to produce independent evidence as to the reliability of the boat and the qualifications of the officer.[19] The steamboat men were perhaps unreasonable, because an annual license could not be construed as a guarantee that the boat would not malfunction or that an officer could not be guilty of negligence.

Despite the complaints against the Steamboat Inspection Service by operators on the Upper Missouri, the service did contribute to higher safety standards. Owners were encouraged to keep their boats in good repair, since they realized that detention was costly. Regulation also meant that old boilers and hulls would be retired rather than used after they were no longer safe. The Inspection Service also eliminated some poorly qualified personnel.

The standards of the government inspectors were never as high as those of the insurance companies, however. Underwriters always conducted their own inspection of boats rather than relying on permits issued by the government agents.

A third service of the federal government, the one eagerly sought by navigators, was river improvement. Navigation of the Missouri was always an arduous task because the stream was shallow in many places and was filled with numerous floating and half-submerged trees. Then, too, the river had very few good natural harbors because of the loose, sandy banks which were constantly undercut by the stream. Early navigators realized that the Missouri would have to be altered by man in order to be a good navigable stream. Charles P. Chouteau was one of the first influential individuals to suggest federal improvement on the Upper Missouri. Chouteau made his suggestion to Secretary of War John B. Floyd after a trip to the Upper Missouri in 1859.

Chouteau believed that the major obstructions to navigation were the rapids below Fort Benton. He wrote to Floyd that the removal of boulders at the rapids would make navigation on the Missouri as safe and easy as that on the Upper Mississippi or Ohio, and would shorten the journey from St. Louis to Fort Benton by about ten days.[20]

In the decade after Chouteau's trip, improvement of the Upper Missouri was suggested by many navigators and army officers. These men argued that the river was vital to the security of the frontier and that the future commerce of the river would justify the expenditure of government funds. Proponents of improvement also pointed out that river improvement would result in more efficient steamboat service for government posts and agencies, which in turn would cut transportation expenses.

By the time of Chouteau's suggestion, the federal government had already established the precedent of allocating funds for river improvement. Unfortunately, throughout the history of river improvement in the United States, the appropriations provided in various river and harbor acts were seldom granted on the basis of actual need, but were usually allotted according to the political strength of a given region. During the 1860's and early 1870's, when the navigation of the Upper Missouri was essential to the development of the frontier, Congress did not specifically allot any money for the improvement of the Upper Missouri. After 1875, when the river carrying trade was already declining, congressional appropriations for the improvement of the Upper Missouri were comparatively generous. The increased appropriations seem to have reflected the increased political importance of Dakota and Montana territories, as well as the fact that during Harrison's administration, congresses were concerned with expending the government surplus. Great sums of money were used for river and harbor improvement. The largest single appropriation for the Upper Missouri, a sum of $300,000, was made in 1890.[21]

The first congressional appropriation specifically designated for the improvement of the Upper Missouri was the sum of $20,000, granted for the fiscal year 1876. Some years earlier, army engineers had conducted two cursory examinations of the Upper Missouri. In 1867 Major C. W. Howell examined the river from Sioux City to Dauphin's Rapids to determine the extent and nature of possible improvements. Howell's expenses were paid out of a general appropriation made for the entire Missouri River. In 1875 Major Charles

Suter, also of the Corps of Engineers, made another brief study of the Upper Missouri. In addition to these two army engineers, Thomas P. Roberts, a civil engineer hired by the Northern Pacific Railroad, studied that portion of the Missouri above Bismarck during the summer of 1872. Roberts' primary task was to determine if the river could be profitably navigated by steamboats operating in conjunction with the Northern Pacific Railroad. The reports made by Howell and Roberts, although both general in nature, were used as a basis for all future engineers' surveys of the Upper Missouri.[22]

Major Howell recommended a congressional appropriation for the improvement of sections of the Upper Missouri, claiming improvement was necessary because the river was vital to military operations. The major improvement involved Dauphin's Rapids, about 150 miles below Fort Benton. This particular section of the river, Howell reported, could be improved by removal of loose boulders and by the blasting of a direct channel through the reefs. Howell remarked: "I esteem the improvement of the rapids of the Upper Missouri not only a necessity, but a duty the government owes to a Territory that promises to be one of the most flourishing states, and a portion of that mountain belt whose settlement will do more towards settling the Indian question than can be done by a powerful and expensive army."[23] Howell did not believe there was any need for the improvement of that section of the river between Fort Randall and Fort Buford which was obstructed by many sandbars, as he contended that steamboats could force their way through the sandy portion of the river without great danger.

Roberts also believed that the most troublesome portion of the Upper Missouri was the rapids. He singled out two places for immediate improvement, Cow Island (198 miles below Fort Benton) and Dauphin's Rapids. Roberts believed that the potential trade on the river would make feasible a permanent improvement of the river from Sioux City to Fort Benton. This permanent improvement, he claimed, could be easily effected by a series of wing dams and pilings which would protect the banks, keep trees from falling into the stream, and keep the river from meandering. Roberts regarded his plan as "radical" and it was so regarded by subsequent engineers.[24] The Corps of Engineers never attempted to improve the entire river, but instead devoted their efforts to the improvement of specific trouble spots.

Congressional appropriations for the Upper Missouri increased rapidly. After 1876, Sanford B. Coulson, Martin Maginnis, Territorial Delegate of Montana, Isaac P. Baker, and Thomas C. Power were the principal agitators for increased appropriations. These advocates frequently pointed out that improvement would benefit farmers as well as navigators, since valuable farmland could be saved by revetment of river banks.

During the period 1876–1900 Congress appropriated a total of $1,383,000 for the improvement of the Upper Missouri. The federal government also spent $317,500 for the removal of obstructions in the Missouri. At least $100,000 of this was spent on the Upper Missouri, or that portion above Sioux City. The appropriations for the Yellowstone River during the period 1879–1896 amounted to $128,750.[25]

The first improvement on the Upper Missouri was made in 1877 as a result of the appropriation of the previous year. In the late 1800's, army engineers on the river were concerned primarily with improvement of the rapids, bank revetment at several towns, the removal of snags, and the construction of a winter harbor at Rock Haven, North Dakota.

The top priority project on the Upper Missouri was the improvement of Dauphin's Rapids and the channel at Cow Island. Work on Dauphin's Rapids was started in 1877 by Lieutenant Edward Maguire. Maguire's crew concentrated on regularizing the channel through the rapids by blasting, removing boulders, and constructing wing dams above the rapids to calm the stream.[26] By 1880 Maguire had done some work on all of the rapids between Fort Benton and Carroll. After 1885 most of the work done on the rocky portion of the river was devoted to maintenance.

Much of the money appropriated for improvement was used for bank revetment at various towns along the river. The usual reason for revetment was to protect harbors, such as those at Bismarck and Sioux City. The Sioux City harbor was nearly ruined by 1879 because meandering of the river had moved the deep channel away from the levee. The river at the levee in Sioux City was so shallow, in fact, that some Yankton wags facetiously reported that a woman tried to drown herself at the levee, but only succeeded in getting stuck in two feet of mud.[27]

The major job of the engineers at Sioux City was to keep the channel on the Iowa side of the river, and also to prevent bank cave-ins which would ruin the harbor facilities. Work at Sioux City was started in 1878, and there was some work done annually at that port after that time.[28] The early work consisted of laying mattresses woven of willow boughs, but after some years of experimentation, the willow mattresses were replaced by wire mattresses, and later by a system of pile-driven dikes. Initially the work at Sioux City was done because of the commercial importance of the port. After Sioux City was no longer a significant port, the engineers justified the work as being necessary to the safety of the city.

Army engineers also carried on major revetment projects at Vermillion, Elk Point, Pierre, and Bismarck. The work at Vermillion and Elk Point was never to promote navigation, since these towns were not ports, but was rather an attempt at soil conservation and flood control.[29]

The type of river improvement which had the most immediate effect was the removal of snags. In 1882 Major Charles Suter requested funds for a snagboat to be used on the Upper Missouri. By 1892 the army engineers operated three such boats on the river above Sioux City.[30] These boats were used to remove dead trees and rocks from the stream and also to remove trees on the river banks which were in danger of being washed into the stream. The greatest amount of snagging was done on the Missouri at a time when steamboating was sharply declining; in 1895 the army engineers operated three snagboats while only fifteen commercial boats were running. Supposedly a common river joke of the time concerned an individual who noticed a snagboat and asked what it was. He was told that it was a government boat used to remove obstacles from the river and that its main purpose was to remove the obstacles so it and the other snagboats could run.[31]

Another government improvement on the Upper Missouri was the construction of a winter, or ice-harbor, at Rock Haven, North Dakota. The ice-harbor was Baker's favorite project, and over a ten-year period he wrote many letters to congressmen and engineers concerning the project. Appropriations were made for the harbor in 1894. The ice-harbor consisted of ways constructed high enough on the bank to be safe from the spring break-up. Rock Haven, the site of the harbor, was located on the west side of the Missouri about five miles upriver from Bismarck, on the opposite bank. This site was picked because it was one of the few places in the Bismarck area which had a firm bank. The river bank at Rock Haven was underlaid with a layer of rock which gave it sufficient stability to be used as a harbor.[32]

Construction on the Rock Haven harbor was done in 1894 and 1895. The harbor was later used to winter the government snagboats. The government also rented wintering space to Baker for his boats. Some improvements were made on the Rock Haven ways as late as 1912.[33] The harbor was rather elaborate and designed to be permanent, as the ways were constructed of concrete.

The Corps of Engineers attempted to facilitate improvement of the Upper Missouri by conducting a complete survey of the river from its mouth to Fort Benton in the 1880's. The basic purpose of the survey was to measure river distances, map the river completely, install bench marks, and study the major trouble spots. The survey had been made to Fort Pierre by 1884, the year in which the Missouri River Commission was established.[34] The commission had completed the survey by 1887.

The first significant result of the survey was a new set of official distances. Before the survey steamboat men had but rough measurements of the river which always took into account the meanderings of the stream. Thus steamboat owners called the distance from St. Louis to Fort Benton about 3,000 miles. The official distance from the mouth of the Missouri to Fort Benton was only 2,274 miles, since the engineers did not measure the stream curves but simply measured across them.[35] These official distances were quickly adopted by the army and Indian Bureau, since the government let its contracts on the basis of rates per one hundred miles. The surveying and mapping done during the 1880's was basic to all engineering work done after that time, whether it pertained to navigation or flood control.

The improvement of the Upper Missouri was always piecemeal, reflecting pork-barrel legislation rather than need. Proponents of permanent improvement of the entire river channel were disappointed that the federal government did not show more interest in the river. Congress did indicate some interest in complete improvement of the Missouri by creating a Missouri River Commission under the River and Harbors Act of 1884. The commission was composed of army engineers who were to study the possibilities of thorough improvement to make the river a great commercial artery from Fort Benton to the mouth.

The commission, during its eighteen-year history, consistently sought increased federal funds for river improvement. Many of the members argued that although traffic was slight, river improvement was justified because it would stimulate commerce. Congress, however, was never convinced of the validity of this argument. From 1884 to 1890 the commission had charge of the entire Missouri River, but after 1890 the work of the commission was confined to that portion of the Missouri below Sioux City. This change indicated that no hope for comprehensive improvement of the Upper Missouri existed after 1890. The Missouri River Commission went out of existence in 1902 when Congress failed to appropriate funds for it. The abolition of the Missouri River Commission was a vital turning point in river improvement because by this action Congress made clear its sentiments that extensive and complete improvement of the Missouri was not justified. If trade had increased on the Missouri during the period when the commission was active, then there might have been a possibility of thorough improvement.[36] Congress did make some appropriations for the Missouri River in various river and harbor bills, but only for occasional pieces of improvement and maintenance of existing installations.

Advocates of improvement of the entire river attempted to solicit federal aid in the twentieth century through the Missouri River Navigation Congress, which revived the goal of an improved channel from Fort Benton to the mouth of the river. Interest in the Navigation Congress was never high. Only seven people were present to hear the presidential address of Governor John Burke of North Dakota at the third annual meeting of the organization held at Omaha in 1910. Burke made his address in a hall which had a seating capacity of eight thousand.[37]

The Missouri River Navigation Congress was not supported by Baker. Baker contended that the idea of thorough improvement and a river-long trade was ridiculous. He believed that the natural flow of Upper Missouri River products was by railroads to the east rather than by river to the south. The cost of improving the entire channel would have been prohibitive. Army engineers estimated that complete improvement would cost from $38,500 to $50,000 a mile.[38]

The dream of navigation from Fort Benton to the mouth was kept alive until the construction of the Fort Peck Dam in Montana. This federal project, started in 1934, killed the goal of a completely navigable river because the dam did not include a lock. Other major dams constructed on the Upper Missouri as part of the Missouri Valley Authority since World War II have not included locks, and the idea was accepted by congressmen and engineers alike that navigation of the entire course of the river is dead. River improvement work of the past quarter-century has been based on the goals of flood control, irrigation, and power production rather than on the improvement of navigation.

Notes

CHAPTER I

1. Hiram M. Chittenden, *A History of the American Fur Trade of the Far West* (Academic Reprints, 2 vols.; Stanford, 1954), II, 763.
2. *Annual Report of the Chief of Engineers, 1895,* Appendix Z, p. 2229.
3. *Annual Engineer's Report, 1915,* p. 1894.
4. *Ibid.*
5. For a complete description of meandering, see A. K. Lobeck, *Geomorphology: An Introduction to the Study of Landscapes* (New York: McGraw-Hill, 1939), pp. 224–229.
6. *Evening News* (St. Louis), June 30, 1866.
7. *Annual Engineer's Report, 1915,* p. 1891.
8. U.S. Department of Agriculture, *Missouri River Basin Program* (April, 1949), p. 16.

CHAPTER II

1. Charles M. Wiltse, *John C. Calhoun, Nationalist* (New York: Bobbs-Merrill, 1944), p. 168.
2. *Missouri Gazette & Public Advertiser* (St. Louis), July 10, 1818; May 26, 1819.
3. *St. Louis Enquirer,* June 9, 1819.
4. *Ibid.,* June 23, 1819.
5. Edwin James, *An Account of Major Stephen H. Long's Expedition of 1819,* in *Early Western Travels,* ed. Reuben Gold Thwaites (32 vols.; Cleveland: Arthur H. Clark Co., 1905–1907), XIV, 127.
6. *Ibid.,* pp. 157, 172.
7. Phil E. Chappel, *A History of the Missouri River* (Kansas City, Mo.: Bryant & Douglas, 1905), p. 73.
8. Hiram M. Chittenden, *A History of the American Fur Trade of the Far West* (Academic Reprints, 2 vols.; Stanford, 1954), I, 385.
9. Stella M. Drumm, "Kenneth McKenzie," in *Dictionary of American Biography,* ed. Dumas Malone (New York: Charles Scribner's Sons, 1933) XII, 94.
10. Chittenden, *American Fur Trade,* I, 227.
11. Francis A. Chardon, *Journal at Fort Clark 1834–1839,* ed. Annie Heloise Abel (Pierre: Department of History, State of South Dakota, 1932), p. xxvii.

12. Chappel, *Missouri River*, p. 75.

13. *St. Louis Beacon*, April 14, 1831.

14. Chittenden, *American Fur Trade*, I, 338.

15. Chardon, *Journal at Fort Clark*, p. 235n.

16. George Catlin, *North American Indians, Being Letters and Notes on Their Manners, Customs, and Conditions Written during Eight Years Travel amongst the Wildest Tribes of Indians in North America, 1832–1839* (2 vols.; Edinburgh: John Grant, 1926), I, 22.

17. Chittenden, *American Fur Trade*, I, 338.

18. *St. Louis Free Press*, July 18, 1833.

19. Chittenden, *American Fur Trade*, I, 363, 366.

20. *Republican* (St. Louis), July 8, 1850.

21. Frank J. Burkley, *The Faded Frontier* (Omaha: Burkley Envelope & Printing Co., 1935), pp. 311–312.

22. Joseph Taylor Hazard, *Companion of Adventure: A Biography of Isaac Ingalls Stevens* (Portland, Ore.: Binfords & Mort, 1952), p. 17.

23. Bertha L. Heilbron (ed.), "Minnesota as Seen by Travelers: Isaac I. Stevens and the Pacific Railroad Survey of 1853," *Minnesota History*, June, 1926, p. 127.

24. Hubert Howe Bancroft, *History of Washington, Idaho and Montana, 1845–1889* (San Francisco: The History Co., Publishers, 1890), p. 609. "Affairs at Fort Benton from 1831 to 1869, from Lieut. Bradley's Journal," *Contributions to the Historical Society of Montana* (Helena, 1900), III, 268.

25. "Bradley's Journal," *Montana Contributions*, III, 272, 274.

26. *Contract between Pierre Chouteau Jr. & Co. and Alfred Cumming, Superintendent of Indian Affairs, May 29, 1855*, in Bureau of Indian Affairs, Interior Department, National Archives.

27. *Contract between Pierre Chouteau Jr. & Co. and Acting Indian Commissioner Charles Mix, March 15, 1859*, in Bureau of Indian Affairs, Interior Department, National Archives.

28. W. F. Raynolds, *Report on the Exploration of the Yellowstone River* (Washington: Government Printing Office, 1868), p. 4.

29. *Ibid.*, p. 18.

30. "Report of Chas. P. Chouteau to the Secretary of War of a Steamboat Expedition from St. Louis to Fort Benton, 1859," *Montana Contributions*, (Helena, 1910), VII, 253. Michael A. Leeson (ed.), *History of Montana, 1739–1885* (Chicago: Warner, Beers & Co., 1885), p. 392.

31. Louis C. Hunter, *Steamboats on the Western Rivers: An Economic and Technological History* (Cambridge, Mass.: Harvard University Press, 1949), pp. 73–79, *passim*.

32. *Ibid.*, pp. 123–127, *passim*.

33. *Ibid.*, p. 131.

34. *Ibid.* pp. 167–175, *passim*.

35. "Report of Chas. P. Chouteau," *Montana Contributions*, VII, 253.

36. *Ibid.*, p. 254.

37. Leeson, *History of Montana*, p. 392.

38. "Report of Chas. P. Chouteau," *Montana Contributions*, VII, 255.

39. *Ibid.*, p. 256.

40. *Ibid.*

41. Leeson, *History of Montana*, p. 393.

CHAPTER III

1. Constant R. Marks (ed.), *Past and Present of Sioux City and Woodbury County, Iowa* (Chicago: S. J. Clarke Publishing Co., 1904), p. 802.

2. Anon., *History of Sioux City from Earliest Settlement to January, 1892* (Boston: Press of B. Wilkins & Co., 1892), p. 5.

3. Marks, *Sioux City*, pp. 802, 804.

4. *Ibid.*, p. 815.

5. Rose Agnes O'Connor, *Sioux City: A True Story of How It Grew* (Sioux City: The Public Library of Sioux City, 1932), p. 31.

6. *Missouri Republican* (St. Louis), April 19, 1860.

7. Herbert S. Schell, *Dakota Territory during the 1860's* (Vermillion, S.D.: Governmental Research Bureau, University of South Dakota, 1954), p. 4.

8. George W. Kingsbury, *History of Dakota Territory* (2 vols.; Chicago: S. J. Clarke Publishing Co., 1915), I, 118.

9. *Ibid.*

10. Schell, *Dakota Territory*, p. 5.

11. *Ibid.*, p. 9.

12. Kingsbury, *Dakota Territory*, I, 141.

13. Schell, *Dakota Territory*, p. 8.

14. Kingsbury, *Dakota Territory*, I, 144.

15. *Ibid.*, p. 169.

16. *Contract between Pierre Chouteau Jr. & Co. and Clark W. Thompson, Superintendent of Indian Affairs of the Northern Superintendency, April 16, 1863*, in Bureau of Indian Affairs, Interior Department, National Archives.

17. *Ibid.*

18. Kingsbury, *Dakota Territory*, I, 300.

19. *Weekly Dakotian* (Yankton, Dakota Territory), June 16, 23, 1863. Schell, *Dakota Territory*, p. 56.

20. Doane Robinson, "A History of the Dakota or Sioux Indians," *South Dakota Historical Collections* (Aberdeen, 1904), II, pt. 2, 316.

21. *Weekly Dakotian*, June 9, 1863.

22. Kingsbury, *Dakota Territory*, I, 289.

23. War Department, *The War of the Rebellion: Official Records of the Union and Confederate Armies*, Ser. 1, XXII, pt. 2, 434. Hereafter referred to as *Rebellion Records*.

24. Schell, *Dakota Territory*, p. 50.

25. *Weekly Dakotian*, October 8, 1863. Kingsbury, *Dakota Territory*, I, 290.

26. *Rebellion Records*, Ser. 1., XXXIV, pt. 2, 622.

27. *Ibid.*

28. *Democrat* (St. Louis), March 17, 1864.

29. *Rebellion Records*, Ser. 1, XLI, pt. 2, 80.

30. *Ibid.*, XXXIV, pt. 2, 766.

31. *Ibid.*, pt. 3, p. 333.

32. "General Alfred Sully's Expedition of 1864, from the Diary of Judge Nicholas Hilger," *Montana Contributions* (Helena, 1896), II, 314.

33. *Rebellion Records*, Ser. 1, XLI, pt. 2, 80.

34. *Ibid.*, pt. 1, p. 147.

35. *Ibid.*, pt. 2, p. 228. "Diary of Hilger," *Montana Contributions*, II, 314.

36. *Rebellion Records*, Ser. 1, XLI, pt. 1, 147.

37. *Democrat*, August 18, 1864. "Diary of Hilger," *Montana Contributions*, II, 320.

38. *Rebellion Records*, Ser. 1, XLI, pt. 1, 148.

39. *Ibid.*, p. 154.

40. *Ibid.*

41. "Diary of Hilger," *Montana Contributions*, II, 314.

42. "Bradley's Journal," *Montana Contributions*, III, 277; VIII, 127.

43. William Joseph Trimble, *The Mining Advance into the Inland Empire* (Bulletin of the University of Wisconsin No. 638, History Series, Vol. III, No. 2 [Madison, 1914]), pp. 80–82.

44. *Hunt's Merchants' Magazine and Commercial Review*, XLII, 78. Kingsbury, *Dakota Territory*, I, 330.

45. "Bradley's Journal," *Montana Contributions*, VIII, 127.

46. "Diary of James Harkness of the Firm of LaBarge, Harkness & Co.," *Montana Contributions* (Helena, 1896), II, 342.

47. *Ibid.*, p. 346.

48. "Bradley's Journal," *Montana Contributions*, III, 284.

49. "Diary of James Harkness," *Montana Contributions*, II, 349.

50. *Weekly Dakotian*, July 29, 1862.

51. *Contract between Joseph LaBarge and William Dole, Commissioner of Indian Affairs, April 1, 1863,* in Bureau of Indian Affairs, Interior Department, National Archives.

52. *Weekly Dakotian*, June 16, 1863.

53. Kingsbury, *Dakota Territory*, I, 289.

54. "C. J. Atkins' Logs of the Missouri River Steamboat Trips, 1863–1868, with Appendix," reprinted from Vol. II of *Collections of State Historical Society of North Dakota* (1908), p. 7.

55. *Ibid.*, pp. 12, 16.

56. "Bradley's Journal," *Montana Contributions*, III, 285.

57. "Atkins' Logs" reprinted from *Collections of State Historical Society of North Dakota*, pp. 19, 20.

58. *Weekly Dakotian*, May 19, 1863.

59. "Bradley's Journal," *Montana Contributions*, III, 285.

60. *Contract between Pierre Chouteau Jr. & Co. and William Dole, Commissioner of Indian Affairs, March 18, 1864,* in Bureau of Indian Affairs, Interior Department, National Archives.

61. *Contract between Pierre Chouteau Jr. & Co. and William Dole, Commissioner of Indian Affairs, March 25, 1864,* in Bureau of Indian Affairs, Interior Department, National Archives.

62. *Democrat,* July 22; August 18, 1864.

63. *Ibid.,* April 18, July 8, 1864.

CHAPTER IV

1. *Union and Dakotaian* (Yankton, Dakota Territory), March 7, 1868.

2. H. A. Trexler, "Missouri–Montana Highways: The Overland Route," *Missouri Historical Review* (April, 1918), p. 147.

3. Robert E. Strahorn, *Montana and Yellowstone National Park* (Kansas City, Mo.: Ramsey, Millet & Hudson, 1881), p. 19.

4. Herbert S. Schell, *Dakota Territory during the 1860's* (Vermillion, S.D.: Governmental Research Bureau, University of South Dakota, 1954), p. 55.

5. *Union and Dakotaian,* March 7, 1868.

6. Charles Larpenteur, *Forty Years a Fur Trader on the Upper Missouri,* ed. M. M. Quaife (Chicago: The Lakeside Press, 1933), p. 309.

7. Lucile M. Kane, "New Light on the Northwestern Fur Company," *Minnesota History,* Winter, 1955, p. 325.

8. *Democrat* (St. Louis), June 20, July 29, 1865.

9. The Agreement of March 23, 1865, is in the Hubbell Papers, Minnesota Historical Society, St. Paul.

10. Thomas J. Scharf, *History of St. Louis* (2 vols.; Philadelphia: Everts & Co., 1883), I, 616.

11. *Democrat,* February 22, May 16, 1865.

12. *Daily Bulletin* (Leavenworth, Kan.), April 9, 1868.

13. *Democrat,* March 10, 23, 1868.

14. "Steamboat Arrivals at Fort Benton, Montana, and Vicinity," *Montana Contributions* (Helena, 1876), I, 318. *Democrat,* March 10, 1868.

15. "Steamboat Arrivals," *Montana Contributions,* I, 321. *Montana Post* (Helena), June 26, 1868.

16. *Montana Post,* July 3, 1868.

17. E. W. Carpenter, "A Glimpse of Montana," *Overland Monthly,* April, 1869, p. 378.

18. *Ibid.*

19. *Ibid.,* pp. 379–380.

20. Philippe de Trobriand, *Military Life in Dakota,* trans. and ed. Lucile Kane (St. Paul: Alvord Memorial Commission, 1951), pp. 36–37.

21. John Napton, "My Trip on the Imperial in 1867," *Montana Contributions* (Helena, 1917), VIII, 305.

22. *Ibid.,* p. 306.

23. *Ibid.*

24. *Union and Dakotaian,* February 8, 1868.

25. *Ibid.,* April 8, May 27, 1865.

26. *Evening News*, May 28, 1866. *Union and Dakotaian*, September 22, 1866; May 4, June 8, 1867. For a complete list of steamboat wrecks on the Missouri River, see report of Hiram M. Chittenden in "Annual Report of the Missouri River Commission, 1896–1897," 55 Cong., 2 Sess., House Executive Document No. 2, pp. 3870–3871.

27. *Democrat*, July 13, 1865.

28. *Union and Dakotaian*, August 17, 1867.

29. Lyman E. Munson, "Pioneer Life in Montana," *Montana Contributions* (Helena, 1904), V, 204.

30. *Morning Herald* (St. Joseph, Mo.), March 29, 1867.

31. Hiram M. Chittenden, *History of Early Steamboat Navigation on the Missouri River: Life and Adventures of Joseph LaBarge* (2 vols.; New York: Francis P. Harper, 1903), II, 305–310.

32. "Atkins' Logs," reprinted from *Collections of State Historical Society of North Dakota*, pp. 18–19.

33. Chittenden, *Steamboat Navigation*, II, 309.

34. "Atkins' Logs," reprinted from *Collections of State Historical Society of North Dakota*, p. 64.

35. John Mullan, *Miners and Travelers' Guide to Oregon, Washington, Idaho, Montana, Wyoming, and Colorado* (New York, 1865), p. 6. *Union and Dakotaian*, February 1, 1868. *Morning Herald*, March 24, April 7, 1867.

36. Mullan, *Miners and Travelers' Guide*, p. 6. *Union and Dakotaian*, March 7, 1868. *Morning Herald*, April 7, 1867. *Evening News*, June 11, 1866.

37. *Democrat*, July 7, 1866, as quoted in the *Union and Dakotaian*, July 28, 1866.

38. "Bradley's Journal," *Montana Contributions*, VIII, 130; IX, 348.

39. George W. Kingsbury, *History of Dakota Territory* (2 vols.; Chicago: S. J. Clarke Publishing Co., 1915), I, 570. *Union and Dakotaian*, August 18, September 5, October 27, 1866.

40. Ray H. Mattison, "The Army Post on the Northern Plains, 1865–1885," reprinted from *Nebraska History*, March, 1954, p. 3.

41. Ray H. Mattison, "The Military Frontier on the Upper Missouri," reprinted from *Nebraska History*, September, 1956, pp. 165–171, *passim*.

42. Kingsbury, *Dakota Territory*, I, 413.

43. *Report of the Secretary of War* (Washington: Government Printing Office, 1869), p. 48.

44. *Press and Dakotaian* (Yankton, Dakota Territory), June 28, 1879.

45. *Evening News*, May 28, June 18, 1866.

46. *Union and Dakotaian*, September 22, 1866.

47. *Press and Dakotaian*, June 28, 1879.

48. *Contract between Hiram K. Hazlett and Major General J. L. Donaldson, Acting Quartermaster General, U.S.A., February 29, 1868, St. Louis, Missouri,* in Old Army Division, National Archives.

CHAPTER V

1. Robert J. Casey and W. A. S. Douglas, *Pioneer Railroad: The Story of the Chicago and North Western System* (New York: McGraw-Hill, 1948), p. 126.

2. Rose Agnes O'Connor, *Sioux City: A True Story of How It Grew* (Sioux City: The Public Library of Sioux City, 1932), p. 32.

3. Anon., *History of Sioux City from Earliest Settlement to January, 1892* (Boston: Press of B. Wilkins & Co., 1892), p. 6.

4. *Democrat* (St. Louis), July 6, 1865.

5. "Articles of Incorporation of the North West Transportation Company," November 11, 1867, in Office of Secretary of State, state of Iowa.

6. *Union and Dakotaian* (Yankton, Dakota Territory), January 2, 1869.

7. *Montana Post* (Virginia City), January 18, 1868.

8. *Democrat*, March 10, 1868.

9. *Union and Dakotaian*, January 2, 1869.

10. *Democrat*, March 10, 1868.

11. *Montana Post* (Helena), September 18, 1868.

12. Northwest Transportation Company Bills of Lading, 1868, in Miscellaneous Letters Received by Office of Indian Affairs, Bureau of Indian Affairs, Interior Department, National Archives.

13. *Chicago Tribune*, September 4, 1868, as quoted in the *Montana Post*, September 25, 1868.

14. *Montana Post*, September 18, 1868.

15. *Union and Dakotaian*, January 2, 1869.

16. *Montana Post*, September 18, 1868.

17. *Union and Dakotaian*, January 2, 1869.

18. *Contract between G. T. Nutter, Agent for the Northwest Transportation Company and E. S. Parker, Commissioner of Indian Affairs, May 13, 1869* in Bureau of Indian Affairs, Interior Department, National Archives.

19. *Report of the Secretary of War, 1869*, p. 212.

20. *Montana Post*, May 21, 1869.

21. *Helena Herald* as quoted in the *Union and Dakotaian*, April 21, 1870.

22. *Union and Dakotaian*, April 21, 1870.

23. *Helena Daily Herald*, November 23, 1870; April 8, 17, 1871; March 21, 1872.

24. Thomas P. Roberts, *Report of a Reconnaissance of the Missouri River in 1872* (Washington: Government Printing Office, 1875), pp. 27–28.

25. "Steamboat Arrivals at Fort Benton, Montana, and Vicinity," *Montana Contributions* (Helena, 1876), I, 323.

26. William A. Jones, *Report upon the Reconnaissance of Northwestern Wyoming Made in the Summer of 1873* (Washington: Government Printing Office, 1875), p. 56.

27. Herbert S. Schell, *Dakota Territory during the 1860's* (Vermillion, S.D.: Governmental Research Bureau, University of South Dakota, 1954), pp. 54–56, 59.

28. All of this information on military posts is from Mattison, "The Military Frontier on the Upper Missouri," reprinted from *Nebraska History*, September, 1956, pp. 173–174.

29. *Daily Journal* (Sioux City), May 26, June 21, 1871.

30. *Helena Daily Herald,* April 17, June 12, 1871.

31. *Daily Journal,* June 21, 1871.

32. *Contract between C. K. Peck of the Northwest Transportation Company and E. S. Parker, Commissioner of Indian Affairs, May 23, 1871,* in Bureau of Indian Affairs, Interior Department, National Archives.

33. *Ibid.*

34. *Helena Daily Herald,* June 12, 1871.

35. *Yankton Press,* April 12, 1871.

36. *Daily Journal,* June 8, 13, 1871.

37. *Ibid.,* August 4, 5, 25, 1871.

38. *Ibid.,* November 5, 7, 1871.

39. *Ibid.,* February 14, 1872.

40. *Ibid.,* November 18, 1871.

41. *Contract for Missouri River, between Hiram K. Hazlett and Assistant Quartermaster General, Chicago, March 17, 1871,* in Old Army Division, National Archives.

42. *Ibid.*

43. *Yankton Press,* May 28, 1873.

44. *Contract for Missouri River, between Hiram K. Hazlett and Assistant Quartermaster General, Chicago, March 17, 1871,* in Old Army Division, National Archives.

45. *Daily Journal,* February 6, 1872.

46. "Tabular Statement" from *Contract between Hiram K. Hazlett and Brevet Major General D. H. Rucker, Assistant Quartermaster U.S.A., Chicago, February 17, 1870,* in Old Army Division, National Archives.

47. *Daily Journal,* July 8, September 29, 1871. *Yankton Press,* August 23, October 4, 11, 1871.

48. *Daily Journal,* February 6, 1872.

49. *Ibid.,* February 6, March 2, 1872.

50. *Contract between Durfee & Peck and F. A. Walker, Commissioner of Indian Affairs, June 14, 1872,* in Bureau of Indian Affairs, Interior Department, National Archives.

51. *Daily Journal,* March 29, April 21, 1872.

52. *Yankton Press,* April 10, 1872. *Daily Journal,* April 14, June 9, 1872.

53. *Daily Journal,* August 8, 1872.

54. *Ibid.,* April 18, 1872.

55. *Ibid.,* May 26, 1872.

56. *Ibid.,* May 1, 1872.

57. *Ibid.,* March 25, 1872.

58. *Ibid.,* July 19, 1872.

CHAPTER VI

1. James S. Foster, "Outlines of History of the Territory of Dakota and Emigrants Guide to the Free Lands of the Northwest," *South Dakota Historical Col-*

lections (Pierre, 1928), XIV, 128, 130. Herbert S. Schell, "Early Manufacturing Activities in South Dakota, 1857–1875," *South Dakota Historical Review*, II (January, 1937), 75–84, *passim*.

2. George W. Kingsbury, *History of Dakota Territory* (2 vols.; Chicago: S. J. Clarke Publishing Co., 1915), I, 601.

3. Herbert S. Schell, "The Dakota Southern: A Frontier Railway Venture of Dakota Territory," *South Dakota Historical Review*, II (April, 1937), 109.

4. *Ibid.*, p. 111.

5. *Ibid.*, p. 99.

6. John Brennan, *Condition and Resources of Southern Dakota: Prospective Trade and Travel of the Dakota Southern Railroad* (Sioux City: Daily Journal Printing House and Bindery, 1872), p. 41.

7. *Ibid.*, p. 42.

8. *Contract for Missouri River between Colonel D. H. Rucker, Assistant Quartermaster, U.S.A., and John B. Dallas, February 21, 1873,* in Old Army Division, National Archives.

9. *Daily Journal* (Sioux City), March 6, 9, 1873.

10. *Ibid.*, March 9, 1873. *Yankton Press*, March 19, 1873.

11. *Daily Journal*, March 11, 1873.

12. *Ibid.*

13. *Yankton Press*, May 21, 1873. *Daily Journal*, March 15, 18, 1873.

14. *Daily Journal*, April 18, 25, 1873.

15. *Daily Journal*, June 12, 14, 1873.

16. *Contract between W. Cass, President of N.P.R.R. Co. and Edward Smith, Commissioner of Indian Affairs, May 13, 1873,* in Bureau of Indian Affairs, Interior Department, National Archives.

17. *Daily Journal*, May 3, 1873.

18. *Yankton Press*, June 25, July 2, 1873.

19. *Bismarck Tribune*, July 11, 1873.

20. *Daily Journal*, August 24, 1873.

21. *Bismarck Tribune*, August 20, 1873.

22. *Bismarck Tribune*, July 23, August 20, 1873.

23. *Bismarck Tribune*, August 30, September 24, 1873.

CHAPTER VII

1. *Yankton Press and Dakotan* (Yankton, South Dakota), May 27, 1896.

2. *Press and Dakotaian* (Yankton, Dakota Territory), April 7, 1882.

3. *Daily Journal* (Sioux City), November 10, 1874.

4. Ralph E. Nichol, "Steamboat Navigation on the Missouri River," *South Dakota Historical Collections* (Pierre, 1952), XXVI, 202.

5. *Daily Journal*, July 6, 1872.

6. *Press and Dakotaian*, December 2, 1878.

7. *Press and Dakotaian*, February 19, 1881. *Yankton Press and Dakotan*, May 27, 1896.

8. *Press and Dakotaian*, September 1, 1881; October 30, 31, 1882.

9. *Daily Journal*, November 10, 1874. *Bismarck Tribune*, April 26, 1882.

10. *Press and Dakotaian*, August 2, 1879. *Daily Journal*, August 27, 1872.

11. *Bismarck Tribune*, December 11, 1903; January 4, 1916. Joseph Mills Hanson, *Conquest of the Missouri* (Chicago: A. C. McClurg & Co., 1909), pp. 35–61, *passim*. This work is a biography of Marsh.

12. Hanson, *Conquest of the Missouri*, pp. 65–115, *passim*.

13. *Andreas' Historical Atlas of Dakota* (Chicago: A. T. Andreas, Publisher, 1884), p. 230. *Bismarck Tribune*, November 27, December 11, 1903.

14. *Bismarck Tribune*, August 27, September 24, 1873.

15. *Ibid.*, September 16, 1874.

16. *Ibid.*, August 11, 1875.

17. *Ibid.*, September 17, 1885.

18. *Ibid.*

19. *Ibid.*, October 5, November 10, 1882.

20. *Pittsburg Post*, April 22, 1904. *Republican* (St. Louis), April 30, 1853.

21. Theodore R. Parker, "William J. Kountz, Superintendent of River Transportation under McClellan, 1861–62," *Western Pennsylvania Historical Magazine,* December, 1938, pp. 237–238.

22. *Daily Journal*, March 18, 1874. *Pittsburg Post*, April 22, 1904.

23. *Democrat* (St. Louis), September 30, 1864. *Daily Journal*, October 8, 1872.

24. *Press and Dakotaian*, July 2, 1874.

25. John H. Charles to Sanford B. Coulson, March 21, 1877, in I. P. Baker Collection, Historical Society of North Dakota, Bismarck. (The largest collection of Coulson Papers is found in the Baker Collection. In 1884 when Coulson closed out his business in Bismarck, he sold a warehouse to the Fort Benton Transportation Company. Maratta had had his business office in the warehouse, and evidently letters and business records were simply left in the building by Maratta and Coulson.)

26. *Press and Dakotaian*, March 11, 1876.

27. *Ibid.*, June 10, 1881.

28. Howe, Carroll and Powell to Sanford B. Coulson, June 9, 1877 in Baker Papers.

29. *Ibid.*, August 24, 1877.

30. *Bismarck Tribune*, August 1, 1882.

31. Percy Frazer Smith, *Notable Men of Pittsburg and Vicinity* (Pittsburg: Pittsburg Printing Co., 1901), p. 132. *Directory of Pittsburgh and Allegheny for 1877–8* (Pittsburgh: Published and Compiled by Thurston & Deffenbacher, 1878), p. 342. *Pittsburg Post*, April 22, 1904.

32. *Press and Dakotaian*, April 2, 1877; April 13, 1878; April 16, May 5, August 2, 1879; January 14, June 14, 1881.

33. S. B. Sperry, U.S. Indian Agent, to Messrs. Durfee & Peck, dated Fort Berthold, August 20, 1874, in Letters Received Fort Berthold Agency, 1873–1874, Microfilm Roll 294, Bureau of Indian Affairs, National Archives. Michael A. Leeson (ed.), *History of Montana, 1739–1885* (Chicago: Warner, Beers & Co., 1885), p. 112. Harry H. Anderson, "A History of the Cheyenne River Agency and Its Military Post, Fort Bennett, 1868–1891," *South Dakota Historical Collections* (Pierre, 1956), XXVIII, 510.

34. *Bismarck Tribune,* September 5, 16, 1882.

35. "C. J. Atkins' Logs of the Missouri River Steamboat Trips, 1863–1868, with Appendix," reprinted from Vol. II of *Collections of State Historical Society of North Dakota* (1908), p. 111.

36. *Who's Who in America, 1920–21* (Chicago, A. N. Marquis Co.), XI, 131. For the story of Power's merchandising career see Paul F. Sharp, *Whoop-Up Country* (Minneapolis: University of Minnesota Press, 1955), pp. 213–228.

37. *River Press* (Fort Benton, Montana), February 13, 1901.

38. *Andreas' Atlas of Dakota,* p. 238. *Bismarck Tribune,* July 28, 1875.

39. *Bismarck Tribune,* April 19, 1876; July 12, 1879. *Press and Dakotaian,* July 15, 1879.

40. *Bismarck Tribune,* September 10, 1877; July 23, 1880. *Press and Dakotaian,* May 3, 1879.

41. *Andreas' Atlas of Dakota,* p. 238. *Press and Dakotaian,* November 15, 1880. *Bismarck Tribune,* November 11, 1881.

42. *Andreas' Atlas of Dakota,* p. 238.

43. "Atkins' Logs" reprinted from *Collections of State Historical Society of North Dakota,* pp. 71–72, 81.

44. *Bismarck Tribune,* May 3, 1882; December 17, 1885.

45. *Press and Dakotaian,* May 5, 1879.

46. Constant R. Marks (ed.), *Past and Present of Sioux City and Woodbury County, Iowa* (Chicago: S. J. Clarke Publishing Co., 1904), p. 32.

47. *Ibid.,* p. 35. Anon., *History of the Counties of Woodbury and Plymouth, Iowa, including an Extended Sketch of Sioux City* (Chicago: A. Warner & Co., 1890–1891), p. 246. *Press and Dakotaian,* February 24, 1876.

48. *St. Paul Sunday Pioneer Press,* February 22, 1948, p. 8, 2nd News Section. "Minnesota Biographies 1655–1912," *Collections of the Minnesota Historical Society* (St. Paul, 1912), XIV, 856. *Contract between Amherst H. Wilder and Edward P. Smith, U.S. Indian Agent, November 8, 1872,* in Bureau of Indian Affairs, Interior Department, National Archives.

49. Contracts between Amherst H. Wilder and Edward P. Smith, Commissioner of Indian Affairs, May 20, June 4, July 19, 1873, in Bureau of Indian Affairs, Interior Department, National Archives.

50. *Sioux City Register,* August 17, 1867, as quoted in the *Union and Dakotaian* (Yankton), August 24, 1867.

51. *Bismarck Tribune,* August 16, 1876; October 19, 1877. *Press and Dakotaian,* November 2, 1877; June 20, 1879; July 22, November 12, 1880.

52. *Press and Dakotaian,* July 8, 1878; July 22, 1880.

53. *Bismarck Tribune,* July 1, 1881.

54. Information taken from Mrs. R. E. Walpole's Notes. Mrs. Walpole, who resides in Yankton, South Dakota, is a granddaughter of John Coulson. *Press and Dakotaian,* March 14, 1877; March 12, 1878.

55. *Annual Engineer's Report, 1883,* pt. 2, pp. 1343–1344. *Bismarck Tribune,* May 30, 1877.

56. Walpole Notes.

57. *Press and Dakotaian,* February 26, March 10, April 29, 1879. Walpole Notes. *Annual Engineer's Report, 1883,* pt. 2, pp. 1343–1344.

58. *Press and Dakotaian,* April 29, 1879. *Annual Engineer's Report, 1883,* pt. 2, pp. 1343–1344.

59. *Bismarck Tribune,* July 5, 1879; June 27, 1884.

60. Walpole Notes.

61. *Press and Dakotaian,* July 19, 1882.

CHAPTER VIII

1. *Press and Dakotaian* (Yankton), April 4, 1877.

2. *Daily Journal* (Sioux City), May 23, 1874.

3. *Ibid. Press and Dakotaian,* October 31, 1876.

4. *Press and Dakotaian,* February 13, 20, 1877.

5. William Evans to Sanford B. Coulson, April 11, 1877, in Baker Papers.

6. *Press and Dakotaian,* April 12, 1877.

7. D. W. Maratta to Coulson, December 10, 1877, in Baker Papers.

8. Maratta to J. C. McVay, February 4, 1878, in Baker Papers.

—9. *Contract for Missouri River Transportation, Commencing March 20th, and Ending October 31st, 1878, between Sanford B. Coulson and Chas. H. Tompkins, Deputy Quartermaster General, U.S.A., March 12, 1878,* in Old Army Division, National Archives.

10. *Press and Dakotaian,* June 17, 1878.

11. *Ibid.,* April 8, 1878.

12. *Contract for Transportation on the Missouri and Yellowstone Rivers between Sanford B. Coulson and Chas. H. Tompkins, Deputy Quartermaster General, U.S.A., March 14, 1879,* in Old Army Division, National Archives.

13. *Ibid.*

14. "Tabular Statement," from *Contract for Missouri River Transportation from March 20 to October 31, 1874, between Sanford B. Coulson and D. H. Rucker, Assistant Quartermaster General, U.S.A., March 14, 1874,* in Old Army Division, National Archives.

15. "Tabular Statement," from *Contract for Missouri River Transportation from March 29, 1876, to October 31, 1876, between Walter A. Burleigh and S. B. Holabird, Deputy Quartermaster General, U.S.A., March 29, 1876,* in Old Army Division, National Archives.

16. *Bismarck Tribune,* June 21, 1876.

17. *Ibid.,* July 12, 1876.

18. *Ibid.*

19. Ray H. Mattison, "The Military Frontier on the Upper Missouri," reprinted from *Nebraska History* (September, 1956), p. 178.

20. Chief Quartermaster, Department of Dakota to Second Lieutenant Drubb, July 24, 1876, in *Letter Register March 20, 1875, to August 10, 1879,* p. 86, in Old Army Division, National Archives.

21. *Bismarck Tribune,* September 13, 1876.

22. John B. Davis to William F. Davidson, March 16, 1877, in Davidson Papers, Minnesota Historical Society, St. Paul.

23. *Press and Dakotaian,* March 30, 1877. *Contract between John B. Davis and Peyton S. Davidson and B. C. Card, Chief Quartermaster, Department of Dakota, March 20, 1877,* in Old Army Division, National Archives.

24. John W. Reaney to William F. Davidson, March 28, 1877, in Davidson Papers.

25. Davis to Captain P. S. Davidson, April 30, 1877, in Davidson Papers.

26. *Ibid.*

27. Mark D. Flower to William F. Davidson, June 30, 1877, in Davidson Papers.

28. Maratta to Coulson, April 10, 1877, in Baker Papers.

29. *Ibid.,* September 30, 1877.

30. *Bismarck Tribune,* August 24, October 10, 1877.

31. William Rhodes to P. S. Davidson, January 20, 1878, in Davidson Papers.

32. *Press and Dakotaian,* October 12, 1878.

33. *Daily Journal,* July 12, 1874.

34. *Ibid.,* March 18, 1874. *Press and Dakotaian,* January 22, 1876.

35. *Bismarck Tribune,* August 11, 1875.

36. *Press and Dakotaian,* May 4, 29, 1877.

37. *Ibid.,* May 11, June 19, 1878.

38. *Ibid.,* April 25, 28, 1879. *Bismarck Tribune,* May 3, 1879.

39. *River Press* (Fort Benton, Mont.), August 21, 1946. *Bismarck Tribune,* March 17, June 2, October 20, 1875.

40. *River Press,* August 21, 1946.

41. *Bismarck Tribune,* July 18, 1877.

42. "Steamboat Arrivals at Fort Benton, Montana, and Vicinity," *Contributions to the Historical Society of Montana* (Helena, 1900), III, 353.

43. *Ibid.,* 351.

44. *Annual Report of the Chief of Engineers, 1878,* pt. 1, p. 693.

45. "Steamboat Arrivals" in *Montana Contributions,* III, 353. *Annual Report of the Chief of Engineers, 1879,* pt. 2, p. 1095.

46. *Bismarck Tribune,* May 7, 1880.

47. Maratta to Coulson, April 17, May 10, September 26, 1877, in Baker Papers.

48. *Press and Dakotaian,* May 10, 1879.

49. *Bismarck Tribune,* May 7, 1880.

50. *Press and Dakotaian,* May 20, 1879. *Bismarck Tribune,* May 7, 1880.

51. *Press and Dakotaian,* August 24, 1880.

52. *Ibid.,* January 19, 1876; May 19, 1877.

53. *Ibid.,* October 17, 28, 1876.

54. Statement of the steamer *Black Hills,* November 18, 1877, in Baker Papers.

55. *Press and Dakotaian,* April 26, 1877; January 1, 1879. *Bismarck Tribune,* June 8, November 12, 1877; May 7, 1880.

CHAPTER IX

1. *Press and Dakotaian* (Yankton), April 30, 1880.
2. *Ibid.*, December 28, 1880.
3. *Democrat* (Chamberlain, Dakota Territory), July 27, 1883.
4. *Ibid.*
5. *Ibid.*, November 27, 1884.
6. *River Press* (Fort Benton, Mont.), June 16, 1937. The list of steamboat arrivals in the *River Press* is based on lists published earlier in Montana Historical Society *Contributions*. The two compilations are substantially in agreement through 1880. The *River Press* shows many more arrivals in the 1880's than are shown in the *Contributions*. The list for the *Contributions* from 1880 to 1888 was supplied by T. C. Power & Bro., whereas the list in the *River Press* was collated primarily from newspaper files.
7. *Bismarck Tribune*, February 11, 1881.
8. *Ibid.*, February 18, March 25, May 13, 1881; April 7, 1882.
9. *Ibid.*, May 13, 1881.
10. *Ibid.*, April 7, October 28, 1882. Michael A. Leeson (ed.), *History of Montana, 1739–1885* (Chicago: Warner, Beers & Co., 1885), p. 396.
11. This is not a direct quote, but is a condensation of provisions contained in "Memorandum of Agreement made between T. C. Power, Manager of the Benton Line of Steamers for the Benton Line and D. W. Maratta, General Superintendent of Coulson Line of Steamers for the Coulson Line, and the Northern Pacific Railroad Company for the transportation of freight during the season of navigation on the Missouri River for 1883," St. Paul, Minnesota, March 4, 1883, in Letter Press Book, October 13, 1882–June 14, 1883, p. 266, in Baker Papers.
12. *Annual Engineer's Report, 1883*, pt. 2, p. 1362.
13. *Bismarck Tribune*, November 19, 1880.
14. *Bismarck Tribune*, January 28, 1938, p. 1, col. 8. *Who's Who in America* (Chicago: P. N. Marquis Co., 1934–1935), XVIII, 228.
15. J. C. Barr to T. C. Power, February 12, 1880, in Baker Papers.
16. Baker to Power, August 23, 1881, in Baker Papers, Letter Press Book, April 21, 1880–January 19, 1882, p. 31.
17. *Bismarck Tribune*, March 22, April 11, 1882.
18. *Ibid.*, April 2, 1882.
19. The Sioux City *Daily Journal* as quoted in the *Bismarck Tribune*, April 6, 1882.
20. *Press and Dakotaian*, April 28, 1882.
21. *Ibid.*, March 6, May 24, 1883. *Bismarck Tribune*, April 28, 1883.
22. Baker to Power, May 27, 1883, in Baker Papers, Letter Press Book, October 13, 1882–June 14, 1883, p. 205. Baker to Colonel Charles Bird, Chief Quartermaster of Dakota, May 19, 1883, in *ibid.*
23. *Bismarck Tribune*, March 18, 1884.
24. Baker to John H. Charles, May 31, 1884, in Baker Papers, Letter Press Book, April 28, 1884–August 25, 1884, p. 116.

25. *Bismarck Tribune*, April 15, October 30, 1885. Baker to S. F. Covington, May 2, 1885, in Baker Papers, Letter Press Book, April 9, 1885–November 15, 1885, p. 77. *Yankton Press and Dakotan*, May 27, 1896, p. 1, col. 3.

26. *Bismarck Tribune*, November 27, 1903, p. 1, col. 3; December 11, 1903, p. 5, col. 3.

CHAPTER X

1. "Articles of Incorporation of the Benton Transportation Company," in *Charters and Articles of Incorporation, Dakota Territory*, X, 408, Office of the Secretary of State, state of North Dakota.

2. Baker to Power, October 21, 1903, in Baker Papers, Letter Press Book April 23, 1902–January 11, 1904, p. 412.

3. *Ibid.*

4. Baker to Walsh and Newman, January 17, 1904, in Baker Papers, Letter Press Book December 15, 1903–March 15, 1907, p. 25.

5. Baker to C. H. Hood, March 9, 1890, in Baker Papers, Letter Press Book January 16, 1890–June 9, 1890, p. 161. *Annual Engineer's Report, 1893*, pt. 3, p. 2302. *Annual Engineer's Report, 1902*, pt. 2, p. 1691.

6. *Bismarck Tribune*, April 7, 1887.

7. *River Press* (Fort Benton, Mont.), June 16, 1937.

8. *Annual Engineer's Report, 1887*, pt. 2, p. 1600. *Annual Engineer's Report, 1889*, pt. 4, p. 2761.

9. Baker to John F. Baker, September 3, 1887, in Baker Papers, Letter Press Book June 27, 1887–September 7, 1887.

10. *River Press*, June 16, 1937; August 21, 1946.

11. Compiled from financial statements of individual steamers in Statement Book 28, pp. 610–628, Benton Transportation Company, in Baker Papers.

12. *Daily World* (Omaha), June 12, 1888. *Bismarck Tribune*, August 21, 1888. Baker to Power, December 11, 1888 in Baker Papers, Letter Press Book November 24, 1888–May 16, 1889, p. 85.

13. Baker to McKnight, December 27, 1889, in Baker Papers, Letter Press Book September 22, 1889–January 16, 1890, p. 456. Baker to McKnight, February 24, 1890, in Baker Papers, Letter Press Book January 16, 1890–June 9, 1890, p. 120.

14. *Annual Engineer's Report, 1890*, pt. 4, p. 3371.

15. Baker to Captain Charles F. Powell, February 23, 1892, in Baker Papers, Letter Press Book December 10, 1891–June 13, 1892, p. 204. *Annual Engineer's Report, 1889*, pt. 4, p. 2761.

16. *Annual Engineer's Report, 1891*, pt. 4, p. 2236.

17. Baker to Powell, February 23, 1892.

18. *Annual Engineer's Report, 1891*, pt. 4, p. 2234.

19. *Annual Engineer's Report, 1893*, pt. 3, p. 2302. Baker to J. D. Harkins, August 4, 1894, in Baker Papers, Letter Press Book November 24, 1893–August 7, 1894, p. 482.

20. Baker to W. W. Pickens, May 21, 1896, in Baker Papers, Letter Press Book December 18, 1895—June 22, 1896, p. 326.

21. Baker to Charles Sprecker Nagle, April 1, 1896, in Baker Papers, Letter Press Book March 27, 1896—July 20, 1896, p. 10.

22. Frank R. Morrissey, "Motor Packets of the Upper Missouri" in *Motorboat*, January, 1913, p. 2.

23. Baker to Oscar E. Maurer, July 18, 1911, in Baker Papers. Baker to E. Pennington, general manager, Soo Line, Minneapolis, October 28, 1904, in Baker Papers, Letter Press Book December 15, 1903—March 15, 1907, p. 131.

24. Morrissey, "Motor Packets," *Motorboat*, January, 1913, p. 3. *Bismarck Tribune*, November 5, 1917.

25. *Annual Engineer's Report, 1902*, pt. 2, p. 1691.

26. Baker to Captain H. M. Chittenden, Corps of Engineers, Sioux City, February 26, 1901, in Baker Papers, Letter Press Book February 2, 1901—June 17, 1901, p. 56. Baker to McKnight, April 3, 1900, in Baker Papers, Letter Press Book April 23, 1902—January 11, 1904, p. 211.

27. Charles to Baker, April 2, 1898, in Baker Papers.

28. Baker to Power, October 21, 1903, in Baker Papers, Letter Press Book April 23, 1902—January 11, 1904, p. 412.

29. "Articles of Incorporation of Benton Packet Company" in *Book of Corporations*, Book 6, p. 545, Office of the Secretary of State, state of North Dakota.

30. *Bismarck Tribune*, June 21, 1926, p. 3, col. 2. Personal Interview with Mrs. Melvin Welsh, Blunt's daughter, Bismarck, August 16, 1958.

31. Freight Book, boat *Deapolis*, Benton Packet Company, 1908–1921, in Baker Papers.

32. Baker to Pennington, general manager, Soo Line, October 28, 1904, in Baker Papers, Letter Press Book December 15, 1903—March 15, 1907, p. 131.

33. *Annual Engineer's Report, 1913*, p. 941. Baker to M. R. Devaney, general manager, Occident Elevator Company, October 3, 1913, in Baker Papers.

34. *Annual Engineer's Report, 1913*, p. 941.

35. Baker to Pennington, general manager, Soo Line, October 28, 1904, in Baker Papers, Letter Press Book December 15, 1903—March 15, 1907, p. 131. *Annual Engineer's Report, 1916*, p. 1147.

36. *Fargo Forum and Daily Republican*, December 7, 1910. Baker to Maurer, July 18, 1911, in Baker Papers.

37. Baker to R. N. Mathwick, May 11, 1914, in Baker Papers. Benton Packet Company, Book 18, Freight Book, *Gros Ventre*, 1913–1917, in Baker Papers.

38. *Annual Engineer's Report, 1920*, extract entitled "Commercial Statistics, 1920," pp. 930, 3786.

39. Baker to Byrne-Allensworth Agency, July 17, 1916, in Baker Papers. Baker to Chicago Steamboat Exchange, July 13, 1917, in Baker Papers. "Profit and Loss Statement for 1918," in Benton Packet Company Book 5, Journal, May 1, 1915—December, 1918, p. 299. *Annual Engineer's Report, 1921*, extract entitled "Commercial Statistics, 1921," p. 830.

40. Profit and Loss Statement in Benton Packet Company Book 5, Journal, May 1, 1915—December, 1918, pp. 242, 299. Profit and Loss Statement in Benton Packet Company Book 6, Journal, 1919–1924, pp. 59, 101, 147, 193–194, 247, 272.

41. "Domestic Corporation Report for 1928 of Benton Packet Company," Domestic Corporation Report No. 1256, in Office of Secretary of State, state of North Dakota.

42. "Articles of Incorporation of the Benton Transportation Company," in Book of Corporations, Book 23, p. 515, in Office of Secretary of State, state of North Dakota. "Domestic Corporation Report for 1937 of Benton Transportation Company," Domestic Corporation Report No. 1254, in Office of Secretary of State, state of North Dakota.

43. Personal Interview with Willard A. Leach, August 16, 1958. Copy of Annual Report of Benton Transportation Company, Bismarck, North Dakota, to the Interstate Commerce Commission for the Year Ended December 31, 1934, in personal papers of Mrs. Willard A. Leach, daughter of Isaac P. Baker, Bismarck, North Dakota. Copies of Corporation Income and Excess-Profits Tax Returns for the Calendar Years 1933 and 1934, in papers of Mrs. Leach.

44. *Washburn Leader* (Washburn, N.D.), July 9, 1937, p. 1, col. 7.

45. Interview with Leach.

CHAPTER XI

1. Laurence Schmeckebier, *The Customs Service, Its History, Activities and Organization* (Baltimore: Johns Hopkins Press, 1924), p. 7.

2. *Ibid.*, p. 64.

3. *Ibid.*, p. 65.

4. *Ibid.*, p. 10.

5. *Bismarck Tribune,* September 19, 1877; March 21, 1878; July 5, 1879.

6. Schmeckebier, *Customs Service,* p. 17. W. W. Copeland, Surveyor, Customs House, Omaha, to McVay, Yankton, September 26, 1877, in Baker Papers.

7. Baker to W. E. Smith, Assistant Secretary, U.S. Treasury, Washington, D.C., May 10, 1886, in Letter Press Book, April 9, 1886–May 24, 1886, p. 153.

8. Schmeckebier, *Customs Service,* p. 59.

9. Lloyd M. Short, *Steamboat-Inspection Service, Its History, Activities, and Organization* (New York: D. Appleton & Co., 1922), p. 2.

10. *Ibid.*, p. 6.

11. *Proceedings of the Eighteenth Annual Meeting of the Board of Supervising Inspectors of Steam Vessels,* held at Washington, D.C., January, 1870 (Washington: Government Printing Office, 1870), p. 15.

12. *Proceedings of the Twentieth Annual Meeting of the Board of Supervising Inspectors of Steam Vessels,* held at Washington, D.C., January, 1872 (Washington: Government Printing Office, 1872), p. 157.

13. *Proceedings of the Thirty-Second Annual Meeting of the Board of Supervising Inspectors of Steam Vessels,* held at Washington, D.C., January, 1884 (Washington: Government Printing Office, 1884), p. 85.

14. *Proceedings of the Twenty-Fifth Annual Meeting of the Board of Supervising Inspectors of Steam Vessels,* held at Washington, D.C., January, 1877 (Washington: Government Printing Office, 1877), p. 142.

15. Short, *Steamboat-Inspection Service*, p. 4. *Press and Dakotaian* (Yankton), September 28, 1878.

16. *Press and Dakotaian*, April 6, 1877.

17. Baker to Power, March 9, 1892, in Baker Papers, Letter Press Book, December 10, 1891–June 13, 1892, p. 267.

18. Baker to Monaghan & Chalk, Local Inspectors of Steam Vessels, Duluth, Minnesota, July 13, 1906, in Baker Papers.

19. *Press and Dakotaian*, September 19, 1877.

20. "Report of Chas P. Chouteau to the Secretary of War," in *Montana Contributions*, III, 256.

21. *Analytical and Topical Index to the Reports of the Chief of Engineers and Officers of the Corps of Engineers, United States Army, 1866–1900* (3 vols.; Washington: Government Printing Office, 1903), II, 740.

22. *Annual Engineer's Report, 1877*, pt. 1, p. 520. *Annual Engineer's Report, 1875*, pp. 517–520, *passim*. Thomas P. Roberts, *Report of a Reconnaissance of the Missouri River in 1872* (Washington: Government Printing Office, 1875), p. 5.

23. *Annual Engineer's Report, 1868*, pp. 627, 630.

24. Roberts, *Report of a Reconnaissance*, pp. 34, 41.

25. *Index to Engineer's Reports, 1866–1900*, II, 740, 1336.

26. *Annual Engineer's Report, 1877*, pt. 1, p. 519.

27. *Press and Dakotaian*, July 26, 1880.

28. *Annual Engineer's Report, 1879*, pt. 2, p. 1078.

29. *Annual Engineer's Report, 1915*, p. 1895.

30. *Annual Engineer's Report, 1882*, pt. 2, p. 1675. *Annual Engineer's Report, 1893*, pt. 3, p. 2299.

31. Nichol, "Steamboat Navigation on the Missouri River," *South Dakota Historical Collections*, XXVI, 193.

32. *Annual Engineer's Report, 1894*, pt. 3, p. 1742.

33. *Annual Engineer's Report, 1913*, p. 941.

34. *Annual Engineer's Report, 1884*, pt. 3, p. 1538.

35. *Annual Engineer's Report, 1887*, pt. 4, p. 2913.

36. *Annual Engineer's Report, 1902, Supplement*, pp. 174–180. This supplement to the *Annual Report of the Chief of Engineers* was written by the Missouri River Commission, and contains a summary of the aims and work of the Commission.

37. *Chicago Sunday Tribune*, February 27, 1910.

38. *Annual Engineer's Report, 1915*, p. 1894.

BIBLIOGRAPHY

I. PRIMARY SOURCES

A. MANUSCRIPTS

Baker Papers, North Dakota Historical Society, Bismarck. The papers and records of I. P. Baker were the most important single source used in this study. Chronologically, the collection covers the period 1877 through 1925. Most of the items deal with matters of the 1880's and 1890's. The papers in the Baker Collection are kept in 119 legal-size document boxes, with about 2,000 pieces per box. About half of these manuscripts pertain to river transportation, the remainder deal with such Baker interests as the Bismarck Bank and the various elevator companies. The collection includes not only Baker letters, but letters of T. C. Power, John H. Charles, Daniel Maratta, and Sanford B. Coulson. (The Coulson letters that appear in the Baker Papers were found in the office of a warehouse that Coulson sold to Baker in 1884.) In addition to the boxed manuscripts, the Baker Papers contain 239 journals, ledgers, and steamboat record books, and sixty-five bound volumes of telegrams and letters. Approximately one-half of this material pertains to river transportation.

Davidson Papers, Minnesota Historical Society, St. Paul. The papers of William S. Davidson are contained in several hundred manuscript boxes. These records pertain mostly to Davidson's activities in Mississippi River steamboating, the wheat business, and real estate. The only portion of the Davidson Papers used in this study were the manuscripts pertaining to the Upper Missouri River government transportation contract awarded to Davidson and John B. Davis in 1877.

Hubbell Papers, Minnesota Historical Society, St. Paul. The Hubbell Papers consist of a few dozen items pertaining to the formation and activities of the Northwestern Fur Company. This material covers the period 1865 through 1869. Of particular interest are the Articles of Agreement of the Northwestern Fur Company and some correspondence of James Hubbell and Alpheus Hawley.

Leach Papers, Mrs. Julia B. Leach, Bismarck, North Dakota. Mrs. Leach has some material not contained in the records of her father, I. P. Baker. She has several reports made by the Benton Transportation Company to the Interstate Commerce Commission, and also some income tax reports. Mrs. Leach also has some photographs and miscellaneous correspondence concerning her father's career.

Walpole Notes, Mrs. R. E. Walpole, Yankton, South Dakota. Mrs. Walpole, a granddaughter of John Coulson, has spent many years collecting material pertaining to Missouri River steamboating. Mrs. Walpole has taken notes from the customs records at Pittsburgh which contain valuable information regarding the size and titles of some of the Coulson Line steamers.

B. NEWSPAPERS

Bismarck Tribune, 1873–1888. Scattered items 1889–1938.
Chicago Sunday Tribune, February 27, 1910.
Daily Bulletin (Leavenworth, Kan.), 1868.
Daily Dispatch (St. Louis), 1866.
Daily Journal (Sioux City), 1871–1874.
Daily World (Omaha), June 12, 1888.
Dakotaian (Yankton), 1861–November 17, 1864.
Democrat (Chamberlain, Dakota Territory), 1883–1885.
Democrat (St. Louis), 1864–1868.
Evening News (St. Louis), 1866.
Fargo Forum and Daily Republican, December 7, 1910.
Helena Daily Herald (Montana Territory), 1870–1872.
Hunt's Merchants' Magazine and Commercial Review (July–December, 1862).
Missouri Gazette & Public Advertiser (St. Louis), 1818–1819.
Missouri Republican (St. Louis), 1828; 1850–1853; 1860.
Montana Post (Helena), June, 1868–May, 1869.
Montana Post (Virginia City), January 18, 1868.
Morning Herald (St. Joseph, Mo.), 1867.
Pittsburg Post, April 22, 1904.
Press and Dakotaian (Yankton), November 12, 1873–1885.
River Press (Fort Benton), February 13, 1901, June 16, 1937, August 21, 1946.
St. Louis Beacon, 1829–1831.
St. Louis Enquirer, 1819.
St. Louis Free Press, 1833.
St. Paul Sunday Pioneer Press, February 22, 1948.

Union and Dakotaian (Yankton), November 18, 1864–November 11, 1873.
Washburn Leader (Washburn, North Dakota), July 9, 1937.
Yankton Press, 1871–August, 1873.
Yankton Press and Dakotan, May 27, 1896.

C. GOVERNMENT PUBLICATIONS AND RECORDS
1. *National Government*
Analytical and Topical Index to the Reports of the Chief of Engineers and Officers of the Corps of Engineers, United States Army, 1866–1900, Vol. II. Washington, 1903.
Annual Report of Chief of Engineers, 1868; 1878–1916; 1921–1934.
Missouri River Basin Agricultural Program. United States Department of Agriculture. April, 1949.
Proceedings of the Eighteenth Annual Meeting of the Board of Supervising Inspectors of Steam Vessels. Washington, 1870.
Proceedings of the Twentieth Annual Meeting of the Board of Supervising Inspectors of Steam Vessels. Washington, 1872.
Proceedings of the Twenty-Fifth Annual Meeting of the Board of Supervising Inspectors of Steam Vessels. Washington, 1877.
Proceedings of the Thirty-Second Annual Meeting of the Board of Supervising Inspectors of Steam Vessels. Washington, 1884.
Report of the Secretary of War. Washington: Government Printing Office, 1869.
The War of the Rebellion: Official Records of the Union and Confederate Armies, Ser. 1, Vols. XXII, XXXIV, XLI.
Contract between Pierre Chouteau Jr. & Co. and D. D. Mitchell, Superintendent of Indian Affairs, May 2, 1849, in Bureau of Indian Affairs, Interior Department, National Archives.
Contract between Pierre Chouteau Jr. & Co. and Alfred Cumming, Superintendent of Indian Affairs, May 29, 1855, in Bureau of Indian Affairs, Interior Department, National Archives.
Contract between Pierre Chouteau Jr. & Co. and Acting Indian Commissioner Charles Mix, March 15, 1859, in Bureau of Indian Affairs, Interior Department, National Archives.
Contract between Joseph LaBarge and William Dole, Commissioner of Indian Affairs, April 1, 1863, in Bureau of Indian Affairs, Interior Department, National Archives.
Contract between Pierre Chouteau Jr. & Co. and Clark W. Thompson, Superintendent of Indian Affairs of the Northern Superintendency, April 16, 1863, in Bureau of Indian Affairs, Interior Department, National Archives.

Contract between Pierre Chouteau Jr. & Co. and William Dole, Commissioner of Indian Affairs, March 18, 1864, in Bureau of Indian Affairs, Interior Department, National Archives.

Contract between Pierre Chouteau Jr. & Co. and William Dole, Commissioner of Indian Affairs, March 25, 1864, in Bureau of Indian Affairs, Interior Department, National Archives.

Contract between Hiram K. Hazlett and Major General J. L. Donaldson, Acting Quartermaster General, U.S.A., February 29, 1868, St. Louis, Missouri, in Old Army Division, National Archives.

Contract between G. T. Nutter, Agent for the Northwest Transportation Company and E. S. Parker, Commissioner of Indian Affairs, May 13, 1869, in Bureau of Indian Affairs, Interior Department, National Archives.

"Tabular Statement," from *Contract between Hiram K. Hazlett, and Brevet Major General D. H. Rucker, Assistant Quartermaster, U.S.A., February 17, 1870, Chicago,* in Old Army Division, National Archives.

Contract for Missouri River between Hiram K. Hazlett and Assistant Quartermaster General, Chicago, March 17, 1871, in Old Army Division, National Archives.

Contract between C. K. Peck of the Northwest Transportation Company and E. S. Parker, Commissioner of Indian Affairs, May 23, 1871, in Bureau of Indian Affairs, Interior Department, National Archives.

Contract between Durfee & Peck and F. A. Walker, Commissioner of Indian Affairs, June 14, 1872, in Bureau of Indian Affairs, Interior Department, National Archives.

Contract between Amherst H. Wilder and Edward P. Smith, U.S. Indian Agent, November 8, 1872, in Bureau of Indian Affairs, Interior Department, National Archives.

Contract for Missouri River between Colonel D. H. Rucker, Assistant Quartermaster, U.S.A., and John B. Dallas, February 21, 1873, in Old Army Division, National Archives.

Contract between W. Cass, President of N.P.R.R. Co. and Edward P. Smith, Commissioner of Indian Affairs, May 13, 1873, in Bureau of Indian Affairs, Interior Department, National Archives.

Contract between Amherst H. Wilder and Edward P. Smith, Commissioner of Indian Affairs, May 20, 1873, in Bureau of Indian Affairs, Interior Department, National Archives.

Contract between Amherst H. Wilder and Edward P. Smith, Commissioner of Indian Affairs, June 4, 1873, in Bureau of Indian Affairs, Interior Department, National Archives.

Contract between Amherst H. Wilder and Edward P. Smith, Commissioner of Indian Affairs, July 19, 1873, in Bureau of Indian Affairs, Interior Department, National Archives.

"Tabular Statement," from *Contract between Colonel D. H. Rucker, Assistant Quartermaster, U.S.A., and Sanford B. Coulson, Chicago, March 14, 1874,* in Old Army Division, National Archives.

"Tabular Statement," from *Contract for Missouri River Transportation from March 20 to October 31, 1874, between Sanford B. Coulson and D. H. Rucker, Assistant Quartermaster General, U.S.A., March 14, 1874,* in Old Army Division, National Archives.

"Schedule of Rates," from *Contract between Colonel D. H. Rucker and Sanford B. Coulson, Chicago, March 18, 1875,* in Old Army Division, National Archives.

"Tabular Statement," from *Contract between Lieutenant Colonel S. B. Holabird, Deputy Quartermaster, U.S.A., and Sanford B. Coulson, Chicago, March 20, 1876,* in Old Army Division, National Archives.

"Tabular Statement," from *Contract for Missouri River Transportation from March 29, 1876 to October 31, 1876, between Walter A. Burleigh and S. B. Holabird, Deputy Quartermaster General, U.S.A., March 29, 1876,* in Old Army Division, National Archives.

Contract between John B. Davis and Peyton S. Davidson and B. C. Card, Chief Quartermaster, Department of Dakota, March 20, 1877, in Old Army Division, National Archives.

Contract for Missouri River Transportation, Commencing March 20, and Ending October 31, 1878, between Sanford B. Coulson and Chas. H. Tompkins, Deputy Quartermaster General, U.S.A., March 12, 1878, in Old Army Division, National Archives.

Contract for Transportation on the Missouri and Yellowstone Rivers between Sanford B. Coulson and Chas. H. Tompkins, Deputy Quartermaster General, U.S.A., March 14, 1879, in Old Army Division, National Archives.

Northwest Transportation Company Bills of Lading, 1868, in Miscellaneous Letters Received by Office of Indian Affairs, in Bureau of Indian Affairs, Interior Department, National Archives.

Bureau of Indian Affairs Letters Received, Fort Berthold Agency, 1873–1874, Microfilm Roll 294, in Bureau of Indian Affairs, Interior Department, National Archives.

2. *North Dakota State Government*
"Articles of Incorporation of the Benton Transportation Company," in Vol. X of Charters and Articles of Incorporation, Dakota Territory, Office of Secretary of State, Bismarck.

"Articles of Incorporation of Benton Packet Company," in Book of Corporations, Book 6, Office of Secretary of State, Bismarck.

"Articles of Incorporation of the Benton Transportation Company," in Book of Corporations, Book 23, Office of Secretary of State, Bismarck.

"Domestic Corporation Report for 1928 of Benton Packet Company," Domestic Corporation Report No. 1256, Office of Secretary of State, Bismarck.

"Domestic Corporation Report for 1937 of Benton Transportation Company," Domestic Corporation Report No. 1254, Office of Secretary of State, Bismarck.

3. *Iowa State Government*
"Articles of Incorporation of the North West Transportation Company," November 11, 1867, Office of Secretary of State, Des Moines.

II. SECONDARY SOURCES
A. Books
Andreas' Historical Atlas of Dakota. Chicago: A. T. Andreas, 1884.

Anon. *History of the Counties of Woodbury and Plymouth, Iowa, including an Extended Sketch of Sioux City.* Chicago: A. Warner & Co., 1890–1891.

Anon. *History of Sioux City from Earliest Settlement to January, 1892.* Boston: Press of B. Wilkins & Co., 1892.

Armstrong, Moses K. "History of Dakota, Montana, and Idaho." In Vol. XIV of *South Dakota Historical Collections.* Pierre, S.D., 1928.

Bancroft, Hubert Howe. *History of Washington, Idaho and Montana, 1845–1889.* San Francisco: The History Co., Publishers, 1890.

Brennan, John. *Condition and Resources of Southern Dakota: Prospective Trade and Travel of the Dakota Southern Railroad.* Sioux City: Daily Journal Printing House and Bindery, 1872.

Burkley, Frank J. *The Faded Frontier.* Omaha: Burkley Envelope & Printing Co., 1935.

CASEY, ROBERT J.; and DOUGLAS, W. A. S. *Pioneer Railroad: The Story of the Chicago and North Western System.* New York: McGraw-Hill, 1948.

CATLIN, GEORGE. *North American Indians,* Vol. I. Edinburgh: John Grant, 1926.

CHAPPEL, PHIL E. *A History of the Missouri River.* Kansas City: Bryant & Douglas, 1905.

CHARDON, FRANCIS A. *Journal at Fort Clark, 1834–1839,* ed. ANNIE ABEL. Pierre, S.D., Department of History, 1932.

CHITTENDEN, HIRAM M. *Early Steamboat Navigation on the Missouri River: Life and Adventures of Joseph LaBarge.* New York: Francis P. Harper, 1903.

———. *History of the American Fur Trade of the Far West.* 2 Vols. Stanford, Calif.: Academic Reprints, 1954.

DE TROBRIAND, PHILIPPE RÉGIS. *Military Life in Dakota: The Journal of Philippe Régis de Trobriand,* trans. and ed. LUCILE M. KANE. St. Paul: Alvord Memorial Commission, 1951.

Directory of Pittsburgh and Allegheny for 1877–8. Pittsburgh, 1878.

FOSTER, JAMES S. "Outlines of History of the Territory of Dakota and Emigrants Guide to the Free Lands of the Northwest." In Vol. XIV of *South Dakota Historical Collections.* Pierre, 1928.

HANSON, JOSEPH MILLS. *Conquest of the Missouri.* Chicago: A. C. McClurg & Co., 1909.

HAZARD, JOSEPH TAYLOR. *Companion of Adventure: A Biography of Isaac Ingalls Stevens.* Portland, Ore.: Binfords & Mort, 1952.

HUNTER, LOUIS C. *Steamboats on the Western Rivers: An Economic and Technological History.* Cambridge, Mass.: Harvard University Press, 1949.

JAMES, EDWIN. *An Account of Major Stephen H. Long's Expedition of 1819.* In Vol. XIV of *Early Western Travels,* ed. REUBEN GOLD THWAITES. Cleveland: Arthur H. Clark Co., 1905.

JONES, WILLIAM A. *Report upon the Reconnaissance of Northwestern Wyoming, Including Yellowstone National Park, Made in the Summer of 1873.* Washington: Government Printing Office, 1875.

KINGSBURY, GEORGE M. *History of Dakota Territory,* Vol. I. Chicago: S. J. Clarke Publishing Co., 1915.

LARPENTEUR, CHARLES. *Forty Years a Fur Trader on the Upper Missouri,* ed. M. M. QUAIFE. Chicago: The Lakeside Press, 1933.

LEESON, MICHAEL A. (ed.). *History of Montana, 1739–1885.* Chicago: Warner, Beers & Co., 1885.

LOBECK, A. K. *Geomorphology: An Introduction to the Study of Landscapes.* New York: McGraw-Hill, 1939.

MARKS, CONSTANT R. (ed.). *Past and Present of Sioux City and Woodbury County, Iowa.* Chicago: S. J. Clarke Publishing Co., 1904.

MULLAN, JOHN. *Miners and Travelers' Guide to Oregon, Washington, Idaho, Montana, Wyoming, and Colorado.* New York, 1865.

O'CONNOR, ROSE AGNES. *Sioux City, a True Story of How It Grew.* Sioux City, Iowa: The Public Library of Sioux City, 1932.

RAYNOLDS, W. F. *Report on the Exploration of the Yellowstone River.* Washington: Government Printing Office, 1868.

ROBERTS, THOMAS P. *Report of a Reconnaissance of the Missouri River in 1872.* Washington: Government Printing Office, 1875.

ROBINSON, DOANE. "A History of the Dakota or Sioux Indians." In Vol. II of *South Dakota Historical Collections.* Aberdeen, 1904.

SCHARF, THOMAS J. *History of St. Louis,* Vol. I. Philadelphia: Everts & Co., 1883.

SCHELL, HERBERT S. *Dakota Territory During the 1860's.* Vermillion, S.D.: University of South Dakota Governmental Research Bureau, 1954.

SCHMECKEBIER, LAURENCE E. *The Customs Service, Its History, Activities and Organization.* Baltimore: Johns Hopkins Press, 1924.

SHARP, PAUL F. *Whoop-Up Country.* Minneapolis: University of Minnesota Press, 1955.

SHORT, LLOYD M. *Steamboat-Inspection Service, Its History, Activities, and Organization.* New York: D. Appleton & Co., 1922.

SMITH, PERCY FRAZER. *Notable Men of Pittsburg and Vicinity.* Pittsburgh: Thurston & Deffenbacher, 1901.

STRAHORN, ROBERT E. *Montana and Yellowstone National Park.* Kansas City, Mo.: Ramsey, Millet & Hudson, 1881.

Trade and Commerce of St. Louis. St. Louis, 1870.

TRIMBLE, WILLIAM JOSEPH. *The Mining Advance into the Inland Empire.* University of Wisconsin Bulletin. Madison, Wis., 1914.

WALSTER, H. L., and NYSTUEN, P. A. *North Dakota Wheat Yields.* Fargo: North Dakota Agricultural College, 1948.

Who's Who in America, Vols. XI and XVIII. Chicago: A. N. Marquis Co., 1920–1921, 1934–1935.

WILTSE, CHARLES M. *John C. Calhoun, Nationalist.* New York: Bobbs-Merrill, 1944.

B. ARTICLES

ANDERSON, HARRY H. "A History of the Cheyenne River Agency and Its Military Post, Fort Bennett, 1868–1891." In Vol. XXVIII of *South Dakota Historical Collections.* Pierre, S.D., 1956.

ATKINS, C. J. "C. J. Atkins' Logs of the Missouri River Steamboat Trips, 1863–1868, with Appendix." Reprinted from *Collections of State Historical Society of North Dakota*. Bismarck, N.D., n.d.

BRADLEY, JAMES H. "Affairs at Fort Benton from 1831 to 1869, from Lieut. Bradley's Journal." In Vols. III, VIII, and IX of *Contributions to the Historical Society of Montana*. Helena, 1900, 1914, 1923.

CARPENTER, E. W. "A Glimpse of Montana," *The Overland Monthly*, Vol. II (April, 1869). San Francisco.

CHOUTEAU, CHARLES P. "Report of Chas. P. Chouteau to the Secretary of War of a Steamboat Expedition from St. Louis to Fort Benton, 1859." In Vol. III of *Contributions to the Historical Society of Montana*. Helena, 1900.

DRUMM, STELLA M. "Kenneth McKenzie." In Vol. XII of *Dictionary of American Biography*. New York, 1933.

HARKNESS, JAMES. "Diary of James Harkness of the Firm of LaBarge, Harkness & Co." In Vol. II of *Contributions to the Historical Society of Montana*. Helena, 1896.

HEILBRON, BERTHA L. (ed.). "Minnesota as Seen by Travelers: Isaac I. Stevens and the Pacific Railroad Survey of 1853." *Minnesota History*, June, 1926.

HILGER, NICHOLAS. "General Alfred Sully's Expedition of 1864, from the Diary of Judge Nicholas Hilger." In Vol. II of *Contributions to the Historical Society of Montana*. Helena, 1896.

KANE, LUCILE M. "New Light on the Northwestern Fur Company," *Minnesota History*, Winter, 1955. St. Paul.

MATTISON, RAY H. "The Army Post on the Northern Plains, 1865–1885." Reprinted from *Nebraska History*, Vol. XXXV (March, 1954). Lincoln.

———. "The Military Frontier on the Upper Missouri." Reprinted from *Nebraska History*, Vol. XXXVII (September, 1956). Lincoln.

"Minnesota Biographies 1655–1912." In Vol. XIV of *Collections of the Minnesota Historical Society*. St. Paul, 1912.

MORRISSEY, FRANK R. "Motor Packets of the Upper Missouri," *Motorboat*, January 25, 1913.

MUNSON, LYMAN E. "Pioneer Life in Montana." In Vol. V of *Contributions to the Historical Society of Montana*. Helena, 1904.

NAPTON, JOHN. "My Trip on the Imperial in 1867." In Vol. VIII of *Contributions to the Historical Society of Montana*. Helena, 1917.

NICHOL, RALPH E. "Steamboat Navigation on the Missouri River." In Vol. XXVI of *South Dakota Historical Collections*. Pierre, S.D., 1952.

PARKER, THEODORE R. "William J. Kountz, Superintendent of River Transportation under McClellan 1861–62," *Western Pennsylvania Historical Magazine*, Vol. XXI (December, 1938). Pittsburgh.

SCHELL, HERBERT S. "The Dakota Southern: A Frontier Railway Venture of Dakota Territory," *South Dakota Historical Review*, Vol. II (April, 1937). Pierre, S.D.

——. "Early Manufacturing Activities in South Dakota," *South Dakota Historical Review*, Vol. II (January, 1937). Pierre, S.D.

"Steamboat Arrivals at Fort Benton, Montana, and Vicinity." In Vols. I and III of *Contributions to the Historical Society of Montana*. Helena, 1876, 1900.

TREXLER, H. A. "Missouri–Montana Highways: The Overland Route," *Missouri Historical Review*, Vol. XII (April, 1918). Columbia, Missouri.

Index

211